A DISABILITY HISTORY OF THE UNITED STATES

OTHER BOOKS BY KIM E. NIELSEN

Beyond the Miracle Worker: The Remarkable Life of Anne Sullivan Macy and Her Extraordinary Friendship with Helen Keller

The Radical Lives of Helen Keller

Helen Keller: Selected Writings

Un-American Womanhood: Antiradicalism, Antifeminism, and the First Red Scare

**OTHER BOOKS IN THE REVISIONING
AMERICAN HISTORY SERIES**

A Queer History of the United States by Michael Bronski

A
DISABILITY
HISTORY
OF THE
UNITED STATES

KIM E. NIELSEN

ReVisioning American History

BEACON PRESS BOSTON

BEACON PRESS
Boston, Massachusetts
www.beacon.org

Beacon Press books
are published under the auspices of
the Unitarian Universalist Association of Congregations.

24 23 22 21   13 12

*Beacon Press's ReVisioning American History series consists
of accessibly written books by notable scholars that reconstruct
and reinterpret U.S. history from diverse perspectives.*

The poem "Disabled Country" is printed here with permission of the author.

This book is printed on acid-free paper that meets the uncoated paper
ANSI/NISO specifications for permanence as revised in 1992.

Text design and composition by Kim Arney

Library of Congress Cataloging-in-Publication Data

Nielsen, Kim E.
A disability history of the United States / Kim E. Nielsen.
p. cm. — (Revisioning American history)
Includes bibliographical references and index.
ISBN 978-0-8070-2204-7 (paperback: alk. paper)
1. People with disabilities—United States--History. 2. Sociology of
disability—United States—History. 3. People with disabilities—Legal status,
laws, etc.—United States—History. I. Title.
HV1553.N54 2012
362.40973—dc23   2012014236

TO NATHAN,

*in celebration of twenty-five marvelous, joyful,
sometimes bittersweet, event-filled, unforeseen years.
And to Morgan and Maya: two of the stunning events.*

DISABLED COUNTRY

If there was a country called disabled,
I would be from there.
I live disabled culture, eat disabled food,
make disabled love, cry disabled tears,
climb disabled mountains and tell disabled stories.
If there was a country called disabled,
I would say she has immigrants that come to her
From as far back as time remembers.
If there was a country called disabled,
Then I am one of its citizens.
I came there at age 8. I tried to leave.
Was encouraged by doctors to leave.
I tried to surgically remove myself from disabled country
but found myself, in the end, staying and living there.
If there was a country called disabled,
I would always have to remind myself that I came from there.
I often want to forget.
I would have to remember . . . to remember.
In my life's journey
I am making myself
At home in my country.

—NEIL MARCUS

CONTENTS

INTRODUCTION

When I crossed the stage to receive my PhD in history in 1996, I had no plans to become a historian of disability. I love history: the captivating stories and the satisfying intellectual bite of a vigorous analysis. At the time, if asked, and if I'd been honest, I'd have considered the topic of disability too "soft"—all that pity and empathy—too boring, and too far removed from the *real* "hard" stories of history. Was I wrong!

I've learned that disability pushes us to examine ourselves and the difficult questions about the American past. Which peoples and which bodies have been considered fit and appropriate for public life and active citizenship? How have people with disabilities forged their own lives, their own communities, and shaped the United States? How has disability affected law, policy, economics, play, national identity, and daily life? The answers to these questions reveal a tremendous amount about us as a nation.

A Disability History of the United States places the experiences of people with disabilities at the center of the American story. In many ways, this is a familiar telling. In other ways, however, it is a radical repositioning of US history. As such, it casts new light on familiar stories (such as slavery and immigration), while also telling new stories (such as the ties between nativism and oralism in the late nineteenth century). It also makes clear that there has been no singular disability experience. Although people with disabilities share social stigmatization, and sometimes are brought together by common experiences and common goals, their lives and interests have varied widely according to race, class, sexuality, gender, age, ideology, region, and type of disability—physical, cognitive, sensory, and/or psychological.

While telling the history of people with disabilities, *A Disability History of the United States* will also tell the history of the concept of disability. These are two very different tasks. Throughout US history, disability has been used symbolically and metaphorically in venues as diverse as popular culture (freak shows, for example) and language ("That's so lame"; "What a retard"; "special"). When "disability" is considered to be synonymous with "deficiency" and "dependency," it contrasts sharply with American ideals of independence and autonomy. Thus, disability has served as an effective weapon in contests over power and ideology. For example, at varying times, African Americans, immigrants, gays and lesbians, poor people, and women have been defined categorically as defective citizens incapable of full civic participation.

The story of US history is often told as a story of independence, rugged individualism, autonomy, and self-made men (and occasionally women) who, through hard work and determination, move from rags to riches. Just as the colonists sought and gained independence from Great Britain in order to create a successful and powerful country, so must individual citizens seek and gain independence in order to create successful and powerful selves. The idealized notion holds that we are a nation of Horatio Algers, perpetual train engines chugging our way (*I think I can, I think I can*) up to the city on the hill, insisting that we can do it ourselves. And, of course, the US democracy is founded on the premise that citizens *are* capable. It is the responsibility and privilege of citizens to vote, contribute economically, and have a say in their government. As citizens, as good citizens, we are to "stand on our own two feet" and "speak up for ourselves" (ableist phrases, if ever there were). In this version of the national story, independence is good and dependency is bad. Dependency means inequality, weakness, and reliance on others.

When disability is equated with dependency, disability is stigmatized. Citizens with disabilities are labeled inferior citizens. When disability is understood as dependency, disability is posited in direct contrast to American ideals of independence and autonomy.

In real life, however, just as in a real democracy, all of us are dependent on others. All of us contribute to and benefit from the care of others—as taxpayers, as recipients of public education, as the children of parents, as those who use public roads or transportation, as beneficiaries of publicly funded medical research, as those who do not participate in wage work during varying life stages, and on and on. We are an interdependent people. As historian Linda Kerber wrote, critiquing the gendered nature of the American ideal of individualism, "The myth of the lone individual is a trope, a rhetorical device. In real life no one is self-made; few are truly alone."[1] Dependency is not bad—indeed, it is at the heart of both the human and the American experience. It is what makes a community and a democracy.

The use of disability as an analytic tool matters in our national story because it forces consideration of the strengths, weaknesses, and contradictions of American ideals. Taking note of race, class, and gender, scholars have examined the historical expansion of democracy. It is time to do the same for disability. Additionally, a richer understanding of US history demands that we use disability to better understand the interdependent nature of democratic communities.

Disability is not the story of someone else. It is *our* story, the story of someone we love, the story of who we are or may become, and it is undoubtedly the story of our nation. It is, quite simply, the American story in all of its complexities. The story of US history is one of many efforts to define, contest, and enshrine a specific national body as best for the nation—a national body both individual and collective.

But . . . what is disability? Who are people with disabilities? And conversely, what does it mean to be nondisabled? When the US Supreme Court struggled to define obscenity in 1964, Justice Potter Stewart threw up his hands in frustration and wrote, "I know it when I see it."[2] It's temptingly easy to do the same about disability. We generally assume that disability is a clearly defined category, unchanging and concrete. Closer inspection, however, reveals that disability is often elusive and changing. Not only do people with disabilities have a history, but the concept of disability has a history as well.

The dominant method of defining disability assumes disability to be a medical "problem" with a clear "cause" that must be "treated" in an effort to find a "cure." This framework considers disability to stem from bodily-based defects and tends to define disabled people almost exclusively by those diagnostic defects (and supposedly nondisabled people by their lack of such defects). It erroneously presumes disability to be ahistorical—that is, to have always had the same, unaltering definition. Such a narrow conception erases the widely diverse and rich lives of so many people with disabilities—for whom disability likely matters, but who also define themselves according to and whose lives are shaped by race, sexuality, gender, class, political ideology, athleticism, their favorite hobby, whether or not they like yappy dogs, and the like. Disability can include disease or illness, but it often does not, and nondisabled people can be ill. Illness sometimes leads to disability (but it often does not), and when it does the illness can go away but the disability remain. Illness, disease, and disability are not synonymous.

Defining disability is difficult—and that's part of my argument. Although the definition theoretically has been based on bodies, the categorization of bodies as disabled has been shaped by factors such as gender, race, sexuality, education, levels of industrialization or standardization, access to adaptive equipment or privacy, and class. With age and medical care, as well as the vagaries of life, or simply daily context, one can move in and out of the category of "people with disabilities." One can be temporarily disabled due to accident or illness. Disabilities can be easily "read" by others (signified by the presence of a wheelchair or the sounds of a speech impediment), or more difficult to discern (such as some psychological disabilities or neurological disabilities).

Disability can be contextual, and its meanings have changed over time. A simplistic example: a fellow historian and I once spent a delightful few days in Montreal at an academic conference. Those around me read my body as nondisabled. The white cane of my friend led others to read her as blind and disabled. Waiters and cab drivers always looked to me to take the lead. However, and to their dismay, I don't speak French. Luckily, my colleague is fluent in French. In that context, my linguistic deficiencies became far more of an impediment, far more disabling, than her blindness. Disability is not just a bodily category, but instead and also a social category shaped by changing social factors—just as is able-bodiedness.

This is not to argue that we should all hold hands and cheerfully insist that we're all disabled in some way or another. That ignores the lived reality that disability can bring physical discomfort or difficulty. It also ignores the historical reality that being defined as disabled has made access to power and resources limited or difficult; and that hierarchies of power contribute to definitions of disability. For example, in the nineteenth century, medical experts argued that menstruation and reproduction so impaired women's bodies (those of middle- and upper-class white women, at least) that their exclusion from higher education and employment was absolutely necessary, for themselves and for the greater good of society. And in the early twentieth century, if public transportation was not accessible, and employers refused to hire a man with only one leg, then exclusionary ideas and resources—not the condition of being one-legged—generated social segregation and unemployment. These are real consequences.

Real consequences include poverty. People with disabilities disproportionately live in poverty and have lower rates of higher education. One of the most troubling aspects of researching this book was reading the historiography on poverty. Many historians of poverty simply assume that it's an inevitability that people with disabilities live disproportionately in poverty. But the feminization and racialization of poverty in the United States are not natural and unavoidable consequences. Neither is it natural and unavoidable that Mississippi has a higher rate of poverty than Wisconsin. These are the results of specific social structures: specific histories, legal practices, industrialization and development policies, educational-access histories, tax structures, ideologies, and more. This book will make clear that people with disabilities have lived and continue to live with disproportionately higher rates of poverty because of specific social structures, ideologies, and practices that hinder their social advancement.

Ideologies and practices that belittle and/or limit people with disabilities arise from ableist attitudes. Ableist attitudes are those that reflect a fear of, an aversion to, or discrimination or prejudice against people with disabilities. They can be as blatant as a refusal to hire someone with an apparent disability, or as subtle as the assumption that everyone attending a concert can stand for two hours. Like racism, sexism, or homophobia, ableism is directed at individuals and built into social structures; it is lived out purposefully, accidentally, and unknowingly. Ableist ideologies shape our media, for example, when people with disabilities are either completely absent or portrayed only as tragic and sad figures. They permeate our dominant standards of beauty and sexiness, definitions of what it means to dance, and measures of healthfulness. They also shape our expectations for leadership and success.

Human variability is immense. We see and hear in varying degrees, our limbs are of different lengths and strengths, our minds process information differently, we communicate using different methods and speeds, we move from place to place via diverse methods, and our eye colors are not the same. Some of us can soothe children, some have spiritual insight, and some discern the emotions of others with astounding skill. Which bodily and mental variabilities are considered inconsequential, which are charming, and which are stigmatized, changes over time—and that is the history of disability.

Parts of this book unexpectedly saddened me more deeply than I had anticipated. The story of the French slave ship *Le Rodeur,* detailed in chapter 3, conjured mental images that I found and continue to find intensely disturbing—and I hope that readers do too, for it is a human story that should be read as such. I experienced other parts of this story as joyful, funny, a call to action, and invigorating. It is my hope that readers, too, will experience this spectrum of emotions, and be equally exhilarated and stirred by this new perspective on the old American story that many of us know so well. That is the history of disability.

AN OUTLINE

Despite the ever-growing scholarship in disability history and the growing popularity of disability-oriented biographies and memoirs, no one has attempted to create a wide-ranging chronological American history narrative told through the lives of people with disabilities. *A Disability History of the United States,* while not a comprehensive narrative, attempts to fill this gap. This book could not have been completed without the scholarship, activism, and narrative accounts of others; those who knew they were telling the story of disability and those who did not.

Just as other scholars have retold the American story by using gender, class, sexuality, and race as tools of analysis, my purpose is to use disability to help us better understand the history of the United States. I hope to provide an example of what it means to consider disability alongside these other analyses as a means of historical inquiry and understanding. I also hope to provide an example of how disability intertwines with race, gender, class, and sexuality. Because disability, as a concept, has been used in many historical time periods to explain and justify definitions of these other social categories, using disability as an analytical tool is one means by which historians and other scholars can attempt simultaneous and multiple analyses.

My purpose also is to galvanize much needed additional scholarship. In many ways, *A Disability History of the United States* poses more historical questions than answers. There are, undoubtedly, questions, topics, and insights that scholars have not yet even begun to consider. For example, historian Margot Canaday argued, in her 2009 book *The Straight State: Sexuality and Citizenship in Twentieth-Century America*, that a primary means of the development of the modern bureaucratic American state was through the policing of sexual norms. Similarly, the story of US history told here suggests (and I am hopeful historians will explore this further) that another means by which the modern bureaucratic state developed was through the definition, and implementation of the definition, of disability. My work also suggests that US capitalism and industrialization both literally and conceptually contributed to the creation of disability. Significant scholarship remains to be done.

A Disability History of the United States begins prior to European conquest and colonization. Chapter 1 examines what is known about disability in the widely diverse cultures of indigenous peoples in North America. Chapters 2 and 3 analyze disability's role in shaping and defining the new nation, the lives of newly arrived Europeans and Africans with disabilities, and the consequences of European conquest and diseases upon Native communities. Chapters 4 and 5 explore the solidification of disability as a rhetorical, legal, and social category. As the new nation, experimenting with democracy, sought to define and distinguish between good and bad citizens, political theorists contrasted "idiots," "lunatics," women, and the enslaved with those worthy of full citizenship. The realities of the Civil War, growing urbanization and industrialization, along with the beginnings of the Progressive Era, created expanded institutional spaces for people with disabilities. Such institutions were both devastating and empowering.

Chapter 6 analyzes the contradictions of turn-of-the-century America in which eugenics, the oralist movement, immigration restrictions, state compulsory-sterilization laws, and increased medicalization, and even some of the suffrage movement's rhetoric, emphasized the undesirability of disabled people as citizens. Simultaneously, however, people with disabilities resisted—using vaudeville and freak shows, for example, as places of resistance and community. Chapter 7 shows how people with disabilities increasingly organized throughout the middle of the twentieth century—to create and pass legislation, to expand educational and vocational opportunities, to define disability discrimination as unjust discrimination, and to recognize the beauty and grace of people with disabilities.

Chapter 8 analyzes the period from 1968 to the present, a period that included significant activism and self-definition among people with disabilities and their allies. In the process, disability culture intensified and sometimes entered the mainstream. Just as women critiqued hierarchies based on the physical differences of sex, and just as people of color critiqued hierarchies based on the physical differences of race, so did people with disabilities critique hierarchies based on the physical differences of disability. A new generation embraced education and access as a right, and young people came of age with radically different expectations of what it means to be an American with a disability.

A Disability History of the United States tells an old story from a new perspective by reexamining it through the lives of people with disabilities. The narrative of US history thus revealed pushes us—as individuals, communities, and a nation—to ponder once again our obligations to each other, the national ideals we extol, and the varying ways we define the ideal American citizen.

BRIEF WORDS ABOUT WORDS

"Cripple," "idiot," "retard," "lunatic," "feeble-minded," "freak," "crazy," "handicap," "lame," "special," "slow," "differently-abled" . . . The words used to refer to people with disabilities have changed over time as ideas about disability have changed over time; indeed, changing words reflect historical change. Authority figures as well as neighbors and family routinely used, and sometimes still routinely use, words now considered tasteless, problematic, condescendingly sweet, or downright offensive. *A Disability History of the United States* uses these words—not to shock readers awake, but to better understand US history and historical change.

As an author I'm careful about the words that I use. Words matter. For example, characterizing someone as "wheelchair bound" or "confined to a wheelchair" is profoundly different than characterizing them as a "wheelchair user" or "wheelchair rider." The differentiation is not political correctness: it is an entirely different ideological and intellectual framework of comprehension. The contemporary disability-rights movement has understood that redefining and reclaiming language is central to self-direction, just as it has been for feminist; lesbian, gay, queer, and transgender; and racial freedom movements.

In ironic and interesting ways, *the absence of words* also has formed this book. As I tell the story of US history, I will argue that disability permeates our national history and our study of it—though we are often unaware or have failed to acknowledge it. The words "disability" and "handicap" often do not show up in book indexes or as database keywords. Historians such as I have had to be creative in our keyword searches—using historically specific terms for specific disabilities (such as "lunatick" or "blind"), as well as reading between the lines of discussions of illness, social welfare, activism, vagrancy, and health.

A PERSONAL NOTE

I fumbled my way into disability history by accident over a decade ago when I ran across a political speech of Helen Keller's. Trained in the history of women and politics, and always interested in how women justified themselves as civic beings in a public world that discouraged their involvement, I became fascinated by Keller's political life and its general erasure from our historical record. I knew nearly nothing about her, had no prior interest in disability, had no immediate family member with a disability, and identified as a nondisabled person. From that moment on, however, I immersed myself in disability history and disability studies scholarship. The rest of my story, as one might say, is history.

Good historical analysis is good historical analysis. Vigorous training, stubbornness, practice, and some skill combine to make me a good historian. It's more complicated, however. I'm female, white, earned a PhD, have a male spouse, am not yet perceived as elderly, live in the United States, and I am a native English speaker. As someone who also identifies and is perceived as nondisabled, I embody privilege. For me, doing smart disability history requires vigorous historical analysis, but it also requires that I acknowledge and wrestle with my privilege. Along the route I've made some mistakes and I have learned a great deal.

Of course, however, to be honest, as I worked with Beacon Press to prepare the proposal for this book, at heart I thought that I knew everything.

Then, of course, life happened.

A week or two after signing the contract for *A Disability History of the United States,* and after I'd been in the field for over a decade, my then sixteen-year-old daughter suddenly became seriously ill. As a result she became a disabled young woman.

Being a historian, a feminist scholar, and a disability studies scholar makes this both easier and harder for me. My daughter struggles with how to reconcile her own desire *not* to be a wheelchair user, *not* to be different, with her own experiences of people with disabilities as normative human beings who live full lives. As do I. While I and others in disability studies have critiqued the framework that defines disability as a medical issue, the initial lack of a diagnosis (and doctor disagreement about it) forced me to wrestle with how emotionally reliant I am on that part of the medical model of disability. The stereotypical responses of some extended family members and friends that disability-is-tragedy have not been helpful. People have used the word "inspiration" regarding my family's experience (and I'm just the mother)—the very word I've fought to avoid using regarding Helen Keller and Anne Sullivan Macy. I'm experiencing how disability profoundly affects an entire family. And I've learned that an unexpectedly large number of strangers feel it is appropriate to ask, "What's a pretty girl like you doing in a wheelchair?"

This experience has affected *A Disability History of the United States* in tangible and intangible ways. Most immediately, it delayed and prolonged the writing process. Intellectually and emotionally, it deepened the book and made it better. Most profoundly, I expect, it significantly but subtly altered the questions I ask.

This is a different book than the one I started, for I am a different person, and I live in a different family, than existed several years ago.

Making my daughter laugh until she tips over and falls down is really, really funny. Her core body muscles are so weak that strong laughter makes her fall over. My husband, Nathan, did it first. As my youngest daughter prepared to be Mary in the church Christmas program, my husband tried to convince her to yell, "My God, it's a girl!" at the pivotal moment. My newly disabled daughter laughed so hard that she fell on the kitchen floor and couldn't get up. That day medication had puffed up her back and arms, making them tender to the touch. Picking her up from the floor caused more pain, which somehow made the maneuver so precarious that we laughed even more. As we've lifted her from the floor I've learned a great deal.

The wonderful, delightful, confusing, and frustrating paradox of disability is that I am also the same person, and I live in the same family, that existed several years ago.

ONE

THE SPIRIT CHOOSES THE BODY IT WILL OCCUPY

Indigenous North America, Pre-1492

The stories, wisdom, and history of the Iroquois, passed down by family and clan members, tell us that long before the arrival of Europeans to North America, a Huron man brought the Great Law of Peace to the Iroquois—first to the Mohawks, then the Oneidas, the Cayugas, the Senecas, and ultimately to the Onondagas. The Peacemaker shared the Kaianere'kó:wa, the Great Law, as the Mohawks refer to it, as a pathway to restore peace, compassion, righteousness; and as a way to develop the strength necessary to live out the law. The Peacemaker gave the Kayanl'hsla'kó, as the Oneida people call it, to all individuals and communities of the People of the Longhouse.[1]

One day, as the Peacemaker was teaching the Mohawks, a sad man named Aionwahta (sometimes referred to as Hiawatha), who had lost his family to death, came to Mohawk country. The Peacemaker consoled him. He was happy to see Aionwahta. In fact, he had been waiting for him. Mohawk accounts indicate that Aionwahta went on to serve as an "interpreter" or "spokesperson" for the Peacemaker, necessary because the Peacemaker had a stutter that made it difficult for people to understand him. Aionwahta understood him, however, and was able to convey his words to the community. With Aionwahta, the Peacemaker reminded the People of the Longhouse of the Creator's desire for harmony.

In the traditional indigenous worldviews of North American peoples, it is believed that every person and thing has a gift (a skill, ability, purpose). When individuals, communities, and the world are in harmony, individuals, often with the help of others, find and embrace their gifts and put them into practice. The Peacemaker, for example, had tremendous insight but needed Aionwahta to successfully transmit his wisdom to the people. A tulip blooms in the spring but provides no beauty in the fall. All that is in the world, when in a healthy balance, have the gifts to accomplish needed tasks. When in harmony, and as members of a shared community who live out reciprocal relationships with one another, individuals share their gifts and benefit from the gifts of others. Defining someone simply by their gift—pottery, for example—or conversely by that which they could not do—climb trees, for example—would never be done. Balance requires that the entirety be recognized and embraced.

INDIGENOUS UNDERSTANDINGS OF DISABILITY

Disability has a history among North American indigenous people—a history, like all histories, profoundly shaped by social factors and basic cultural understandings of the world and its people. There is no doubt that prior to the arrival of Europeans in North America, just as today, bodies varied. Means of mobility, the sensory reception of the surrounding world, cognitive processes, and body mechanics were assorted and changeable. Their meanings were also assorted and changeable.

More accurately, and paradoxically, however, disability *does not* have a history among North American indigenous people. Most indigenous communities had no word or concept for what in American English we today call "disability."[2]

Indigenous scholars and activists Dorothy Lonewolf Miller (Blackfeet) and Jennie R. Joe (Navajo) suggest that some indigenous nations have defined what might be called disability in relational rather than bodily terms. In indigenous cultures, "disability" occurred when someone lacked or had weak community relationships. Though individuals might experience impairment, disability would come only if or when a person was removed from or was unable to participate in community reciprocity. For example, a young man with a cognitive impairment might be an excellent water carrier. That was his gift. If the community required water, and if he provided it well, he lived as a valued community member with no stigma. He participated in reciprocity and lived in balance. His limitations shaped his contributions, but that was true of everyone else in the community as well.[3]

After Europeans arrived in North America and created institutions for people with disabilities, indigenous families were more reluctant than other social communities to hand over their family members to outside care. Miller and Joe attribute this to the relational definition of disability. As long as an individual could sustain meaningful relationships that involved emotional or labor reciprocity—regardless of cognitive, physical, or emotional capacities—and lived out balance, they were not considered disabled. Reciprocity and its consequential ties mattered foremost in defining someone's competency.[4]

Generally, indigenous peoples understood the relationship between body, spirit, and mind very differently than the Europeans who later made their way through North America, the Africans forced in chains to the continent, the Asians who arrived to work the railroads in the nineteenth century, and contemporary peoples. Indigenous worldviews rest on the interwoven nature of body, spirit, and mind. Just as the contemporary word "disability" had no comparable concept, the contemporary phrase "able-bodiedness" would have had little meaning. Because the body was not separate from one's spirit and mind, an "able body" in and of itself would be inconsequential. Only if the spirit, body, and mind were in harmony did indigenous communities consider a person to be well—regardless of whether that person was blind, experienced chronic pain, or walked with a dance-like lilt. Most indigenous communities did not link deafness, or what we now consider cognitive disabilities, or the shaking bodies of cerebral palsy, with stigma or incompetency. Stigma and a need for community intervention came only when one's body, mind, and spirit were in disharmony. Thus, one's body or mind could lack what is today called disability, could lack what is today called illness, but still be considered imbalanced.[5]

For example, Navajo peoples of what is now the southwestern United States believed that bodily differences at birth (for example: a flipper-like limb, a cleft palate) were caused by parental actions resulting in imbalance, such as touching objects struck by lightning; incest; marrying within one's clan; or other taboo transgressions. A proper response thus involved discerning the cause of the impairment and restoring balance to the spirit with an appropriate healing ceremony. The "problem" was not the impairment, but whatever imbalance had caused it. The cleft palate would not go away, but its problematic nature could be resolved, and thus balance would be restored.[6]

The Hopi believed that improper actions could result in bodily differences for oneself or one's family members. Injuring an animal without prayers of apology, or ridiculing an animal's weakness, could cause disharmony manifested in the body. As told to Native scholar Carol Locust, one Hopi woman "was born with a club foot because her father had trapped a porcupine and cut off its forefeet."[7]

Similarly, Apache peoples believed that crooked legs or arms could result from parental violation of taboos regarding bears. Speech problems could be induced if a pregnant woman ate quail eggs. Palsy or a difficulty controlling facial or mouth muscles could come after a pregnant woman ate deer or elk meat. Among the Apache, surviving to old age meant that one had managed to stave off the "malevolence of the supernatural world" that could make physical survival difficult. Because avoiding taboo acts or places, and steering clear of witches, was not always possible, stigma did not always accompany the physical consequences of such contact.[8]

Furthermore, as Locust explains it, most tribes teach that "the spirit chooses the body it will occupy. Thus each person is responsible for who and what he is; he cannot blame others for the shortcomings of his body." Spirits choose their physical bodies in order to accomplish their purpose. If an individual does not meet his or her purpose, it is not the fault of the body—regardless of what that body can or cannot do.[9] When a balanced spirit is what matters, varying bodies matter less.

Similarly, indigenous nations had little or no concept of mental illness prior to European contact, only the recognition of unhealthy imbalance. Separating the mental from the physical or spiritual made no sense in this cultural context. Some groups viewed the behaviors and perceptions of what today we call psychological disability as a great gift to be treasured and a source of community wisdom. Others considered them a form of supernatural possession, or evidence of the imbalance of an individual's body, mind, and spirit. Because blindness and what is today called a psychological disability, for example, or a psychological disability and chickenpox, might be caused by similar disharmonies or the breaking of taboos, their treatments might also be similar and would have the same goal of restoring an individual's harmony.[10]

The human variabilities today referred to as disability certainly existed and have histories among the vastly disparate indigenous nations of North America. Eyesight, mental acuity, hearing, and the means of mobility varied among individuals; some bodies had one arm rather than two, and some had one leg significantly shorter than the other leg. Spiritual insight, leadership skills, and the ability to make pots that did not leak also, however, varied from person to person. Most indigenous communities considered all of these variations—whether physical, intellectual, spiritual, or functional—part of the same spectrum. Not surprisingly, the ways in which indigenous North American peoples understood themselves and their world shaped their understandings of physical, spiritual, and mental differences.

These understandings varied widely because the indigenous nations of North America understood themselves and the world around them in disparate ways. When Europeans arrived on the continent, they did not find a group of people who we today refer to as American Indians. At the time of contact, the tens of millions of North American indigenous peoples composed separate cultural and political groupings, speaking as many as twenty-five hundred distinct languages.[11] They lived in diverse climates, in political groupings from the small to the very large and powerful, with widely divergent belief systems, and in physical terrains ranging from plains to woodlands to deserts. In no way did these peoples consider themselves as sharing a cultural identity—that of *the* American Indian. There was no singular experience of disability, just as there was no singular definition of disability, among indigenous nations.

THE LIVING OF DAILY LIFE

The daily life of someone who was deaf, blind, moved with the rhythms of cerebral palsy, or who could not walk or had difficulty walking, is hard to discern for the centuries prior to European arrival in North America. While fundamental differences existed among the vast numbers of tribal nations, there are some commonalities that can help us understand daily life in this period. It is likely that being disabled had little impact on the measurement of an individual's capacity. For example, a young child born deaf in an indigenous North American nation grew up nearly always being able to communicate with her community. She would not be physically segregated. The expectation would be that if she survived the vagaries of life to which all were exposed, she could find and enjoy a partner, and she would eventually grow old as a treasured elder who tickled and guided the children around her. If all were in balance, she would find her gift—perhaps weaving, perhaps gathering particularly delicious herbs—and share that gift with her community, who would then share their gifts with her. A successful healing ceremony, if one was thought needed, would balance and resolve whatever unease might have existed—but certainly no one would expect the young girl to hear, for such a result was not necessary.

Nearly every indigenous-language group used signed communication to some degree, and many nations shared signed languages despite their verbal linguistic differences. Europeans documented use of signed language among North American indigenous peoples as early as the sixteenth century, and anthropologists and linguists generally agree that it was employed long before contact with Europeans. Signed language has been identified within at least forty different verbal linguistic groups. Today we know about indigenous signed languages because of its continued use by some elders, the anthropological work of scholars such as the Smithsonian's Garrick Mallery in the late nineteenth century, films made by Hugh L. Scott in 1930 at the Indian Sign Language Council, and the tenacious scholarship and activism of contemporary linguists such as Jeffrey E. Davis.

The most widely used signed language spread across an extensive region of the Great Plains, from Canada's North Saskatchewan River to the Rio Grande, from the Rocky Mountain foothills to the Mississippi-Missouri valley. What is now referred to as the Plains Indian Sign Language (PISL) enabled communication across communities regarding trade, in critical political negotiations, and even in courtship. Great Plains peoples used this "signed lingua franca," as Davis has characterized it, within their communities as an alternative to spoken language for ritual or storytelling purposes—and, of course, as a primary language for deaf people and those around them. Its use intensified after the European introduction of horses and the increased language contact that accompanied nomadic life. Though proficiency varied among individuals and among nations, the existence and steady use of signed languages meant that deaf and hard of hearing people had a language ready and, quite literally, at hand.[12]

The young girl born deaf could have relied on signed communication. Her hearing family members, too, knew that if their hearing diminished as they grew older, they could rely on signed communication. As this girl grew to adulthood, she could express pleasure at a good meal, signify a fair exchange of weaving, or reassure her own daughter that she had collected enough reeds. Nearly wherever one went in North America in the period prior to the arrival of Europeans, its indigenous peoples, whether deaf or hearing, could signify satisfaction by holding their right hand at their throat, palm down, and then moving it forward several inches. She likely would have done so too.

The social context of a widely used signed language shaped the meanings and implications of deafness. Given that both hearing and deaf people used this language, and given its integration into daily life and indigenous practices, deafness from birth or the loss of hearing at any point in one's life would not have meant social isolation. It would not have excluded someone from leadership or meaningful and reciprocal relationships with hearing people. If one became deaf, one could remain connected to the community with few changes.

The harsh conditions of life in indigenous communities routinely scarred and altered bodies, despite individual skill or carefulness, such that bodily variabilities were the norm. The physical requirements of a nomadic life such as that lived by Great Plains indigenous peoples, for example, would have taken their toll. Fiercely cold weather resulted in frostbite and the loss of fingers or toes. Conflicts or accidents could mean the loss of limbs or eyesight, or cause head trauma or impaired mobility. Illnesses and disease also altered bodies. Men, women, and children minding or hunting animals might be bitten, trampled, or accidentally cut by arrows or knives. Pregnancy or birth complications could cause chronic pain, and occasionally prolapsed uteruses and resulting mobility limitations. All bodies likely and eventually became transformed, and thus bodily differences were unremarkable. Noted one Native scholar writing of mountain lion and bear attacks, smallpox, conflict, and disease, "Acquired handicaps were so common that little attention was paid them."[13]

Because indigenous worldviews rested on the core belief that all had gifts, aging and the bodily changes that accompanied it did not lead to an assumption of diminished capacity (as it often does today in the dominant US culture). Elders, like all others, had gifts to share—though, like all others, their gifts might change throughout life stages. Communities assumed that elders could and *should* exercise leadership and guidance—regardless of age-related diminishment; regardless of limbs altered by accidents, conflict, or cold weather; and regardless of minds perhaps not as quick as they once were. Indigenous communities embraced aged bodies and minds that other cultures disregarded as inconsequential.

This is not to imply that the physical differences today referred to as disability were without consequence in indigenous societies prior to the arrival of Europeans. On a fundamental level, the consequences could be very stark. The realities of weather, geography, periods of conflict, and the physical requirements of hunting and gathering societies meant that newborns and individuals with physical trauma sometimes simply died. A disability that today could be successfully managed over the course of a long and healthy life might, under the physical conditions of indigenous groups, result in death.

And communities did make distinctions with respect to variance. In the Hopi nation, disabilities that emerged any time after birth were understood to come as a result of a deviation from the Hopi way of life. Anything from diminished vision to poor bladder control to a paralyzed limb meant that the individual had digressed, even ever so slightly, from Hopi ideals. Blindness, for example, like all other disabilities, "may have occurred at age eighty-five, but was still considered un-Hopi because the natural state of Hopi life is perfect health, no matter what the age."[14] In consequence, no one could avoid the physical changes wrought by deviating from the Hopi way.

The Hopi and other indigenous nations could also ascribe negative cultural values to disability. If balance and harmony were the goal, and if imbalance and disharmony could be manifested via bodily and mental differences, stigma—or at least unease—could be and sometimes was associated with the bodily and mental differences that we today call disability. Even if balance was restored during a healing ceremony, the physical sign of an individual's prior imbalance remained literally marked on the body.

As the historian Tom Porter (Sakokweniónkwas) details, in the Iroquois Constitution taught by the Peacemaker, people who were deaf or hard of hearing, blind, or had limited mobility could not become chief. Chiefs who became disabled while serving as leaders did not lose their positions, but it then became the duty of sub-chiefs to assist them.[15] As Porter explains it, this was due not to stigma but to the tasks demanded by the position. The ideal, of course, was one of balance. Ideals, however, are often hard to live out; and it is important not to unduly romanticize indigenous-nations communities. Despite the teachings of one's communities, human beings do stray. The fundamental mind-set of indigenous nations emphasizing balance and reciprocity, however, later contrasted sharply with that of Europeans.

———

Prior to European conquest, the worldviews of indigenous peoples understood body, mind, and spirit to be one. These beliefs allowed for fluid definitions of bodily and mental norms, and fundamentally assumed that all had gifts to share with the community—and that for communities to exist in healthy balance, each individual needed to do so. A young man who no longer controlled the movements of his arm after falling from a tree or cliff while scouting neighboring peoples would learn other means by which to hunt, fish, drum, and please his sexual partners. His gift might be that of sharing and teaching the community's past. If the community was flourishing and resources were plentiful, he would eat well. If times were hard, he, like all others, would go without. Perhaps his sister frequently spoke to beings that others did not see, and her frequent and unpredictable vocalizations made successful hunting and fishing difficult. She may have been considered to have great insight into that which others did not understand, and others would come to her for guidance. Both individuals would have lived with family members, contributed to the community, and benefited from the community.

Outside forces, however, would irrevocably and profoundly change North American communities—beginning with the arrival of Europeans in the fifteenth century and continuing for many centuries. The invasions of Europeans, the diseases they brought with them, and the increased military conflicts those invasions created, dramatically altered the experiences and bodies of indigenous people. Western concepts of wellness and medicine directly and tragically conflicted with the indigenous embrace of body, mind, and spirit as one. Any sense of mutuality between European and Native cultures was extinguished by disease, greed, and notions of cultural superiority. Within all of the cultures involved in this fateful meeting, cultural conflicts and influences forged new experiences and definitions of disability.

TWO

THE POOR, VICIOUS, AND INFIRM

Colonial Communities, 1492–1700

From the very beginning of the European colonization of North America, before the ships making the ocean passage even left European ports, disability and definitions of appropriate bodies and minds shaped the experience. Those directing the long voyages across the Atlantic excluded individuals with bodies or minds deemed undesirable or unlikely to survive the voyage, which could be arduous even for the most robust. Adventurers, wealth seekers, and colonists who died during the treacherous and generally unpleasant journey were simply thrown overboard. The determination of "able-bodied" depended largely on the perception that one conformed to communal expectations regarding class, gender, race, and religion.

The Spanish were the first Europeans to explore the New World. Sponsored by the Spanish crown, Christopher Columbus led an expedition of three ships, landing in 1492 in what is now the Bahamas, and then Cuba. By 1592 explorers and colonists from Spain, France, and England had made their way by ship and foot around North America's Atlantic coast, the Gulf of Mexico, and much of the Pacific coast, pushing ever inland. Some sought trading relationships, some sought slaves and riches, and others sought to establish permanent settlements. Everywhere Europeans went they encountered indigenous peoples of different languages, cultures, and histories. The first long-lasting foothold was that of the Spanish along the Floridian coast. Later, in the 1600s, the English and French began more permanent settlements in what is now Canada, New England, and as far south as Virginia. As settlements and trade expanded, the numbers of Europeans in North America grew.

FIRST CONTACT

To the indigenous people of North America, the arriving Europeans were odd and curious creatures indeed. The Jesuit missionary Pierre Biard and the Franciscan priest Gabriel Sagard assumedly were average-looking French men, but both wrote of the disgust with which indigenous peoples of New France (Nova Scotia) considered them and their bodies in the early 1600s. Sagard recorded how those of the Huron nation believed that his beard made him ugly and rendered him stupid. Biard made this observation: "They have often told me that at first we seemed to them very ugly with hair both upon our mouths and heads; but gradually they have become accustomed to it, and now we are beginning to look less deformed."[1]

Less deformed? The hairy face a sign of intellectual weakness and disfigurement? Indigenous definitions of normative bodies, at least those among the Huron of New France, definitely did not include hairy mouths and heads.

It's hard to exaggerate the cultural confusions and misunderstandings between European and North American peoples in the first centuries of European arrival. The peoples of the two continents interpreted the workings of the world, and each other, in radically different frameworks. Even good intentions could be and often were profoundly misinterpreted. It's also hard to exaggerate the violence, cruelty, and fears that permeated most encounters.

Communication difficulties exacerbated tensions and contrasting goals, but each group used their bodies and hands to communicate. Members of indigenous nations were accustomed to communicating with those speaking other languages by hand gestures or, more successfully, the signed languages that spread across much of North and Central America. Bernal Díaz del Castillo and Álvar Núñez Cabez de Vaca reported using hand signs to communicate with indigenous peoples, but neither man recorded the specifics of these signals. When the Spanish expedition led by Pánfilo de Narváez embarked around what is now Tampa Bay, Florida, in 1528, his chronicler Cabeza de Vaca wrote of the people they encountered, "They made many signs and threatening gestures to us and it seemed that they were telling us to leave the land, and with this they departed from us." The signed communication must have been relatively complex as well as comprehensible, for when Cabeza de Vaca washed ashore near today's Galveston Island, the indigenous peoples told him via sign "that they would return at sunrise and bring food, having none then." Cabeza de Vaca recorded encountering people accustomed to using manual communication as far away as the Gulf of California. Francisco Vásquez de Coronado wrote similar accounts in 1541.[2]

The Spanish explorers assumed they encountered discrete gestures—not a language. Today's scholars confidently argue that signed language among indigenous nations served deaf and hard of hearing people as well as the communication needs of peoples of different languages. European explorers benefited from already existing signed languages or signed communications, but dismissed them as unsophisticated hand signals. Spanish explorers were contemporaries of the Spanish Benedictine monk Pedro Ponce de León (1520–1584), who was just beginning to argue that deaf people could be educated and is credited with developing the first manual alphabet. North American indigenous sign languages thus existed long prior to any signed language in Europe. (France, the home of other early explorers, became a leader in deaf education, but not until the 1700s.) Members of indigenous nations believed that people born deaf had intellect and personal capacity. European peoples tended to believe the opposite. The European assumption of the inferiority, the primitive savageness, of the North American peoples they encountered made it additionally unlikely that they would recognize that indigenous peoples had developed something Europeans had yet to accomplish.[3]

Signed language, however, was not enough to bring cultural harmony.

DISRUPTION, DISEASE, AND DISABILITY: EFFECTS OF EUROPEAN INCURSION

Those who survived the grueling ocean passage from Europe tromped with relief and trepidation onto the unfamiliar landscapes of North America, carrying with them household items and clothing as well as weapons and disease. Disease, more than weapons, profoundly affected and decimated the bodies, and thus the societies, of peoples already living on the continent. The smallpox, measles, influenza, bubonic plague, cholera, whooping cough, malaria, scarlet fever, typhus, and diphtheria that Europeans carried with them brought massive death as well as blindness, deafness, disfigurement, and the loss of caregivers to indigenous North Americans. The lack of acquired immunological resistance and a relatively homogeneous gene pool among Native peoples, as well as malnutrition and environmental stressors, facilitated the spread of disease. The social chaos caused by massive death rates forced changes in community interactions and reciprocity, and profoundly altered lives. Colonial efforts to expand settlements, the enslavement of Native peoples by the Spanish, and the consequential slave trade that emerged in the southeastern parts of North America, as well as the movements of peoples and goods along the commercial trade routes used by the French, Spanish, and British, also sped the spread of disease.[4]

Disease epidemics were widespread. The first recorded epidemics swept through New England in 1616–1619, killing an estimated 90 to 95 percent of the indigenous Algonquian peoples living there. Throughout the 1630s and 1640s smallpox claimed approximately 50 percent of the Huron and Iroquois people living in the Saint Lawrence River and Great Lakes region. Scholars estimate that along what became the southeastern US coastal areas of Virginia, the Carolinas, and Louisiana, less than five thousand indigenous people remained by 1700. Of the more than seven hundred thousand indigenous people in Florida in 1520, only two thousand surviving descendants remained by 1700.[5]

In the 1630s, disease swept once again through the New England indigenous communities already decimated by the 1616–1619 epidemic. William Bradford wrote of the Algonquians near Plymouth Colony:

> They fell down so generally of this disease as they were in the end not able to help one another, nor not to make a fire nor to fetch a little water to drink, nor any to bury the dead. But would strive as long as they could, and when they could procure no other means to make fire, they would burn the wooden trays and dishes they ate their meat in, and their very bows and arrows. And some would crawl out on all fours to get a little water, and sometimes die by the way and not to be able to get in again.[6]

Thomas Morgan wrote of the same community in 1637 that they "died on heaps as they lay in their houses . . . in a place where many inhabited, there hath been but one left a live to tell what became of the rest . . . the bones and skulls upon the severall places of their habitations made such a spectacle."[7] Neither Bradford nor Morgan recorded their own responses to such a horrible plight.

The arrival of an epidemic weakened a community's physical and cultural environment, making it even more vulnerable to further epidemics. When disease disrupted community labor cycles because few people were left to do the planting, or because those remaining alive moved in hopes of avoiding further epidemics, villages, according to the historian William Cronon, "often missed key phases in their annual subsistence cycles—the corn planting, say, or the fall hunt—and so were weakened when the next infection arrived."[8]

The environmental changes brought on by European incursion and disease also disrupted subsistence. As historian David Jones has written, colonists deforested traditional living areas, which "led to wider temperature swings and more flooding." Colonists' livestock grazed and overran the crops of indigenous communities, which exacerbated tensions and often resulted in the attempted seizure of Native lands. Jones also notes that Europeans "introduced pests, including blights, insects, and rats. All of these changes fueled rapid soil erosion and undermined the subsistence of surviving Indian populations."[9] Weakened by an initial round of disease, and subject to environmental changes wrought by colonists, and, in some cases, depletion in their numbers as a result of massacres and the slave trade, many indigenous communities faced subsequent waves of disease with few resources.

When viral epidemics such as smallpox, measles, chickenpox, and mumps arrived in a village, those between the ages of fifteen and forty experienced the brunt of the outbreaks and had the highest death rates. Their fully developed immune systems responded most aggressively, meaning that they experienced the most virulent reactions—pustules, swelling, fever, weakness, and fatigue. With those most responsible for physical labor incapacitated, "the everyday work of raising crops, gathering wild plants, fetching water and firewood, hunting meat, and harvesting fish virtually ceased." The young, the old, and those physically unable to engage in such labor likely received little food or care. Many who might otherwise not have died of disease did so simply because they had no one to provide them with food and water. In such physically and culturally depleted communities, caring for one another, engaging in community reciprocity, and sustaining vital cultural traditions became nearly impossible. As one European colonist wrote of the indigenous peoples near Charleston in 1710, "They have forgot most of their traditions since the Establishment of this Colony, they keep their Festivals and can tell but little of the reasons: their Old Men are dead."[10] Understandably, such devastation wrought spiritual and cultural crises.

For those with physical or mental disabilities, and for those whose bodies or minds made physical escape, gathering food or firewood, and finding water difficult, disease epidemics frequently and simply meant death. Though they may have possessed excellent storytelling or basket-making skills, wisdom, the ability to nurture children, these things meant little in the face of overwhelming communal stress. Those with disabilities likely were disproportionately affected by the arrival of Europeans in North America.

Epidemics often left disability in their wake. Survivors of smallpox experienced high rates of blindness and physical disfigurement. Scarlet fever could leave those afflicted blind, deaf, or deafblind. The consequences of European colonization and conquest not only altered the ways in which indigenous peoples experienced what is now called disability, but it disproportionately killed people with disabilities and also produced disability.

The period of European conquest in North America reveals much about the relationship between disability and disease. While the two are not synonymous, disease can lead to disability. Sometimes the resulting disability has little social or economic consequence, sometimes the consequences are significant. The large-scale onset of disease, however, when coupled with war, racism, environmental decline, and displacement, was extremely debilitating and brought significant levels of disability to people of indigenous nations. It also made the material realities of disability profoundly harsher.

Disease brought disability to European settlers as well, but the material realities were less significant and less widespread than for the indigenous peoples of North America. Physical disability was relatively routine and unremarked upon among colonists unless it resulted in an inability to labor in gender-, class-, and racially appropriate ways. European settlers paid far greater attention to those with mental or cognitive disabilities, and provided community care as they saw fit.

EUROPEAN NOTIONS OF "ABLE-BODIED," AND COMMUNAL RESPONSE TO DISABILITY

The Spanish, French, British, and other Europeans who traveled to North America did so with many different goals. Some dreamed of establishing orderly and permanent colonies of like-minded individuals and families, others sought slaves, gold, and long-term trading relationships from which wealth and power would result. A few sought fame. Nearly all who organized such expeditions sought able-bodied and able-minded peoples to carry out and support these formidable tasks. They generally excluded people considered to have disabilities from the groups that boarded the wooden ships in European ports.

But what did it mean to Europeans to be able-bodied and able-minded in the 1600s? In 1616 Jesuit missionary Pierre Biard recorded that many of the men with him had "some defect, such as the one-eyed, squint-eyed, and flat-nosed."[11] Neither France, nor England, nor Spain offered physically easy lives in the early 1600s; nor did traveling by ship to North America. Bodily variations due to disease, accident, or birth were common and included in definitions of able-bodied. Thus, while those Europeans arriving in North American might have met seventeenth-century standards of able-bodiedness, their bodies varied substantially. Within the early capitalist systems beginning to dominate Europe during the seventeenth century, the primary definition of disability was an inability to perform labor.

European colonists paid relatively little attention to physical disability, but substantial attention to cognitive or mental disabilities. This reinforces the argument that bodily norms were relatively fluid and that bodies themselves varied immensely. One-armed men and women, or those with slight palsies or limps, or those who could not hear, and on and on, could plant fields, mind children, sail, build a barrel or a hunting trap, fish, shoot a gun, or spin and weave. Unlike the physically disabled, however, those that today we would categorize as having psychological or cognitive disabilities attracted substantial policy and legislative attention by Europeans attempting to establish social order, capitalist trade networks, and government in sixteenth- and seventeenth-century North America.

Just as there was considerable variability in the experience of Native communities, English settlements also varied. The English Puritans who settled in New England did so as families and households who sought to establish permanent settlements built on religious ideals. Their leaders thus considered female bodies appropriately able-bodied for their colonial hopes. The English who settled in the Chesapeake Bay region did so largely as individuals who sought economic advancement on a commercial outpost, either as landholders or as indentured servants, or because they were coerced into doing so. The desired body for working tobacco fields was young, male, and able to perform significant physical labor.

Because the English, far more than the French or Spanish, sought permanent settlements of men, women, and children (rather than military, trading, or religious outposts), they focused more attention than did the Spanish or French on community and social policy. The Puritans of New England thus more quickly established their own legal structures. Those of the Chesapeake Bay region, in comparison, tended to rely on English courts.

The Puritan social ethic pervaded all aspects of life in early New England. Believing that God had created the world to be orderly and hierarchical, the Puritans sought to replicate that design in their social structure and community covenants. Intending originally to settle in Virginia but landing much farther northward, English Puritans led by William Bradford settled in 1620 in what is now Plymouth, Massachusetts. They chose a site already cleared and farmed by Patuxet Indians, who had abandoned it after a disease epidemic swept through in 1617. The members of Plymouth Colony came to be known as Pilgrims, in remembrance of whom US children now often create hats at Thanksgiving time. The colonial settlers established a male-disabled-veterans' benefit in 1636, promising that "if any that shall goe returne maimed [and] hurt he shalbe mayntayned competently by the Colony during his life." In 1641 the Massachusetts "Body of Liberties" guaranteed that no one would be made to perform public service if they were unable to due to "want of years, greatness of age, defect in mind, failing of senses, or impotency of Limbs." It also established legal protections for those considered mentally incapable of making sound financial decisions—"any woman that is married, any child under age, Idiot or distracted person." A subsequent edition of the Body of Liberties omitted the previous statement, but provided that "Children, Idiots, Distracted persons, and all that are strangers, or new commers to our plantation, shall have such allowances and dispensations in any Cause whether Criminall or other as religion and reason require."[12]

Massachusetts law, and generally that of other colonies, distinguished between "idiots" and "distracted persons" throughout the seventeenth and eighteenth centuries. Idiots were those, according to the poor law of 1693, who were "naturally wanting of understanding, so as to be uncapable to provide for him or herself." Idiots were generally born idiots, and their condition was lifelong and permanent. A distracted person (sometimes referred to as a "lunatick"), in comparison, "by the Providence of God, shall fall into distraction, and become *Non compos mentis*"—for whom perceived mental instability occurred later in life and could be temporary.[13] The relatively large amount of colonial law dedicated to what we now call cognitive and psychological disabilities remained consistent until the American Revolution.

Early colonial legal frameworks protected from punishment those who could not understand the law. Massachusetts, as stated earlier, guaranteed in 1639 that "Children, Idiots, Distracted persons, and all that are strangers, or new commers" would not be punished for failing to adhere to the law—adopting an already firmly established English practice. Rhode Island adopted a similar provision in 1647. It stated that in cases of manslaughter, punishment would not be given to "a natural foole that hath not knowledge of good or evil; nor a felonious intent . . . neither doth it concerne a madd man, who is a man, as it were, without a mind; for the saying is: an act makes not a man herein guiltie, unless the mind be guiltie."[14]

The final concern of New England law regarding mental or cognitive disabilities was financial. Families always bore primary responsibility for those who could not labor and thus care for themselves—whether due to youth, old age, or mental, cognitive, or physical disabilities. Communities considered both idiots and the distracted undesirable inhabitants, particularly those without families, because of their general inability to provide for their own financial support. Beginning in 1693, poor laws allowed local officials to use the estates of either idiots or the distracted to defer the cost of community support.[15] Laws also sought to protect and manage property owned or inherited by those considered idiots or the distracted, ensuring that the larger community would not end up financially responsible for their daily needs.

The implementation of laws regarding idiocy required standards, and those standards generally involved work, self-care, perceived intellectual capacity, and the maintenance of property. Massachusetts resident Mighill Smith voted three times in the same election, but the 1647 colonial court decided not to fine him: "His putting in of three beans at once for one mans election, it being done in simplicity, & he being pore & of harmless disposition." Mary Phipps was determined "void of common reason and understanding that is in other children of her age [and] . . . next to a mere naturall in her intellectuals."[16] Both adults were thus idiots not culpable for their actions, considered innocent and harmless and in need of protection.

Just as people with cognitive disabilities today are vulnerable to physical and sexual assault or economic exploitation, so were colonial idiots. The cases of Benomi Buck and his sister Mara Buck are one example. Their father, the Reverend Richard Buck, was hired by London's Virginia Company to provide spiritual guidance to the several thousand indentured servants and masters of the company. Buck and his second wife, whose name in the historical record is given as "Mrs. Buck," left England in 1609 only to be marooned for nine months in Bermuda before finally arriving in Virginia in 1611. Mara, whose name means "bitter," was born in 1611, and Benomi, "son of my sorrow," in 1616. (Between those births, in 1614, Buck officiated at the marriage ceremony of John Rolfe and Pocahontas.) The reverend and his wife died in 1624. At his death, Buck owned substantial property, at least several indentured servant contracts, personal property such as livestock and tobacco, and other goods valued at 320 pounds of tobacco.[17]

What we know of Benomi and Mara Buck largely comes from the legal battles regarding their portions of their father's estate. Death and the attempted crimes of others put them in the historical record. Benomi, considered an idiot and "in no way able to governe himself, or to manage that small estate left him by his said father," lived until 1639, having both in childhood and adulthood always been under legal guardianship. When Governor John Harvey investigated Benomi's case, he found that several of Benomi's guardians "had much inriched [themselves] from the stocks" intended to support the young man. Mara received the Crown Court's attention after rumors surfaced that a man sought to marry her, at age thirteen, in order to gain access to her portion of her father's estate. The court determined her to be disabled and in need of guardianship. She was, her guardian in 1624 testified, "very Dull to take her lerninge."[18]

Mary Phipps also only entered the historical record after a crime. In 1689 the unmarried nineteen-year-old granddaughter of Thomas Danforth (the judge of the Salem witch trials) of Charlestown, Massachusetts, gave birth to a child. Phipps twice named John Walker, a forty-nine-year-old bricklayer, the father. He had, she told the midwife, "took several opportunities to abuse her body in his wicked lustfull manner" while preventing her from crying out by covering her mouth. Servant Hannah Gilson described Walker as "so nasty & his language so base that she would not have been alone in a house with him for all the world hee was so wicked." Mary's father reported that she had been "enslaved . . . with fear that if she did tell anybody he [Walker] would kill her."[19]

Though clearly Phipps had been raped, she and her child came to the courts only because the child was a bastard. The courts sought to determine fiscal responsibility and found John Walker responsible. Perhaps the legal situation was made worse by Phipps's idiocy and palsy. She was, court depositions stated, "void of common reason and understanding that is in other children of her age, not capable of discerning between good and evil or any morality . . . but she knows persons and remembers persons. She is next to a mere naturall in her intellectuals . . . She is incapable of resisting a rape hav[ing] one side quite palsied . . . [we] have to help her as a meer child."[20] Walker's punishment was to provide for the child financially. When the baby died, Walker had no more involvement. Phipps's famous grandfather later died in 1699 and left her a portion of his estate, but what happened to Phipps is unclear.

Just as communities expected families to provide care and finances for idiots, so did communities expect families to care for the distracted and the lunatic. Those from well-to-do families lived with family members and, as long as they had financial support, generally didn't enter the public record. Ann Yale Hopkins, the wife of the governor of Connecticut in the mid-seventeenth century, had "fallen into a sad infirmity, the loss of her understanding and reason." Colonial leader and family friend John Winthrop recorded her condition, blaming it on her husband's indulgence of her intellectual pursuits. Despite the medicinal water that Winthrop prescribed for her, she remained considered insane for over fifty years.[21]

Poor people deemed insane, and those violent or uncontrollable, became a community responsibility. A 1694 Massachusetts statute guaranteed that each community had the responsibility "to take effectual care and make necessary provision for the relief, support and safety of such impotent or distracted person." If the insane person was destitute, they became the town's fiscal responsibility. Connecticut, New York, Rhode Island, Vermont, and Virginia followed with similar statutes. When Jan Vorelissen of Pennsylvania could no longer support his son Erik, "bereft of his naturall Senses and [who] is turned quyt madd," the city provided support. The colony of New Haven provided funds for the town marshal to care for distracted Goodwife Lampson, "so far as her husband is not able to do it."[22]

When those considered insane threatened public safety, communities attempted to restrain them. A Virginia court ordered that the sheriff restrain John Stock, who in 1689 "keeps running about the neighborhood day and night in a sad Distracted Condition to the great Disturbance of the people." The sheriff was to restrain Stock in "some close Roome, where hee shall not bee suffered to go abroad until hee bee in a better condition to Governe himselfe."[23]

Local responsibility appears to have been accepted, but colonial communities strongly resisted caring for the stranger. Laws with titles such as "For the Preventing of Vagabonds" or "For the Preventing of Poor Persons" required newcomers to guarantee their economic viability. Strangers unable to do so would be "warned out," with the threat of a lash. Historian Albert Deutsch notes that towns might have even, under the cover of night, rid themselves of their own insane paupers by dumping them in other communities or locales. A man named "Mad James" apparently wandered throughout Kings County, New York, in 1695, leaving the deacons of each town to eventually meet together to share the costs of maintaining him. "Warning out" came from fiscal concerns, not a fear of insanity—and, as Gerald Grob writes, "the fate of the insane was not appreciably different from that of other dependent groups."[24]

Grob's analysis is helpful in many respects. The treatment and comprehension of those considered insane was not "appreciably different from that of other dependent groups" because insanity, just like idiocy, was not believed to be particularly shameful. The influential Puritan theologian Cotton Mather considered insanity, just as his own stuttering, a punishment for sin. The temptations and struggles of sin, however, beset everyone and, as one historian characterized it, "the failure to win the struggle was not necessarily a cause for shame."[25]

In this period of early colonization and conquest, bodily variabilities pervaded families, communities, and daily life. Europeans thus made little comment on such anomalies—*as long as one could labor.* Early European colonists defined disability in such a way that emphasized economic productivity in a manner appropriate to one's race, class, gender, and religion. If well-to-do families could economically gloss over the laboring inability of their lunatic, idiot, or distracted family member, that individual's disability generally remained irrelevant to community proceedings. If the blind, if the slow to walk, if the lame individual could still produce labor, which they were generally able to do in preindustrial North America, physical disability remained unnotable.

Disability, however, remained a central organizing principle. In 1701, as increased settlement pushed each of the Colonies toward increasingly sophisticated regulations, Massachusetts passed the first of many similar statutes. The laws, designed to prevent the "poor, vicious, and infirm" from embarking onto North American ground, required the master of each seagoing vessel to post bonds if any of their passengers embarked as "lame, impotent, or infirm persons, incapable of maintaining themselves." If the captain was unable to provide such a guarantee, he had to return the passenger to their port of embarkation at his own cost.[26] Disability was defined as the inability to "maintain" oneself economically, and those unable to do so were discouraged from ever boarding ship for North America.

DISABILITY, MONSTROUS BIRTHS, AND GENDER DISSIDENTS

There is one sharp exception to the laboring and economic focus of the definition of disability in the early history of North American Europeans: monstrous births. Like the members of some indigenous nations, many Europeans believed that pregnant women with inappropriate thoughts, women who engaged in deviant actions, could produce deviant offspring. Theological and popular literature common in sixteenth- and seventeenth-century England warned that monstrous births signified divine displeasure, and such children were commonly displayed at local fairs. Fetuses or children considered monstrous, whether born alive or dead, were those with extreme bodily variabilities.

In all of the colonial historical record from this period, the births considered most horrific and momentous were those of Mary Dyer and Anne Hutchinson.

Puritan theology emphasized hierarchy and order: just as God lovingly and wisely ruled the people of His kingdom (the Puritan God was male), so must male household heads lovingly and wisely rule their households. While humanity's profoundly sinful nature always tempted one away from God, those who carried out good works and adhered to the community covenant could become one of God's elect. Puritans traveled to North America seeking space to create new communities ordered on their theological framework. Anne Hutchinson, a highly educated woman and the eventual mother of fifteen children, left England as one of many. She, her husband, and their children arrived in Massachusetts in 1634. Onboard ship she and other immigrants had often discussed the sermons they heard. Once in Boston she began hosting theological discussions in her own home. Hutchinson, however, began to emphasize the redemptive nature of God's grace rather than the importance of an individual's good works, and the ability of all to communicate directly with God (rather than through clerical intermediaries) and receive God's forgiveness.

At Hutchinson's heresy trial in November 1637 a minister stated bluntly to her, "You have stept out of your place, you have rather bine a Husband than a Wife and a preacher than a hearer; and a Magistrate than a Subject."[27] Via her actions and her theology, she and those who followed her, including Mary Dyer, subverted clerical hierarchy and by so doing subverted gender and political hierarchies.

In the midst of this, Massachusetts Bay Colony governor John Winthrop accused both Mary Dyer and Anne Hutchinson of monstrous births. Dyer had delivered a stillborn child in October 1637, after which Winthrop testified as follows:

[Dyer] was delivered of a woman Child still-borne (having life a few howers before) two Monthes before the tyme, yet as large as ordinary Children are. The face of it stood soe low into the breast, as the Eares, (which were like an Apes) grewe upon the Shoulders, the Eyes and Mouth stood more out then other Childrens, the Nose grew hooking up-wards, the face had noe parte of heade behind, but a hol-lowe place, yet unbroken. It had no forehead, but in the place thereof, were fower pfect hornes, whereof two were above an Inch long, th-other two somewhat shorter. The breast and Shoulders were full of Scales, & sharpe pricks, like a Thornebacke. The Navell and all the belly, with the distinccon of the Sex were behind the Shoulders, and the backparte, were before the Armes, & legs were as other Children, But instead of toes it had on each foote 3 Clawes with sharpe Talents like a fowle. In the upper parts of the backe behind, yt had two greate Mouthes, and in each, a peece of red flesh sticking out.[28]

In 1638 Hutchinson also had what Winthrop characterized as a monstrous birth. She, he later wrote, "brought forth not one, (as Mistris Dier did) but (which was more strange to amaze-ment) 30 monstrous births or thereabouts, at once . . . some of one shape, some of another; few of any perfect shape, none at all of them . . . of humane shape."[29] Each of the thirty births repre-sented one of Hutchinson's heresies.

After the heresy trial in late 1637, religious leaders excommu-nicated Hutchinson. She, her family, and her remaining follow-ers were exiled to Rhode Island. Years later, in 1660, Dyer was hanged in Boston Commons as a Quaker dissident, likely the first European female hanged in the colonies.

Many women in this period experienced stillbirths or gave birth to children with nonnormative bodies. Indeed, few child-bearing women did not. What, however, does it mean that in this period the two bodies of European descent described as most anomalous, most horrific, and most frightening issued from the bodies of two theologically dissident females? Other women who gave birth to nonnormative children received very little public or theological attention. Of all European women in North America, Hutchinson and Dyer most threatened religious, political, and gender hierarchies. Their supposed monstrous sin manifested itself on the supposed monstrous beings that literally developed in their wombs; and as Joseph Winthrop charged, the act of giving birth to these beings proved the women's sinfulness. As Winthrop insisted, deviant bodies signified maternal sin—the more monstrous the sin, the more monstrous the birthed body. Female challenges to patriarchy and theological power combined to render the bodies of Dyer's and Hutchinson's stillborn children, as well as the bodies of Dyer and Hutchinson, deeply deviant and threatening. Disability was material reality for many European colonists, but it also served as a potent metaphor and symbol.

The colonial theologian Cotton Mather may have considered his stuttering a sign of sin, but like the disabilities of many, it was not thought to have resulted from a sin of great shame, nor was it a matter of great consequence. The same could not be said of Dyer and Hutchinson, female theological dissidents whose stillborn children, in their bodily variability, were considered indicative of dangerous moral deviance.

THREE

THE MISERABLE WRETCHES WERE THEN THROWN INTO THE SEA

The Late Colonial Era, 1700–1776

Samuel Coolidge and his parents must have had big dreams for his future. Born in 1703 in Watertown, Massachusetts, the fifth son of Richard and Susanna Coolidge, the young white man preached in various pulpits and graduated from Harvard in 1738. We remember him, however, not as a great preacher or as a great intellect, but as someone who exemplifies the life of one with psychological disabilities—insanity, as those around him called it—in late colonial America. First and foremost, families provided care. As European colonists became greater in number, however, and more established in their community structures, care for those who needed assistance in caring for themselves, and whose families could not or did not provide it, became the responsibility of individual villages and towns.

THE LIMITS OF COMMUNITY CARE

Coolidge's unruly and unpredictable behavior got him banished from Cambridge, Massachusetts, and sent home to Watertown in 1743. There, Coolidge largely depended on the goodwill of neighbors for food and lodging, but in 1744 he left—"being far gone in Despair, sordidness and viciousness." He wandered back into Watertown in 1749 and the community once again agreed to care for him, but only if he would serve as the town's schoolmaster. Coolidge remained the town's charge for the rest of his life, and taught school when able to do so. When struggling, he wandered the streets of Watertown and Cambridge half-naked, yelling profanities, and disrupting classes at his alma mater. Neighboring towns repeatedly returned him to Watertown. Town officials paid community members to house and feed Coolidge, and sometimes locked him in the schoolhouse at night to make sure that he would be there to teach the next day. In 1763 he worsened, and Watertown residents refused to board him. Selectmen then found someone who agreed to house him if he remained locked up in a room, the room where he stayed until his death in 1764.[1]

Like others with disabilities who could not support themselves and had no family support, Coolidge became the responsibility of his hometown—indeed, other locales refused to care for him and forcibly returned him to Watertown. Watertown was not the only community to "warn out" indigents—with both physical and verbal threats—who were not its own, avoiding fiscal responsibility. Indeed, Onondaga County in upstate New York eventually became known for smuggling paupers into neighboring regions under cover of nightfall. Similarly, in 1785, a blind man named John Skyrme was transferred from one local official to another twenty-four times as he traveled the twenty-one-day journey from Eastchester, New York, back to his home of Providence, Rhode Island.[2]

Only when Coolidge became unmanageable (and clearly a wide spectrum of behavior was tolerated as manageable) did town leaders isolate him in a locked room. Before then townspeople considered him troublesome enough to lock him in the schoolhouse at night but harmless and lucid enough to teach their children. Townspeople expected him to use the skills he had—in his case, an education—to support himself by teaching, and indeed forced him to do so.

Like Coolidge, revolutionary thinker and hero James Otis Jr. (credited with the phrase "taxation without representation is tyranny"), also of Massachusetts, was believed to have developed insanity, but his prior political leadership, and his family's money and stability, meant that he experienced a less traumatic community response. From childhood on, Otis's behavior included actions that others considered unpredictable and incomprehensible. In late 1769, a British tax collector attacked Otis and Otis suffered a significant head wound. After the attack he became, others believed, even less lucid, more violent, and less predictable.

By January 1770, Otis's longtime friend and comrade, future United States president John Adams, wrote, "Otis is in confusion yet. He looses himself. He rambles and wanders like a Ship without an Helm . . . I never saw such an Object of Admiration, Reverence, Contempt and Compassion all at once as this. I fear, I tremble, I mourn for the Man, and for his Country. Many others mourne over him with Tears in their Eyes." Otis's language, Adams said, was full of "Trash, Obsceneness, Profaneness, Nonsense and Distraction." That March, Otis's behavior included what friends termed "mad freaks": he broke windows and fired guns on the Sabbath.[3]

The response of Otis's family was to remove him to their country home in Barnstable. In 1771 the family successfully had Otis declared incompetent, which meant that others had control of his legal and financial affairs. Ultimately the family at Barnstable (in all practical matters, probably the family's servants or slaves) could not cope with Otis's occasional violence. It was not unheard of for respectable men to earn money by housing and caring for those considered insane at their rural homes, and until his death in 1783 Otis generally lived in the care of such men: a Mr. Osgood in Andover and a Captain Daniel Suther of Hull. In Hull,

Otis even taught school for a period—just as Samuel Coolidge had done.[4]

While Otis was still at the family home of Barnstable, Otis's father, James Otis Sr., wrote him a classic letter of parental admonishment. In it the older man not only revealed himself to be an expert in fatherly manipulation but disclosed his beliefs about insanity. Otis's condition, he implied, came because his son succumbed to inner weaknesses that could be shunned by exercising a stronger will and self-control. "Loeving Son," he wrote, "what a dreadful example you are." He insisted that if Otis would only "reform your manners [and] curb that unruly passion which you indulge too much," and pray sincerely to God, all could be well. If Otis would simply "seek to him [God] *sincerely and heartily* for his Grace" a "Reformation of Life and Manners" would result. Considering the "pains and costs I have been at to educate my first born," the father went on, and considering all of the "good prayers you have been the subject of and especially from your good Mother now in *Heaven*," Otis needed to "sett down and seriously consider the way you are now in." Otis Sr. signed the letter, "Afflicted Father."[5]

Otis's colleague and fellow patriot Patrick Henry also lived with psychological disability, but that of his wife. After the 1771 birth of her sixth and last child, Sarah Shelton Henry's behavior became so unmanageable to her family that "she was confined in a cellar room, bound in a straitjacket, and attended by a servant [slave]." (Family memoirs called it "one of the airy, sunny rooms in the half basement" of Scotchtown, the Henry estate in Hanover County, Virginia.) Her family and friends believed her to be insane. She died after several years of confinement at Scotchtown.[6] Her husband's money protected her from the consequences of the poor laws, and we know tantalizingly little about her plight. Given the situation of his wife, one wonders what Patrick Henry thought of the fate of his fellow activist James Otis.

Thomas Jefferson's sister Elizabeth, believed to be an idiot, similarly was protected by familial resources. Her famous brother cared for her financially and she lived in his household.[7] Those in need of community care more frequently entered the domain of the poor laws and public records. Elizabeth Jefferson, protected by family resources and perversely by her legal status of *feme covert* (which meant that she could not own anything and thus had no need to be under adult guardianship), largely remained out of the public record.

In comparison, without family to care for him sufficiently, Thomas Rathburn of Rhode Island entered the public record due to his need for community resources. He avoided the asylum and stayed in his home only by receiving a tax exemption from his local community. For sixteen years he had been unable to "walk one step on foot without crutches or two staves," and had not found work.[8] It is likely that Rathburn, like so many others today (as evidenced by the independent-living movement of the late twentieth century) and in the past, preferred staying in his own home to life in an asylum. It is also likely, however, that Rathburn did not have significant say in the policy decisions of public poor-relief programs.

Rathburn was lucky not to end up institutionalized. Historian Karin Wulf found that in colonial Philadelphia, poor-relief officials were more likely to force men into institutions like an almshouse, but fund women in private homes. This even included paying others to care for them. "Crazy" Mary Charton, for example, could have been sent to an almshouse but instead lived in the home of Elizabeth Heany, who received two shillings and six pence a week to care for her. Wulf also found that in poor-relief applications, men were more likely to be described as having a permanent disability, such as blindness or paralysis, and their disability linked to their inability to work. Women tended to be described simply as poor, though we can assume that many were disabled. Indeed, as mariners, construction workers, horse drivers, and simply as people who spent more time on the streets, exposed to more risks, men had far greater opportunity to be seriously hurt in an industrial accident, and their disabilities became more public. With no form of workers' compensation, such accidents generally ushered the entire family of an injured worker into poverty.[9]

Prior to the Revolution, in the communities of European settlers, those like Coolidge and Otis, like Sara Shelton Henry and Elizabeth Jefferson, who were believed insane or idiots, were confined only if such was considered absolutely necessary. Those exhibiting madness were social irritants and annoying, but madness itself was typically not considered a dangerous threat to be isolated and ostracized at all costs—nor, as in the case of James Otis and Samuel Coolidge, did it keep one from being hired as a schoolteacher. As James Otis Sr. laid it out for his son, individuals could be held accountable for their own madness, but significant social shame did not come from it. As the famed religious leader Cotton Mather wrote regarding his wife in 1719, "I have lived for near a Year in a continual Anguish of Expectation, that my poor wife by exposing her Madness, would bring a Ruin on my ministry. But now it is exposed, my Reputation is marvelously preserved among the People of God."[10]

Indeed, significant evidence exists to suggest that unorthodox behaviors were simply part of everyday life. Unless violent, those considered insane were accepted in society. In Brampton, Massachusetts, residents went about their daily business despite the disruptive behavior of one Jack Downs. Downs regularly enjoyed plucking wigs off the heads of church worshippers with a string and a fishhook, and was well known for throwing rotten apples at the minister during the sermon. Bill Buck, of Hopkinton, lived in the town's almshouse but was not confined there. Townsfolk apparently endured and even enjoyed the insulting speeches he gave residents, as well as the local cornfields, while he roamed the community.[11]

Hopkinton's almshouse was not the only such institution in the rapidly developing Colonies. Almshouses, which began to be in regular use by the end of the colonial period, met many community needs and were a general dumping ground for all those unable to support themselves financially. They also served as correctional institutions. Connecticut's first such institution, for example, established in 1727, was intended to house "all rogues, vagabonds and idle persons going about in town or country begging, or persons . . . feigning themselves to have knowledge in physiognomy, palmistry, or pretending that they can tell fortunes, or discover where lost or stolen goods may be found, common pipers, fidlers, runaways . . . common drunkards, common night-walkers, pilferers, wanton and lascivious persons . . . common railers or brawlers . . . as also persons under distraction and unfit to go at large, whose friends do not take care for their safe confinement."[12] A perception of the need for care or confinement, rather than diagnosis (for one could be a "fidler," a vagabond, or "persons under distraction"), drove this early development of institutionalization.

Similar institutions developed in Rhode Island in 1725, in New York in 1736, and in Pennsylvania in 1752. The Pennsylvania Hospital was intended for "the Reception and Relief of Lunaticks: and other distemper'd and sick Poor within this Province." The New York "Poor-House, Work-House, and House of Correction" similarly welcomed a broad spectrum of people. Virginia opened the doors of the first asylum exclusively for those with mental and cognitive disabilities—"ideots, lunatics, and other persons of unsound minds"—in 1773. The institution sought to "care . . . [for] those whose cases have not become quite desperate . . . [and restrain] others who may be dangerous to society."[13]

Those with cognitive or mental disabilities may have been confined only if considered necessary, but confinement was not pleasant—either at home or in an institution. Sometimes confinement was horrific. Patrick Henry's wife died locked in her cellar. All individuals who entered Connecticut's institution were automatically whipped on the back "not exceeding ten lashes." Those institutionalized as insane in the Pennsylvania Hospital were confined in the institution's cellar and chained by the waist or ankle to the wall. Many wore a "madd-shirt": "a close-fitting cylindrical garment of ticking, canvas, or other strong material without sleeves, which, drawn over the head, reached below the knees, and left the patient an impotent bundle or wrath, deprived of effective motion."[14]

Though horrid in contemporary terms, such conditions are evidence of early efforts to provide curative treatment. The decades surrounding the American Revolution were a period of transition for those with mental and cognitive disabilities, in which some were referred to experts outside of the family and some were not. The little that physicians had to offer generally included bleeding, purging, and blistering, but turning to physicians implied that those involved considered "cure" to be possible. For James Otis Jr., cure involved a simple firming up of self-control—at least according to his father. Increasingly, however, finding a solution (which assumed an identified problem) meant seeking the assistance of individuals outside the family. Those considered available to provide assistance variably were midwives, ministers, and educators, but increasingly physicians.

This was one more manifestation of the American Enlightenment's turn to education and reason, science, and the belief in human capacity (or at least the capacity of some people). The Revolution and the new nation itself would come to be founded on the radical argument of the Enlightenment that citizens, however limited in breadth the category might be, had rights and were capable of reasoned decision making and could be trusted with the vote. As the Declaration of Independence stated, "all men are created equal . . . [and] endowed by their Creator with certain unalienable rights." Given such human potential, and trust in human reason, the new scientific method of thinking held tremendous sway. Advances and attempted advances in medicine and technology presumed that order could be found, solutions achieved, and increased enlightenment would result.

When Cotton Mather (the very same Puritan minister who had considered his stuttering a sign of sin) encouraged smallpox inoculations, and those inoculations resulted in far fewer deaths, many saw it as one more example of an enlightened society's ability to conquer nature. Few recognized or knew that Mather had learned of the beneficial consequences of inoculation from an African-born slave. If science and reason, however, could advance technology, bring forth new political imaginings, and find medical solutions to perceived physical problems, perhaps it could be relied upon for others as well.

The most popular home medical manuals of the period also offered suggestions for the treatment of mental and cognitive disabilities. John Wesley's 1747 *Primitive Physic* suggested treating "lunacy" with a daily ounce of vinegar or applying a boiled blend of ivy, oil, and white wine to one's shaved head every other day for three weeks. "Raging madness" could be treated by applying cold water to the head or eating only apples for a month. (Baldness would be treated by rubbing first an onion and then honey on the afflicted area twice a day.)[15]

The general lack of discussion and institutional acknowledgment of physical disabilities suggests that they simply were not noteworthy among communities of European colonists in the period before the Revolution. Indeed, it suggests that such bodily variations were relatively routine and expected—and accommodations were made, or simply didn't have to be made, to integrate individuals into community labor patterns. And some people simply died. Smallpox and other epidemics routinely ran through colonial towns and villages, resulting in increased deafness, blindness, and skin disfigurements. Undoubtedly, axes occasionally caused one to lose either finger or limb, trees toppled in the wrong direction, children were burned in fires, and guns misfired.

First and foremost, families cared for individuals in the late colonial period—and could do so relatively easily in their own homes: those considered insane, for example, might need only a daily dose of vinegar. Communities of European colonists moved to provide organized care only when and if individuals came to be considered overly disruptive, and when and if families could or did not provide care.

INDIGENOUS NATIONS AND COMMUNAL RESPONSE

The desire and ability to provide consistent familial or community care generally depended on some level of stability, resources, and security. European colonization in North America left few indigenous nations with the ability to provide care on a meaningful and significant scale.

Nearly half the Cherokee nation died when smallpox hit in 1738, as did half the Catawbas of the southeastern coastal region in 1759. When British explorer and navigator George Vancouver first reached Puget Sound in 1792, he met members of the southern Coast Salish nation who already had been scarred and lost vision due to smallpox. In the race among European nations to best one another in gaining greater colonial control of North America, the disease had beaten the Europeans to the continent's northwest coast.[16]

People of the Kiowa nation in what are now Texas, Oklahoma, and New Mexico tell a story in which a Kiowa man encounters Smallpox, riding a horse through the plain.

> The man asks, "Where do you come from and what do you do and why are you here?" Smallpox answers, "I am one with the white men—they are my people as the Kiowas are yours. Sometimes I travel ahead of them and sometimes behind. But I am always their companion and you will find me in their camps and their houses." "What can you do?" the

Kiowa asks. "I bring death," Smallpox replies. "My breath causes children to wither like young plants in spring snow. I bring destruction. No matter how beautiful a woman is, once she has looked at me she becomes as ugly as death. And to men I will not bring death alone, but the destruction of their children and the blighting of their wives. The strongest of warriors will go down before me. No people who have looked on me will ever be the same."[17]

It's likely that indigenous nations that highly valorized the warrior were more rigid in their bodily ideals, and thus less accepting of disability, than groups primarily agricultural or nomadic. The ever-increasing number of European settlers, and their ever-expanding geographical reach, also intensified large- and small-scale military conflicts between indigenous nations and the colonists. In those cases, and in those regions, the ability to battle became far more important for both Native and European men. A successful warrior generally required physical strength, agility, and keen eyesight, hearing, and analytical skills; and while some women excelled at war, most tribes masculinized the ideal. Some individuals simply could not live up to, or it was assumed they could not live up to, the physical and mental demands of the warrior ideal because of their bodies. In nations such as the Aztec and the Iroquois, ideals of leadership thus were more likely to exclude people whose bodies did not meet the high standard set for the community's most esteemed positions. Such exclusion would have resulted in stigma—sometimes harsh, sometimes mild—being attached to those impairments.

"REFUSE" SLAVES AND THE SLAVE TRADE

At the same time indigenous peoples were dying in large numbers and being pushed from the regions of European settlement, Europeans were bringing Africans to North America by force.

The first Africans arrived in North America in 1619, nineteen in number and bearing the legal status of indentured servants—not slaves. By the 1640s, however, European colonists had built slavery into the legal frameworks of colonies both north and south, and Africans landed in the New World as chattel. In 1700, twenty thousand enslaved Africans lived in North America, and by 1790 there were almost seven hundred thousand; by 1860 there were nearly four million. The transportation of slaves into the United States was abolished as of January 1808, but slavery continued legally in some parts of the United States until the Union prevailed in the Civil War in 1865.

The racist ideology of slavery held that Africans brought to North America were by definition disabled. Slaveholders and apologists for slavery used Africans' supposed inherent mental and physical inferiority, their supposed abnormal and abhorrent bodies, to legitimize slavery. Indeed, slaveholders argued that the bodies and minds of those they enslaved were disabled to such an extent that slavery was a beneficial kindness owed to those in need of care. Disability permeated the ideology, experience, and practices of slavery in multiple and profound ways.

Estimated US Slave Population, 1619–1860

Year	Estimated US slave population
1619	19
1700	20,000
1790	697,897
1800	893,041
1810	1,191,364
1820	1,538,038
1830	2,009,050
1840	2,487,455
1850	3,204,313
1860	3,953,760

Source: US Census Bureau

European slave traders built on an already existing slave trade and market within Africa. While important differences existed between the internal and transatlantic African slave trades, the two became intertwined. Within Africa, for example, slavery did not pass from parent to child. Children born of an enslaved mother were born free. Slave traders were in the business to make money. This meant that they sought to enslave people with bodies and minds considered fit for work, people who could command a good price.

In 1701 one slave-trading company wrote directly to the king of Whydah (Ouidah), on the coast of western Africa, characterizing the bodies and minds of those the king's traders should seek out:

> We . . . do desire your Majestie . . . will be pleased to direct ye Buyers never to buy a Negro to be offered to us to sale above 30 years of Age nor lower than 4 ½ foot high . . . nor none Sickly Deformed nor defective in Body or Limb, for we want Negroes as Chargeable in Carriage as ye best. And ye Diseased and ye Aged have often been ye Distruction of ye whole Adventure, so that we must desire that our Negroes be every way perfect & fit for Service and had much Rather at proportionate prices have a boy & a Girle not under 3 ½ foot high to every 5 Men and 5 Women than have any above 30, sickly & deformed.[18]

Age, height, evidence of past disease, or the state of one's limbs thus protected some individuals from being abducted and sold into slavery but did not protect them from violence.

What happened to those whose bodies were considered too disabled for enslavement? The historian Hugh Thomas notes that in slaving raids "old men and women, as well as children, were considered valueless and often killed." This likely included those with physical disabilities that made them ineligible for slavery. On the other hand, Africans with physical abnormalities considered extreme, whose bodies could be exhibited for money, were prized.[19]

Once captured or sold into the slave market, the enslaved began the deadly journey to Africa's western coast. Historians estimate that as many as half of those pressed into slavery suffered the effects of disease, exposure, malnourishment, fatigue, or violence on the overland journey. If they reached the coast alive, they were held in wooden structures; again, with little food, subject to high disease rates, and with already traumatized bodies and minds. More died while awaiting transport.[20]

Sailing across the Atlantic in this period was unpleasant even for those who could afford the best of transports, and it could be deadly for anyone. Crewmembers stayed on the ships far longer than slaves did, and made repeated voyages. More than 20 percent of the crewmembers who sailed on English ships from the Bristol and Liverpool trading companies died during their labor.[21]

Without exception, enslaved individuals experienced the voyage from Africa to North America, known as the Middle Passage, as horrific. Already traumatized and physically embattled, crowded into a ship's hold and into the narrow portions between the ship decks, surrounded by strangers who frequently spoke unfamiliar languages, possibly imprisoned with members of enemy tribes and communities, and often tied or in chains, the enslaved endured a journey that could last from fifty-five to eighty days (depending on ports of departure and arrival). Crewmembers raped women and likely sometimes men. Food and water were inadequate.

In such conditions, disease could spread quickly. One of the most horrendous examples of slave-trade cruelty, and of the consequences of disease and disability, is the story of the French slave ship *Le Rodeur*. Fifteen days into its 1819 voyage, the first symptoms of the "frightful malady" of "ophthamalia" (or ophthalmia, a highly contagious eye disease that can cause blindness) appeared. Crewmembers initially paid little attention to the "considerable redness of the eyes" among the enslaved, crediting it to the scarcity of water: slaves received eight ounces per day (later reduced to "half of a wine glass"). Cases of the disease and its resulting blindness increased quickly, and were made worse by dysentery. Eventually crewmembers were also afflicted. Ultimately, almost forty Africans failed to regain eyesight, twelve lost sight in one eye, and fourteen "were affected with blemishes more or less considerable." Twelve of the crewmembers lost their sight, including the ship's surgeon; and five became blind in one eye, including the captain. Any loss of sight among the enslaved would reduce the trader's profit. As a later government report stated, "even those blind of one eye would sell for a mere trifle."[22]

The end of the story of *Le Rodeur* is best told by J. D. Romaigne, a young boy serving on the ship, in the letters he wrote to his mother:

> This morning the Captain called all hands on deck, negroes and all. The shores of Guad[e]loupe were in sight. I thought he was going to return God thanks publicly for our miraculous escape.
>
> "Are you quite certain," said the mate, "that the cargo is insured?"
>
> "I am," said the Captain. "Every slave that is lost must be made good by the underwriters. Besides, would you have me turn my ship into a hospital for the support of blind negroes? They have cost us enough already. Do your duty."
>
> The mate picked out thirty-nine negroes who were completely blind, and, with the assistance of the rest of the crew, tied a piece of ballast to the legs of each. The miserable wretches were then thrown into the sea.[23]

Since the slave trade existed to make money, disability in a slave resulted in a loss of profit. Following the perverse logic of slavery and the prevailing ableist belief that blind people could not labor—and that "even those blind of one eye would sell for a mere trifle"—the crew simply threw overboard those persons who were worth more to them dead than alive. As poet John Greenleaf Whittier wrote in 1834 about the event,

> Fettered and blind, one after one,
> Plunged down from the vessel's side.
> The sabre smote above,
> Beneath, the lean shark lay,
> Waiting with wide and bloody jaw
> His quick and human prey.[24]

As with nearly all slave-trading ships, the sharks followed in the wake. While clearly not all such voyages ended as horrifically as *Le Rodeur*'s, the devaluing of human beings—and particularly of human beings with disability, considered useless—was omnipresent in the slave trade.

When slave ships landed in North America, slaves with discernible physical, psychiatric, or cognitive disabilities were damaged goods. They became, in the parlance of the time, "refuse slaves." Slave company agents noted disease or disability on a sales invoice in order to justify receiving low prices. When first put up for sale, enslaved Africans with visible disabilities often sold slowly, if at all. In 1680 a Barbados slave agent complained that his cargo had not been sold after three weeks because it included "very ordinary Slaves both Old some Poore & Blind and many burst ones . . . made them ly long on our hands & goe off at low prices." Similarly, South Carolina slave trader Henry Laurens complained about "refuse slaves" in 1755: "We have this day sold forty-two to the amount of £7,455 12 shillings [in] currency, in which are included that sold at vendue [auction] for only £35 12 shillings. They seemed past all hopes of recovery. God knows what we shall do with those that remain, they are a most scabby flock . . . Several have extreme[ly] sore eyes, three very puny children and, add to this, the worst infirmity of all others with which six or eight are attended, viz. old age." Entry ports were often riddled with such slaves, who had been abandoned and left to die.[25]

Many owners and slave traders sold refuse slaves northward. One trader, with a "negro man" characterized as "craizie [and who] does little or noe work," was advised to "dispose of him to ye northward." Northern colonies, however, did not want these undesirables. In 1708 Rhode Island passed one of the first laws attempting to discourage the importation of refuse slaves, describing them as "som[e] Sent for murder Som[e] for thifing Som[e] Runaways & most Impudent Lame & distempred."[26]

The brutality of slavery rendered those who maintained it and benefited from it increasingly horrific and inhumane. The poisonous combination of racism, ableism, and economic drive left slaves with disabilities extremely vulnerable.

The experiences of people with disabilities in colonial America varied tremendously according to one's familial resources (economic as well as physical), race, legal status, gender, and class. For those brought to North America by force and trapped in the slave trade, disability often meant being consigned the status of "refuse," which frequently resulted in abandonment and death. For people of indigenous nations, disability often came as the result of the disease and violence that accompanied European arrival. Native Americans had fewer resources to share with the vulnerable in their communities, and physical abilities became more valued. For disabled people of European descent, the economic resources of one's family often mattered tremendously. Unless one was considered threatening, mental disability could be of relatively benign consequence. For those deemed threatening, even family money and care did not make confinement pleasant.

In the century prior to the creation of the American nation, the legal and economic condition of one's family and community shaped the definitions, experiences, and consequences of disability. Conversely, it shaped the standards and consequences of ableism. Given the lack of even a weak nation-state, the well-being of one's community mattered tremendously.

FOUR

THE DEVIANT AND THE DEPENDENT

Creating Citizens, 1776–1865

By the 1770s, the British government and colonists loyal to it had made their intentions clear to those Europeans living in disparate regions throughout North America. King George and the British Parliament intended to maintain and expand British political and economic control. The French and Spanish governments still had influence, but the British wanted them out. What Great Britain saw as masterful leadership, however, a growing number of colonists considered the illegitimate abuse of power. When unfairly exploited, the Declaration of Independence proclaimed, the people had the responsibility to resist.

King George, the colonial revolutionaries proclaimed, desired their continual subservience. In his paternalism, he sought to make decisions for them. He sought their dependency. Revolutionaries such as Thomas Paine, John Adams, James Otis, and, later, Otis's sister, Mercy Otis Warren, argued that they were not children—indeed, as human beings they had basic rights, they desired and were entitled to a say in their government, and they could govern themselves.

In the decades following the American Revolution, the new nation sought to define and distinguish between good and bad citizens. Democracy was a grand and potentially dangerous experiment that presumed its citizens could and would make reasoned political decisions. How could the new republic survive unless the bodies and minds of its citizens were capable, particularly its voting citizens? Political theorists contrasted idiots, lunatics, women of all races, people of indigenous nations, and African Americans with those considered worthy of full citizenship. States increasingly developed disability-based voting exclusions, alongside and often as a part of those of race and gender. Inherent to the creation of the United States was the legal and ideological delineation of those who embodied ableness and thus full citizenship, as apart from those whose bodies and minds were considered deficient and defective.

The process of differentiating between fit and unfit citizens raised many legal, ideological, and practical questions. How could unfitness be determined? When was it threatening? Could the unfit be salvaged? If so, how?

DEMARCATING CATEGORIES

Legal frameworks provided some solutions to those shaping the nation's legal, economic, and civic structures. Racist ideologies defined male and female African Americans as fundamentally inferior specimens with deformed bodies and minds who were best confined to slavery. Indigenous peoples were killed or removed, and generally made ineligible for citizenship. And like these other categories, but often privileged by whiteness, most white women remained as *feme coverts*—legal nonentities determined unfit for civic life. Disability, as a concept, was used to justify legally established inequalities.

The post-Revolutionary years as well as the first part of the nineteenth century brought a rapid expansion of private and public institutions that increasingly categorized and organized those people considered unfit. Historian David Rothman argued in 1971 that the vast multiplication of institutions for "the deviant and the dependent" represents the post-Revolutionary unease with disorder. Driven by a democratic republic's need for a competent voting citizenry, the nation sought to regulate and impose order via institutions. The social changes wrought by the twin forces of early industrialization and urbanization—such as children who no longer had to rely on parents as their only source of economic development, wage laborers who sought greater control over their work, and those who journeyed westward to escape growing regulation—only heightened concern about unruly chaos. The nation sought to transform the questionable citizen into a good one and confine those either refusing or incapable of transformation. While institutions each had varying histories, they shared the underlying assumption that human behavior could be managed and altered through professional intervention.[1]

Whether Rothman is accurate or not, the creation of institutions and the increasing regulation that accompanied them further defined the normal and the abnormal, ableness and disability. White citizens considered insane, idiotic, or unable to support themselves economically due to physical difference were increasingly institutionalized, and voting restrictions based on justifications of mental inadequacy expanded. States and the federal government began to strengthen immigration laws that restricted entrance to those considered disabled. Individuals considered unfit but redeemable or deserving received educational opportunities. Founded in 1817, the Connecticut Asylum for the Education and Instruction of Deaf and Dumb Persons is just one example of institutional creation often experienced as empowering and liberating. Its students and advocates established similar schools in a widening expanse all over the country—and perhaps the leadership of those in its target population, deaf people, further made the difference. Those whose bodies or minds were believed to be beyond redemption were variably warehoused or removed. Their leadership in institutional development was definitely not encouraged. Perceived intellect, bodily capacity, race, class, gender, ethnicity, and circumstance all intersected to determine one's civic competency.

When individuals and groups denied full citizenship sought to claim it, they consequently often used language of disability and able-bodiedness. For example, in 1791 an unnamed contributor to the *Universal Asylum and Columbian Magazine* warned of the deleterious effect of limiting women's education. No one should be surprised, the author wrote, at the "pale-faced, decrepid, weak, deformed women, daily presented to view, who have been tortured into a debility which renders their existence wretched."[2] The nation required women's education, the author insisted, in order to ensure able-bodied women that it might succeed in its grand experiment of democracy. How could women— if deformed and decrepit—help the new nation at such a critical moment? Embedded in these arguments was the unstated premise that good citizens were citizens able and competent in all ways.

When advocates for women met at the Seneca Falls Women's Rights Convention of 1848, they made their claims for equal citizenship by emphasizing their own civic fitness—again, often silently contrasting it with those seen as lacking. Attendees resolved that "the equality of human rights results necessarily from the fact of the identity of the race in its capabilities and responsibilities." Abolitionist and former slave Frederick Douglass agreed, similarly asserting that "the true basis of rights was the capacity of individuals."[3]

The new, expanding, and solidifying republic required the maintenance and policing of competent citizens. Ideologies of racism, sexism, as well as ableism supported and contributed to the demarcation of full citizenship but certainly did not exclude all identified as disabled. Within only a few decades of the Revolutionary War, disabled veterans pleasantly found that as a whole their familial, employment, and economic conditions varied little from those of their able-bodied male neighbors.

REMARKABLE UNREMARKABLENESS: DISABLED WAR VETERANS

When Ebenezer Brown of Newton, Massachusetts, left home to fight in the American Revolution, he was a young man. Like most young people, he had dreams and plans but no idea how his life would play out. By 1820 he was sixty-three years old, had recently married for the second time, and had two children: a daughter, Elizabeth, and a son, Frederick, "who is a cripple." While fighting in the 1777 Battle of Saratoga, Brown had received "a severe wound in the shoulder." Because of his "utter inability to labor," he sought a pension. "Few men," his 1820 pension petition detailed, "served longer in the Revolutionary army suffered more in that service or remain in more destitute circumstances." Like 87 percent of the veterans seeking a pension, Brown's disability resulted from an injury incurred in combat.[4]

Brown survived the Revolutionary War: its diseases (90 percent of those who died in the war died from disease), its medical treatment (a wound in a limb often resulted in amputation; a midthigh leg amputation had a 65 percent mortality rate), and its accidentally exploding guns. Going in, he likely had no idea that he had a better chance of dying than of being wounded and surviving.[5]

It is likely that Brown had never been hospitalized before the war. Most European colonists, whatever their class status, received medical treatment in the home: their own, a neighbor's, or a doctor's. The Continental Army quickly tried to establish both field and general hospitals, converting taverns, town halls, and the confiscated property of those loyal to the Crown. Not only were soldiers unaccustomed to seeking medical care in a hospital, but the hospitals sometimes provided nothing but a roof. They often lacked food, bedding, and even beds, and what medical care they offered was limited. General Anthony Wayne called the Ticonderoga hospital a "house of carnage." William Hutchinson remembered the hospital he entered as "a most horrid sight. The floor was covered with blood; amputated arms and legs lay in different places in appalling array." Often those needing surgery (mostly amputation) waited in the same room where doctors were operating on those before them in line.[6] Thus Brown was likely unaccustomed to the thought of hospitalization, but in addition, he may have actively sought to avoid it.

After receiving his shoulder wound, Brown may have instead returned home for medical care, as did many soldiers and as would have been the norm in nearly all cases of injury. For example, after being shot in the leg during the Battle of Bunker Hill, Benjamin Farnum's friend John Barker dragged him from the battlefield. His family, close by in Andover, received news that he'd been injured. Before the day was over, a horse-drawn carriage, quickly adapted for Farnum's damaged leg, had carried him home. His family provided his medical care. Or perhaps, like fellow soldier Richard Vining, Brown hired someone to convey him to his home after being wounded.[7]

What we do know about Brown is that when he sought a pension, he met the criteria. He proved his military service, a legitimate military cause of disability, and the inability to labor for wages. The Revolutionary War Pension Act of 1818 established disability as a legal and social welfare category. The act assumed that impairments such as blindness, an amputated leg, or a hand mangled in a horse-and-carriage accident did not render one disabled according to early-nineteenth-century definitions. Under the Pension Act, disability was the inability to perform economically productive labor.

Large numbers of disabled veterans, however, found employment: 49 percent as farmers, 27 percent as skilled laborers such as coopers or blacksmiths. A small number with class background sufficient to seek an education became teachers or preachers, skilled labor that required little physical exertion. Disabled veterans worked at the same types of jobs, in roughly the same proportions, as nondisabled veterans. Even more remarkably, as historian Daniel Blackie has found, the work and poverty rates of disabled and nondisabled veterans were markedly similar in 1820.[8]

Ebenezer Brown and his first wife, Catherine, had been married for over twenty-five years when she died. The fact that Brown, our disabled veteran with the shoulder injury, had married and raised two children was unremarkable—which in itself is remarkable. Today people with disabilities have lower marital and family rates than those without disabilities. Disabled Revolutionary War veterans labored, married, had children, and had households typical in size and structures, at rates nearly identical to their nondisabled counterparts.

When Bristol Rhodes left Cranston, Rhode Island, to fight in the Revolution, he too had hopes and expectations, perhaps even greater than Brown's. In 1778 Rhode Island's General Assembly had proclaimed that "every able-bodied negro, mulatto, or Indian man slave" who passed the military's muster would "be absolutely FREE." Born a slave in 1755, the twenty-three-year-old Rhodes would have desired freedom greatly. He joined the army and served for three years before being shot by a cannon and losing a leg and a hand. After being injured, Rhodes returned to Cranston, where he had been a slave, but in 1789 he moved to Providence. He lived on the pension he received from the new Congress, which only issued pensions intermittently; by April 1790, for example, Congress owed Rhodes approximately $26. Rhodes's home became a center of community life for other free African Americans. His military service, and undoubtedly the life he led afterward, generated respect from many in Providence, both black and white. When he died in 1810 the local newspaper eulogized him as "a black man of the Revolution."[9] He never again worked for a living but became an integral part of the community.

The new nation's economic structures, the growing market economy, and the ways in which households worked together to complete tasks meant that people with impairments could and did participate in productive labor. One simply made accommodations or adjustments, and relied on the support of others where necessary. The later concentration of industrialization and capitalism would make that more difficult.

RACE AND (IN)COMPETENT CITIZENSHIP

The post–Revolutionary War period makes clear the legal and intellectual ties between labor and civic expectations. As free men, Revolutionary War veterans (black and white) were expected to engage in economically productive labor. For white women, the expectation was not that universal. If indentured servants, if housemaids, if members of a shoemaking family, their household (and often the law) expected them to labor. What kind of physical, care, and supervisory labor they did and were expected to do varied according to class, age, and marital status. The perceived deficiencies of their bodies and minds, however, made them ineligible for certain kinds of work. The bodies and minds of enslaved African Americans also (but often in different ways) were considered too deformed for some jobs but well suited to manual, reproductive, and household labor.

White women and enslaved African Americans generally could not own their own labor in the ways that white men could. They had few if any legal rights to make decisions about and manage the economic fruits of their labor. Given that disability was defined as the inability to labor, white women, free African American women, and slaves came to be associated with the disabled. Political theory linked the denial of property rights with the embodiment of supposed deficiencies.

Slavery and racism rested on the ideology that Africans and their descendants in North America lacked intelligence, competence, and even the humanity to participate in civic and community life on an equal basis with white Americans. Slave owners, medical experts, theologians, the drafters of the US Constitution, and nearly all parts of the dominant Euro-American society argued that both slave and free African Americans were disabled mentally and physically. The concept of disability justified slavery and racism—and even allowed many whites to delude themselves, or pretend to delude themselves, that via slavery they beneficently cared for Africans incapable of caring for themselves.[10]

Thomas Jefferson, whose contradictory and uneasy relationship with race continues to plague our national identity, wrote in his 1800 *Notes on the State of Virginia* that although "in memory they [slaves] are equal to the whites," they were "in reason much inferior . . . in imagination they are dull, tasteless, and anamolous [*sic*]." Because they "seem to require less sleep," slaves could be made to work long hours.[11]

In the 1839 *Crania Americana*, Samuel George Morton "proved" that European descendants had larger skulls, thus larger brains and greater intelligence, than African Americans. Medical doctor Samuel Cartwright, perhaps one of the most influential proponents of scientific racism, argued in his 1848 "The Diseases and Physical Peculiarities of the Negro Race" that "blacks' physical and mental defects made it impossible for them to survive without white supervision and care." Cartwright even turned the desire not to be enslaved into physical defects to which the inferior black body was predisposed: drapetomania caused the enslaved to attempt escape; hebetude caused laziness, shiftiness, and the damaging of property such as farm tools; and dysaethesia aethiopica was the psychotic desire to destroy an owner's property. According to Cartwright, these conditions all developed due to and within the defective black body. Similarly, in the 1840s prominent surgeon Josiah C. Nott warned that African Americans were not "sufficiently enlightened to qualify . . . for self-government," maintaining that the cold of northern climates "freezes their brains as to make them insane or idiotical."[12]

The "experts" of scientific racism also expressed their racist ideology in gendered terms. In 1843 Knott invited the readers of the *American Journal of Medical Sciences,* a leading medical journal founded in 1820 and read by a variety of intellectuals, to "look first upon the Caucasian female with her rose and lily skin, silky hair, Venus form, and well chiseled features—and then upon the African wench with her black and odorous skin, woolly head and animal features—and compare their intellectual and moral qualities, and their whole anatomical structure." Their intellectual, moral, and physical defects, Knott believed, would be clear. He also pointed out that American Indians had "many peculiarities which are just as striking."[13] The deficiencies of enslaved women supposedly also included animalistic and uncontrollable sex drives.

While slave owners and the intellectuals who supported them used the concept of disability to justify slavery, abolitionists used disability to argue against slavery. White and black abolitionists emphasized the physical and psychological damages wrought by slavery, the abuses experienced by slaves with disabilities, and the debilitating and forced dependency of slavery. The literature and fiery speeches of abolitionists detailed the scars, the incapacitating beatings, and the horrific impairments caused by slavery in order to emphasize its depravity and cruelty. Abolitionists displayed—in text, illustrations, and in person—the crippled, disfigured, and disabled bodies of enslaved persons as moral suasion.

The 1840 Massachusetts Anti-Slavery Society's annual report argued, "He [the slave] is weak and unable to move. Why is he so? Because your dominion has palsied him. Will any man, who pretends to a jolt of philosophy, deny that it is *slavery* that has disabled the slave?" Abolitionists implied that emancipation would heal the bodies and minds of African Americans from the metaphorically and literally disabling consequences of slavery. Freed from coerced dependency and inequality, they would enter society as "independent, hard-working (and by implication, able-bodied) citizens."[14] The palsying, disabling results of slavery would disappear with freedom.

Abolitionists were right that slavery significantly damaged the bodies and minds of enslaved African Americans. Slavery involved significant and often repetitive physical labor, inadequate subsistence and housing, poor working conditions, corporal punishment, and emotional, physical, and sexual abuse. Runaway-slave advertisements include frequent mention of "bowlegged" or "bandy-legged" slaves, sometimes indicating dietary deficiencies, as well as descriptions of deaf slaves, details of gunshot wounds, cropped ears, significantly scarred slaves, those with improperly healed fractures, lame slaves as well as those with fingers or toes lost to frostbite, limbs lost in accident, and those who stuttered. For example, an 1815 advertisement in the *Richmond Enquirer* sought a runaway named Doctor, who "once had his right arm broken, in consequence of which, his arm is smaller & shorter than the left one, and stands a little crooked."[15]

While abolitionists used the advertisements for runaway slaves to note the horrors of slavery, such notices also indicated that slaves with disabilities had not lost their will or ability to resist slavery. For example, Bob, a New Orleans slave who had an amputated leg, stole away from his master in 1840 with the assistance of a crutch. The abolitionist and women's rights activist Sojourner Truth had, in her words, "a badly diseased hand, which greatly diminished her usefulness" to her master but not for future political activism and leadership. A slave named Peggy was "very much parrot toed and walks badly," but similarly ran away from her Virginia master in 1798.[16] Another, Jonathan, was deaf, and yet managed to escape—with a horse—in 1774.

RUN away, about the 20th of July, from the subscriber, in Fauquier, a mulatto man slave named Jonathan, about 26 years old, 5 feet 9 or 10 inches high, is deaf, two of his toes are joined together, reads tolerably well, and had on a brown linen coat, russia drilling breeches, a new felt hat bound, white dowlass shirt, and new store shoes; he also took with him a small black trotting horse, and a middle sized sprightly black mare, which paces and gallops, has a large scar on the near thigh, and branded on the same with HK in a piece. Whoever secures the said slave in any gaol in this colony, north of James river, so that I get him again, shall have 3 l. if on the south side of James river, 5 l. and if in either of the Carolinas, or in any of the other colonies, 10 l. It is expected he will make for the Carolinas. HOUSEN KENNER.[17]

Even those unlikely to run away could and sometimes chose to resist. Abolitionist and escaped slave Lewis Clark told a Brooklyn audience of such an act of resistance by "an old slave, who was the most abused man I ever did see." The man's master had beaten him "till he had hardly a sound joint in his body. His face was all smashed up, and his right leg was broken to pieces." When the enslaved man "got old and a cripple, he wan't worth much," and the master sought to get rid of him. Not wanting to drown the elderly slave himself, the master "thought he'd contrive to make him drown his self." The slave owner "drove" the older man into a pool of water, "and kept throwing stones at him to make him go further in." The slave caught the stones with his hat: "This made the master so mad, that he waded in with a whip, to drive him further." Though the elderly enslaved man had been disregarded as physically ineffectual, "cripple as he was, he seized hold of his master, and kept ducking him, ducking him, without mercy." Clark concluded that the elderly man meant to drown his owner, and may have done so if "the neighbors hadn't come and saved him."[18]

The enslaved man physically strong enough to drown his owner likely would have been characterized as "unsound," for slave owners determined the labor capacity of those that they enslaved based on "soundness." Bills of sale, plantation records, wills, and judicial records frequently listed enslaved people by this quality—a measure of a slave's physical, moral, and mental capacity for laboring in a competent but subservient manner. Laws required those selling slaves to disclose any known or suspected unsoundness, for, as we have seen, any perceived loss of labor capacity diminished a slave's economic worth. Slave trader Samuel Browning, for example, had to provide an exchange for Rose, a woman he had sold, because she was "an Ediot." Blindness or diminished vision was a particular concern for owners, not only because it limited the kinds of duties a slave could perform and reduced their economic value but also because it was possible to fake.[19]

Slave owners feared fakery. Owners and overseers tended to challenge any sensory disability, as well as madness, infertility, or epilepsy ("fits") out of a suspicion that slaves falsely claimed disability in order to avoid labor. Malingering was a related concern. It not only represented economic loss but played on the slave owners' fear that their slaves, those they deemed inferior in every respect, were outwitting them.[20]

Slaves with disabilities, despite often being listed as "unsound," labored. For example, in a list of those that he enslaved in the 1830s, Samuel Barker, of Charleston, South Carolina, noted some as "useless." The "useless," however, performed significant and vital labor: as historian Dea Boster has noted, "Among the slaves identified as 'useless' were Old Stephen, who 'rakes trash'; Old Betty, a nurse and midwife; Peggy, who 'cooks for negroes'; Bess, a 23-year-old 'feeble' woman who 'can cook'; and Old Minda, a 'first rate midwife and nurse.'" Others with disabilities worked in the fields, cared for nurseries that could include up to thirty children, or did household labor. A one-armed carpenter named Aaron engaged in skilled labor on Edmund Ravenel's South Carolina plantation. One memoir of the time even noted a blind slave who daily drove the breakfast cart out to those working in the cotton fields, presumably a route that both he and the draft animals knew well.[21] Clearly, many disabled slaves engaged in valued and skilled labor.

Their reproductive capacities meant that women experienced slavery and disability differently than men. Childbirth often resulted in disability for women regardless of race, but enslaved women forced into physical labor soon after childbirth more frequently endured prolapsed uteruses, a disabling condition in which the uterus partially protrudes from the vagina, causing near-constant pain and painful sex, difficult and limited mobility, and dangerous future pregnancies. The realities of slavery also meant that enslaved women were more likely than other women to endure vesicovaginal fistula, a condition generally resulting from difficult births or the misuse of forceps, in which urine continually leaks from the vagina due to a tear between the vaginal and bladder walls. The smell, mess, and embarrassment often meant that such women were socially isolated.

If an enslaved woman gave birth to a child with a disability, childbirth not only endangered her but meant greater fears for that child's future. Children born with bodies considered significantly abnormal faced an uncertain future, and their mothers' reproductive worth was questioned. Children considered "monsters" or "monstrosities"—either dead or alive—could be taken from parents and their bodies placed on public display for the white community: in disturbingly similar ways to a slave market. One of the most famous examples is that of Millie and Christine McKoy, conjoined twins born enslaved who were displayed for profit by their owner.[22]

One of the vicious tenets of scientific racism was that African Americans did not feel physical pain or anxiety due to their racially defective bodies. Either convinced of this or simply not caring, slave owner and medical doctor James Marion Sims, today often considered a founder of modern gynecology, performed years of "nightmarishly painful and degrading experiments, without anesthesia or consent, on a group of slave women." He eventually perfected the surgery that could alleviate a vesicovaginal fistula, but only after years of physically restraining enslaved women during forced vaginal surgeries. He performed over thirty such surgeries on an enslaved woman named Anarcha and scores more on numerous other individuals.[23]

African American slaves felt a strong obligation to care for all in their community. Absent institutional structures on which to draw, they generally had to rely on one another. Mothers, for example, knew that if they were sold apart from their children or were otherwise unable to care for them, other women in the slave quarters would take on their role. The elderly and those who needed physical or cognitive assistance also had faith that their community would care for them as much as possible.

While the members of enslaved communities tried to provide care for one another, the larger white society often made that extremely difficult. Despite varying state laws against it, it was not unheard of for slave owners to "free" their very elderly or disabled slaves and leave them without support in southern cities. Frederick Douglass remembered his cousin Henny, disabled by severe burns in childhood, being "set adrift to take care of herself . . . a helpless child, to starve and die" after her master gave up on literally beating her into the kinds of labor he desired. Nor was it unheard of for owners to send elderly or blind slaves into isolated cabins in the woods, leaving them to fend for themselves. It galled Douglass that even after a religious conversion, his master Thomas Auld chose to hold "with tight grasp the well-framed and able-bodied slaves . . . who in freedom could have taken care of themselves" but turned "loose the only cripple among them, virtually to starve and die."[24]

Debates about race, disability, and the state of the nation forcefully entered the public arena around the 1840 census. Each year the census had asked additional questions about the bodies of its citizenry. The 1830 census had recorded, for the first time, the numbers of deaf, blind, and "dumb" residents. The 1840 census added a query about "insane and idiot" residents (one category). Census results indicated that free blacks had a rate of insanity and idiocy nearly eleven times more than the enslaved. In Maine, a free state, the census indicated that 1 of every 14 black persons was insane or an idiot; in Louisiana, a slave state, that number was 1 in every 5,650. Indeed, according to the 1840 census, insanity and idiocy seemed to run rampant in the non-slave states: one out of every 162 African Americans in the North were supposedly insane or idiots, but only one out of every 1,558 in the South.[25]

Slavery advocates pounced on this data as proof of the incapacity of African Americans, the deleterious effects of freedom, and the nation's moral obligations to maintain the practice. Slavery, apologists continued to insist, was the humane response to the deficient bodies of African Americans. The most publicized pro-slavery response to the census insisted that "the free negroes of the northern states are the most vicious persons on this continent, perhaps on the earth," with distressingly high rates of insanity and idiocy. Conversely, slaves were "not only far happier in a state of slavery than of freedom, but we believe the happiest class on this continent." Freedom, argued the pro-slavery interpreters of the 1840 census, resulted in insanity and imprisonment for African Americans unfortunate enough to no longer be enslaved.[26]

Mathematician Edward Jarvis pointed out gross errors, likely purposeful, in census calculations beginning in 1842, but the federal government never altered the 1840 census results. Jarvis noted, for example, that at least twenty-one Northern towns with only twelve black residents each were reported to have at least fifty-six insane or idiot black residents.[27] To Jarvis, the point was scientific accuracy. To others, of course, the debate concerned racial ideology (or racism) and the legal and social frameworks necessary to keep a democracy functioning.

Debates regarding the role of indigenous people in a democratic nation were more muted in the dominant public sphere than those regarding African Americans, but only because death became the de facto strategy. Disease epidemics and their consequences continued to kill and disable huge numbers of people from indigenous nations. The numbers are almost too horrifying to comprehend. Indigenous communities repeatedly experienced death and cultural devastation. In 1738 nearly half of the remaining Cherokees died during a smallpox epidemic; similar outbreaks affected the Catawbas in 1759 and the Piegan nation during the Revolutionary War. Approximately two-thirds of the Omahas died after European expansion facilitated by the Louisiana Purchase of 1803, and some historians esti nearly half of the population residing between New M the Missouri River died of smallpox in the same period. In the 1820s, as many as 80 percent of the Columbia River area people died in a fever epidemic.[28] Communities simply could not care for one another in the circumstances, and many who did not die as a result of the epidemic lost their lives in the resulting chaos. Once again, smallpox left many of those who survived blind and scarred.

The areas of devastation spread as Europeans traveled across North America with continued goals of conquest, religious conversion, the acquisition of "unowned" farmland, and economic trade. Permanent Spanish colonizers arrived in the coastal California region of the Tongva people in 1771. Colonial practices, such as forcibly separating female children from their parents and locking them in female barracks called *monjerios,* exacerbated the spread of disease. It's estimated that the Tongva population declined 78 percent in the years after Spanish arrival and that children's life expectancy averaged 6.4 years. Grazing animals introduced by the Spanish, and allowed to roam, depleted Tongva food supplies and further disrupted subsistence. Similarly, the Tongva's neighbors, the Chumash, endured at least seven deadly epidemics in the first forty-nine years of Spanish and Mexican occupation.[29]

INSTITUTIONS, MEDICALIZATION, AND TREATMENT

In the colonial period, disability was only one of many reasons why residents of European settlements might need assistance. Families had the first responsibility to care for those considered dependent. If families could not provide care, such care became the community's responsibility. How, or why, or due to what diagnosis one became indigent mattered little in the colonial period.

In the early national period, however, the diagnostic explanation of indigence mattered profoundly.[30] Indeed, expertise and diagnoses increasingly dominated evaluations of bodies and minds. This happened, not surprisingly, simultaneous to an expansion in the professionalization of medicine. Physician training slowly became standardized throughout the early nineteenth century, as those without access to formal education (such as female midwives) were slowly pushed from the medical trade. Physicians increasingly held diagnostic control, and thus treatment control. Medical determinations increasingly justified inequalities such as slavery and determined citizenship status. For example, medical expertise regarding women's biological deficiencies buttressed the exclusion of white women from higher education, voting, and property ownership. Similarly, between the Revolutionary War and the passage of the 1818 Revolutionary War Pension Act, those administering veteran pensions slowly began to require that doctors (rather than local shop owners, neighbors, or ministers) determine impairments.

Across the new republic, beginning first in New England but spreading south and westward, public and private groups thus nearly fell over one another in efforts to establish insane asylums, schools for deaf and blind people, community hospitals for those in poverty, and schools for the feeble-minded and idiots. Public education expanded quickly. Religious reform movements emphasized the need for good works and human redemption. Even elite boarding schools, for both girls and boys, grew in number.

Solutions were sought. The number of institutions that defined normative and deviant bodies and minds grew dramatically, both public and private, with recipients willing and coerced.

In 1817 Laurent Clerc and Thomas Hopkins Gallaudet founded the nation's first disability-specific institution in the United States, the American Asylum for the Deaf, in Hartford, Connecticut. Among others, its students would include the famous painter John Brewster Jr. As Clerc explained it, using himself as an example, the asylum would transform "those unfortunate beings who . . . would be condemned all their life, to the most sad vegetation" from "the class of brutes to the class of men." "Regenerative hands" would redeem deaf Americans, just as they had done for Clerc himself at the national school for deaf students in Paris. The American Asylum and many other early schools were part of the wave of evangelical Protestantism that flooded the United States in the early nineteenth century, guided by the mission of using sign language to share Christianity with those formerly isolated from its blessings. By the 1850s, deaf churches, publications, advocacy organizations, sports teams, literary societies, and residential schools had fostered a rich and growing deaf culture and community. In 1864, at the encouragement of Thomas and Sophia Fowler Gallaudet's son Edward Gallaudet, the US Congress authorized and formally recognized the National Deaf-Mute College (renamed Gallaudet College in 1894). With the expansion of deaf schools and communities in the nineteenth century, literacy, education rates, and economic success rates for deaf people rose significantly.[31]

Just as Clerc believed that education could transform both individuals and society, physician and abolitionist Samuel Gridley Howe argued that society had an obligation to educate those in its midst to their fullest extent. If society was to progress, and it could, Howe argued, it had to improve the lives of all. "The terrible ills which now infest society are not necessarily perpetual," Howe insisted. "The ignorance, the depravity, the sufferings of one man, or of one class of men, must affect other men, and other classes of men." Therefore, "the interest and the duty of society are common and inseparable." All, even idiots, he argued, could be taught economic productivity and some could become self-sufficient.[32]

Howe led efforts to create schools for blind students, deaf-blind students, and idiots (including Boston's Perkins School for the Blind in 1829, whose students included Laura Bridgman, Anne Sullivan, and Helen Keller, in Massachusetts). Similarly, students from the Connecticut Asylum for the Education of Deaf and Dumb Persons established other such schools in a widening expanse all over the country. Not everyone, however, had the resources, opportunities, or desire to leave home and enter an educational institution. The southern states generally had fewer institutional opportunities, and those available were segregated and of lower quality than those in the North. Parents of elite southern white deaf and blind children, however, often hesitated to send their children northward. Too much overlap existed between abolitionists and the educational reformers leading such institutions.[33]

It thus should be no surprise that understandings of disability transformed profoundly in the post–Revolutionary War period. Theological and supernatural explanations of madness began to be replaced by biological explanations. For example, prior to 1825 the Supreme Court had always referred to madness as "that most calamitous visitation from Providence." After 1825, the Court began referring to it as a "disease."[34] Harvard established the nation's first medical college in 1782 and medicine slowly became standardized. With badges of authority and expertise, doctors and educational experts embraced and then defended the tasks of explaining, diagnosing, and treating physical and intellectual differences. And even when not in institutions, people with disabilities and their families increasingly interacted with and relied on medical authorities.

Although experts became increasingly dominant, cultures continued to clash over definitions of madness. For example, in 1798 members of the Cree nation brought a man whom they considered dangerous to the Hudson's Bay Company settlement of York Factory on the southwestern shore of the bay. The Cree lived in a region that stretched from the Great Lakes into what is now northern Canada and sold furs to the HBC. The fur traders of the York region treated the man, whom they believed was insane, by bleeding him—a common practice among the European colonists. HBC employees deemed the man much improved after the procedure, but he fled against their wishes. To the Cree, insanity was a meaningless concept; they believed the man was a *windigo,* a person possessed by the spirit of winter, made asocial, cruel, and consumed by cannibal desires. HBC traders were concerned that the man's being on the loose would disrupt the upcoming goose hunt (or at least their ability to make money from it). Similarly, in 1816 a Cree man named Achappee warned the HBC's James Clouston of a fellow Cree named Mistaenyu. Achappee likely believed he risked his life by informing Clouston of a man he was convinced was a windigo, who would "kill every person that he could see; [and] that sometimes . . . walks in the air invisible from where he can do Mischief" and feasted on human beings. Clouston believed Mistaenyu to be insane, "afflicted in so distressing a manner."[35] Similar reports of differing perceptions continued to be reported throughout the nineteenth and into the twentieth century.

People of European descent considered to be insane, who likely would have remained unconfined in the colonial period unless considered dangerous, increasingly found themselves restrained in the years following the Revolutionary War—particularly in the northern states. A Massachusetts law of 1796, for example, allowed local authorities to confine the mad, without a formal process, to the local jail for years.[36] Almshouses, prisons, and asylums often served as catch-all institutions; confining moral transgressors (poor pregnant women with no husbands), heavy drinkers, those considered idiotic or insane, people with "fits" (epilepsy), and others about whom local officials felt uneasy.

"Treatment," even when administered while at home, varied considerably. Doctors frequently used purging, bleeding, frights, hard labor, and immersion in cold water. Mary Sewall, treated for insanity at her home in Maine in 1824, was restrained to a specially designed chair for seventy-three days, bled copiously, and given a highly restricted diet. Two local physicians visited the home to supervise the care given to the twenty-five-year-old white woman. No insane asylums existed in Maine. Sewall died six months after her treatment began, possibly because of these interventions.[37] Despite the state's lack of available institutions, Sewall's case is an example of the medicalization of madness.

While Sewall's "cure" clearly did not help her, institutionalization was not necessarily a better alternative. The appalling conditions that Dorothea Dix encountered while touring homes for the indigent insane in Massachusetts pushed her to engage in political reform efforts. While giving religious instruction in asylums, a not uncommon practice among Boston women of her religious background and class, Dix encountered criminals, idiots, and the insane confined together, in "cages, closets, cellars, stalls, pens! Chained, naked, beaten with rods, and lashed into obedience." Dix was shocked by the lewd language, lack of heat in winter, inadequate food, and general abuse that pervaded these institutions. Her 1843 "Memorial to the Legislature of Massachusetts" listed the horrors of every asylum in the state, including the one in Westford: "Grant that I may never look upon another such scene! A young woman, whose person was partially covered with portions of a blanket, sat upon the floor; her hair disheveled; her naked arms crossed languidly over the breast; a distracted, unsteady eye and low, murmuring voice betraying both mental and physical disquiet. *About the waist was a chain,* the extremity of which was fastened into the wall of the house." Using the moral righteousness and authority attributed to her class, gender, and race, Dix made a career for herself, publicizing and attempting to improve asylum conditions.[38]

The efforts of Howe and others to educate and thus institutionalize idiots, and likely many other communities of people with disabilities, had complex consequences. In the 1830s and 1840s most children and adults with cognitive disabilities from families who were not indigent lived at home and were integrated into the community. Kemp Battle of North Carolina remembered going to school in Raleigh in the 1830s: "We had in school a half-witted boy who was not expected to learn anything but was sent to school to keep him out of mischief." In the same decade, Thomas Cameron, a white adult man with cognitive disabilities in rural North Carolina, attended local events, had a job carrying messages and at the local post office, and was adored by the nieces and nephews of his affluent family. And famed writer Margaret Fuller insisted that her younger brother Lloyd go to school, for "[even] if he does not learn much in lessons the influence on his character and manners is better."[39]

Building on the work of French educator Edouard Séguin, in the late 1840s, Samuel Gridley Howe, Hervey Wilbur, and other Americans began to make the argument that idiots could be educated. In 1847 Howe undertook a major survey of Massachusetts, finding 574 "human beings who are condemned to their hopeless idiocy" lived there and had been "left to their brutishness"; if all the state had been surveyed, he argued, the number would be "between twelve and fifteen hundred." He asserted that for both economic and moral reasons the state had an "imperative duty" to help such citizens. "It has been shown," Howe went on, "that they are not only neglected, but that through ignorance they are so often badly treated and cruelly wronged that, for want of proper means of training, some of them sink from mere weakness of mind into entire idiocy; so that, though born with a spark of intellect which might be nurtured into a flame, it is gradually extinguished, and they go down darkling to the grave, like the beasts that perish." The legislature agreed, and the state established the Massachusetts School for Idiotic Children and Youth in 1849. Other states followed.[40] The goal was to integrate those considered idiots into the community via institutionalization.

By the 1870s, however, despite Howe's presumably good intentions, the increased social attention had not universally improved the lives of those with cognitive disabilities or those of their families. In 1873 businesswoman, advocate for women's rights, and 1872 presidential candidate Victoria Woodhull spoke of parenting her teenage son Byron: "I am cursed with this living death." The 1870 census had counted idiots in the same column as convicts. Howe had generally blamed families for their idiot children—the result of alcohol abuse, masturbation, family traits, physical feebleness, or moral weakness. Removing them from their parents and siblings, he argued, would benefit society. Family members of those with cognitive disabilities, once [admired fo]r their devotion and care, now experienced shame.[41] [With incre]ased shame came increased institutionalization.

Institutionalization was not exclusive to whites. In the late 1860s, and with some federal government financial support, the Cherokee nation voted to build the Cherokee Asylum for the Insane, Deaf, Dumb, and Blind. At nearly the same time, the nation voted to establish an orphan asylum; both institutions were outside what is now Tahlequah, Oklahoma. In its first year, residents of the former included one person diagnosed with general debility, two with rheumatism, eleven as blind, four cripples, three insane or idiots, and one with consumption. The Cherokee asylum, like all asylums of the time, cannot simply be dismissed as a horrible place just because it was an institution. A letter from local community leader Wat A. Duncan to the *Cherokee Advocate* suggests that the reality was more complex. Born in Georgia, near a Cherokee village known as Dahlanegah, in 1823, Duncan and his parents survived the deadly and forced exile to

Oklahoma known as the Trail of Tears. As an adult, Duncan became a Methodist preacher.[42]

Using English, the language of the colonizers, Duncan wrote to celebrate the Cherokee asylum.

> This Asylum don't belong to me, nor to you. It don't belong to this church nor the other church. It belongs to the whole Cherokee people. All have an equal interest in it. Every one should do his part to build it up so as to make it to the greatest amount of good. It ought not to be treated like a lone tree in a prairie. One traveller will go by that tree and break a switch. Another one will go along and break a branch. A wagoner will drive along, and chop into the side of it. At last another comes along and builds a big campfire at its roots. And in a short time the tree is dead. But the Asylum should be treated like a flower garden. Every one should do his part to make it grow, flourish and bloom, so as to lend a charm to the entire Nation. It should be warmed with the heart's truest feelings, and made light by gentle smiles and generous words.[43]

Duncan understood the asylum and its residents to be the community responsibility of all Cherokee nation members. More research needs to be done regarding the Cherokee Asylum for the Insane, Deaf, Dumb, and Blind. How similar or dissimilar it was to other manifestations of institutionalization in the United States is unclear; nor is it clear how much leadership came from within the Cherokee nation.

Some individuals experienced institutional life as empowering. Mary L. Day, one of the first graduates of the Maryland Institute for the Blind (which opened in 1854), thought her institutional experience and education vital: "So anxious was I to become a pupil that I made every personal effort to attain so desirable an end," she wrote. "I found unshrinking perseverance necessary to bring it about." The woman, orphaned as a child, defended the importance of education for blind people in terms of their economic production. "The educated blind in their own home are as useful and industrious as are those who have not been deprived of their sight. They are handy and ingenious."[44] Day's experiences and those of others suggest that institutional life was neither inherently empowering nor destructive: among other things, it depended on the level of leadership and the extent of control by those with disabilities.

Day's defense that her education enabled people with disabilities to be "useful and industrious" mattered. Some institutions for people with disabilities sought to address issues of economic production—not by confronting ableism directly, but by finding employment, home industry, or trade opportunities. The regulation and standardization of industrialization, though it increased in uneven stops and starts, had made it more difficult for people with impairments to earn a living. A young woman unable to walk had easily worked in her family's shoemaking industry. She could not, however, continue to make shoes as shoemaking slowly transferred from home industry to the factories of New England. She would not be able to live in the inaccessible dormitories available to female factory workers in mill towns such as Lowell, Massachusetts; she would not be able to walk the distances demanded of her; nor would other factory workers be as willing as her family members to make food available to her nearby her residence or aid in emptying her chamber pot. Additionally, increased industrialization (discussed further in the next chapter) caused increased impairments. Christopher Tomlin suggests that industrial accidents were quite rare in the first four decades of the 1800s, but that death and accident rates rose significantly from the 1830s to the 1860s as employers attempted to speed up and intensify production processes (while being held increasingly less liable by the courts).[45] This had significant consequence in a culture in which disability was defined with respect to the lack of ability to be economically productive.

CITIZENRY IN THE NEW NATION

In the years following the American Revolution, the United States came to grips with its chosen political system: a democracy. Leaders in the original thirteen states hoped that their bold risk would result in political and economic success. Many had sacrificed a great deal to achieve independence. The new nation, many insisted, thus needed the support of a capable and competent citizenry. Disability became one ideological means by which to adjudicate worthy citizenship.

One manifestation of the concern over disability, unfit bodies and minds, was early immigration law. While colonial Massachusetts had tried to prevent the "lame, impotent, or infirm persons, incapable of maintaining themselves" from landing ashore, by 1848 Massachusetts and Alabama used what is now known as an LPC ("likely to become a public charge") clause. Alabama law, for example, required that "any person commanding any vessel which brings into this State any infant, lunatic, maimed, deaf, dumb, aged, or infirm person, who is likely to become chargeable to any county," had to provide a bond of $500. Massachusetts law required each port to have an examiner. If that examiner found "among said passengers any lunatic, idiot, maimed, aged, or infirm person, incompetent . . . to maintain themselves," the shipmaster needed to post a bond of $1,000.[46]

The actual process of implementing LPC clauses in the early years of the nation remains historically sketchy. How could one tell if a blind man, a woman with a limp, or a seventy-year-old would become a public charge? Did class matter? Was any disability or old age, as read by the port official, enough to disqualify someone from landing ashore? Clearly LPC regulations left significant power in the hands of port officials. Evidence from the latter nineteenth century and early twentieth century indicates that wealth and European descent aided successful immigration to the United States. While Revolutionary War pension policy did not assume that impairments resulted in an inability to labor, early immigration policy made such assumptions.

Between the 1820s and the Civil War, states also began to disenfranchise disabled residents by means of disability-based voting exclusions. Massachusetts began by prohibiting men under guardianship (considered *non compos mentis*) from voting in 1821. Virginia excluded "any person of unsound mind" from voting in 1830 (it went without saying that women and African Americans were excluded from the vote). Between 1830 and 1860, Delaware, California, Iowa, Louisiana, Maryland, Minnesota, New Jersey, Ohio, Oregon, Rhode Island, and Wisconsin variably prohibited men considered insane and those under guardianship from voting.[47]

Early exclusions, such as that in Massachusetts in 1821, were based on property: since those under guardianship could not control property, they could not vote. Similar arguments were made for women and the enslaved. In the 1830s and 1840s, however, this changed. The insane and the idiot, legal theorists now argued, were incapable of voting wisely and thus should not vote.[48] Voting exclusions moved from being justified on economic grounds to being justified by racial, gender, or disability inadequacies.

The relationship between disability and citizenship in the first decades of the new nation, however, was complicated and contradictory. The physical disabilities of people such as Revolutionary War veterans mattered relatively little, and could be seen as a physical marker of patriotic devotion and heroism. When George Washington attempted to squelch a possible rebellion among military forces in 1783, his success is still sometimes attributed to his use of spectacles. While addressing the troops, he pulled out his eyeglasses in order to read his speech. In an era in which most people were illiterate and in which few had access to eyewear, most of the men had never seen Washington so attired. The president and former general put his eyeglasses on while saying, "Gentlemen, you will permit me to put on my spectacles, for I have not only grown gray but almost blind in the service of my country." Purportedly such a sign of great sacrifice made grown men cry. Wartime service may have made Washington "gray" and "almost blind," but these would also have been a factor of his fifty-two years of age. His diminished sight, however, was interpreted as a sign of humility and sacrifice.[49]

In the case of George Washington, blindness (or, more realistically, the use of eyeglasses) served as the marker of his worthy leadership. For most other residents of the new nation, however, disability rendered the full exercise of citizenship highly unlikely and unattainable.

FIVE

I AM DISABLED, AND MUST GO AT SOMETHING ELSE BESIDES HARD LABOR

The Institutionalization of Disability, 1865–1890

'Twas in the year of Sixty three,
And on the third of May,
A rebel shell brought harm to me
And took my arm away . . .

They bore me to a hospital
And gave me chloroform;
I slept, and when I woke again
Was minus a right arm.

From hospital to hospital
They carried me about,
And though they watered well the stump
They couldn't make it sprout . . .

That May-day made a maid a jilb!
(Miss Mary Dey was her name.)
May day like that come ne'er again,
So fraught with grief and shame.

To accept my hand she had agreed,
"Her love would ne'er grow cold."

But when I lost my hand, she said,
The bargain didn't hold.

I offered her my other hand
Uninjured by the fight;
'Twas all that I had left, I said,
She said, 'twould not be right.

"Gaze on these features, Dear," I cried,
"They're fair as you will see."
"Without two hands," she made reply,
"You cannot handsome be."[1]

However handsome Thomas A. Perrine of Pennsylvania may
have been, the poor guy got dumped after returning from the
Civil War. It hadn't been a good year. Shrapnel did significant
damage to his arm in his very first battle, at Chancellorsville,
Virginia, in May 1863, resulting in amputation. In early August
the army discharged him, and his fiancée broke their engagement. Aside from his sense of humor and his skill with rhyme,
little is known about him. The young white man signed up for the
140th Pennsylvania Volunteers, likely with two relations, lived
in Ann Arbor, Michigan, for a while after the war, and died in
1890. While Louisa May Alcott, who would go on to write *Little
Women* and other novels, had served as a nurse in a Civil War
hospital, she had reassured one young soldier with a prominent
facial injury that "all women thought a wound the best decora-
tion a brave soldier could wear."[2] Perrine's fiancée, however, ob-
viously thought otherwise.

Charles F. Johnson, who married before the war, had better
luck in love. He and his wife, Mary, had both a son and a daughter prior to his enlistment. In the June 1862 battle of Charles
River Crossroads, he received multiple gunshot wounds in the
thigh and testicles. He went home to heal and then rejoined the

military. Two years later, while he served as a colonel in the Invalid Corps, Charles and Mary exchanged frequent letters, expressing their appreciation and fondness for one another, and revealing their deep involvement in each other's lives. Responding to her mention of a neighbor's new baby, he reflected obliquely on their relationship, future children, and their future sex life. "Mary that thing is 'played out'—or more properly or correctly or definitly [*sic*] speaking '*I* am played out'—I am sorry (for your sake) that I can not accommodate *you*."[3]

As the bloodiest war in US history, the Civil War fought between the federal government and the Southern Confederate States of America, which sought to secede from the Union, redefined lives and forced a rethinking of disability in the United States. Fought between 1861 and 1865, the war killed more than 620,000 people. Like Revolutionary War soldiers, if wounded, Civil War soldiers were more likely to die than survive. Those who survived found themselves in a nation shocked by the devastation of war. The continuation and expansion of pensions begun after the Revolutionary War, the establishment of "homes" for Union and later Confederate veterans, and increased use of photography of veterans generated national conversations about disability. Emancipation meant new experiences of disability for African Americans, and renewed debates about race and the health of the nation. The war and its consequences generated new adaptive devices and medical advances—from the first wheelchair patent in 1869 to improved prostheses—that improved the lives of many, not just disabled veterans. For some, the period was a reminder that people with all kinds of disabilities, including those with psychological disabilities incurred during the war, had a place in the community. For others, the growing visibility of people with disabilities caused fear and suspicion.

Perrine's fellow veterans in the Invalid Corps—the "one-armed corps," as they often called themselves—had varying luck with employment after the war. Albert T. Shurtleff worked as a

watchman in the DC War Department office. John Bryson returned home, "naturally anxious" about how he would provide
for his family. He needn't have worried: his neighbors in Lansing-
burgh, New York, elected him tax collector. He later clerked in
the Adjutant General's Office in DC, where he was working the
night of President Lincoln's assassination. Shurtlett and Bryson
may have been helped by Section 1754, a federal measure passed
in 1865 that gave preference to disabled veterans in civil service
employment. B. D. Palmer found employment as a Kansas hotel
clerk, but only after he learned to write with his left hand due to
the loss of his right. George W. Thomas, on the other hand, had
not yet found employment two years after being mustered out.
The white farmer and fisherman from Nantucket, then twenty-
five years old, did not know what to do to support himself. William Baugh, a Confederate veteran from Danville, Virginia, had
worked as a wheelwright before the war. Wounded during the
Seven Days Battles and at Gettysburg, he could neither farm nor
repair wheels. He sought the assistance of a wealthy cousin in
order to secure the lease on a local toll bridge, as an alternative
means of making a living: "I am Disabled, and must go at something else besides hard Labor. . . . I shall take it as a great favor
if you will see the Parties concerned about this matter."[4] Many
disabled Civil War veterans found that re-creating an economic
and social life with a newly disabled body could be very difficult.

Civil War veteran Robert A. Pinn (1843–1911), in comparison, achieved significant professional success. The grandchild of
slaves, born free in Massillon, Ohio, he had, in his words, "experienced all the disadvantages peculiar to my proscribed race.
Being born to labor, I was not permitted to enjoy the blessings
of a common school education." He and four siblings helped his
parents to farm. He had been "very eager to become a soldier, in
order to prove by my feeble efforts the black man rights to un-
trammeled manhood." At first denied a chance to serve, he joined
Company I of the Fifth US Colored Troops immediately upon its

creation in June 1863. In September 1864, he lost his arm due to a battle wound, and for his valor under fire he earned the Congressional Medal of Honor. After the war he returned to Ohio, and despite his lack of formal schooling he entered Oberlin College, trained as an attorney, and was admitted to the Ohio bar in 1879. At some point during this time he married, had a daughter, and raised her as well as a niece. The disabled veteran was the first African American attorney in his hometown of Massillon.[5] Labor based on intellectual work rather than physical work, made possible by access to one of the few racially integrated institutions of higher education at the time, and undoubtedly by his own personal skills, served Pinn well.

Attempting to solve the employment needs of disabled veterans, while also resolving staffing problems in the federal government and Union military, in 1863 President Lincoln and the War Department had established the Invalid Corps. Eventually including nearly twenty thousand men scattered across the country, the Invalid Corps was designed to release able-bodied men for fighting while using disabled veterans for other labor. The disabled soldiers guarded military prisoners, protected warehouses and railways, squelched antiwar uprisings in both Vermont and Pennsylvania, and enforced the unpopular draft in the face of fierce opposition, including during a series of draft riots in New York City in 1863. Nearly every man in the Invalid Corps, despite the unit's original intentions, encountered violence while in its service.

Charles Johnson, whose wartime injuries, as he'd written to his wife, Mary, had left him sexually "played out," led Invalid Corps troops in major combat with Confederate forces in June 1864 when Confederate general Wade Hampton attempted to raid Union supplies stockpiled at White House Landing, in Virginia. In the midst of battle, Colonel Johnson's commander sought reassurance from Johnson that his men would not retreat: "Will your invalids stand?" the general asked via a messenger. "Tell the general," Johnson replied with deadpan humor, "that my men are cripples, and they can't run." His troops' successes delighted Johnson—especially as their success ran counter to stereotypes about disability. Military officials, he wrote to his wife, "appear to be tickled at the idea that 2000 men *under an 'Invalid'* should repulse between 5 and 6000 picked troops under such leaders as [General Wade] Hampton and [General] Fitz Hugh Lee."[6]

Despite Johnson's pleasure at his troop's performance, the Invalid Corps and its members were frequently ridiculed as cowardly slackers who habitually tried to avoid service. It did not help that "IC" was also the military designation for "Inspected, Condemned"—a label applied to rotten meat, faulty rifles, and rotting ammunition. Their detractors called them the "Condemned Yanks," the "Inspecteds," as well as the "Cripple Brigade."[7] In the Invalid Corps, in pension programs, and on the streets, people with disabilities, even when disabled as a result of military service, were often looked at suspiciously.

How many of the Invalid Corps members eventually filed for veterans' disability pensions is unclear. African American disabled veterans had less of a chance of being awarded pensions than did their white colleagues. If poor, which many blacks were, the travel costs required to file papers and obtain documentation were onerous. If illiterate, filling out paperwork required significant assistance. And even once a pension application was successfully filed, racism and hostility on the part of claims agents approving pensions was likely. Agents looked with greater skepticism on the claims of African American veterans.[8]

Veterans with nonapparent disabilities that resulted from the war—disabilities not easily discerned by those gazing on their bodies—were not only less likely to apply for a pension but, like African Americans, had a decreased chance of their pension being approved. Wartime damage to one's neurological system, brain injuries, or what is now called posttraumatic stress disorder often carried stigma for veterans and sometimes their families.[9] Many men, perhaps all men, could not sustain masculine ideals—unfaltering, a heroic warrior, a successful breadwinner, and able to stand strong despite all—which undermined their status in society.

For some, the war simply generated too much psychological strain—particularly when blended with poverty, a physical disability, family trauma, and previously existing psychiatric disabilities. Confederate soldier Benjamin Carder presumably left his Virginia hometown for the battlefield with both fear and excitement. Carder returned home from a Union prisoner-of-war camp physically disabled and unable to continue his work as a stonemason. Two of his children had died during his absence, and he bore complete fiscal responsibility for his remaining nuclear family, his ill mother, a blind sister, and a sister with five children.[10] His experiences as a prisoner of war likely had been horrific.

Carder became what doctors overseeing his treatment at Virginia's Western State Lunatic Asylum called "delusional." He believed that if President Lincoln would only let him speak to Union troops, he could bring about the war's end. It is unclear what behaviors led to Carder's institutionalization, but his family must have felt desperate. Presumably his behaviors included violence, for his absence would have made harsh family economics even worse. Doctors at Western attributed the psychological problems of at least 10 percent of their patients admitted between 1861 and 1868 to "the War." Some across the country referred to the postwar emotional struggles of veterans as "soldier's heart."[11] It is reasonable to assume that many struggled for decades afterwards.

Forty-five thousand veterans, like the lovelorn Thomas Perrine, the unemployed George Thomas of Nantucket, and the attorney Robert Pinn, survived the war and the amputation of at least one limb. All were more likely than their able-bodied male neighbors to struggle with employment and family issues, but disabled Confederate veterans had less financial and institutional support than disabled Union veterans. As W. H. Carter of Abingdon, Virginia, wrote, "Our Cripple Soldiers is starving & many of them [are] in the poor house. I for one am a one legged man all most on Starvation." Confederate veterans were less likely to have access to prosthetics; even though, for example, Mississippi spent one-fifth of its state budget on artificial limbs in 1866. Women's groups also helped raise funds for prosthetics for Confederate veterans. Disabled Union veterans, however, had potential access to pensions significantly larger—and paid more timely—than did disabled Confederate veterans.[12]

The war, however, spurred technological inventions in adaptive equipment—as have all US wars. While many companies and individuals promoted prosthetics, one of the most successful (and one that still exists) was that created by James E. Hanger—a Confederate veteran who himself had a leg amputated in the war. Veterans routinely traded prosthetics that did not work, trying to help others while seeking a proper fit for their own limbs, and crafted or modified their own. Other disabled veterans sought adaptive equipment such as canes or glass eyes, in order to increase comfort, continue with employment, or for aesthetic reasons. In the years between 1861 and 1871, the number of patents issued for prosthetic limbs and assistive devices increased threefold from the previous fifteen years. Samuel A. Craig, who served in the Invalid Corps after being wounded in the face and neck, improvised his own adaptive equipment: "By fixing a wax plate over the whole in the roof of my mouth," Craig chronicled, "I was enabled to talk and drink soup."[13] The wax plate also allowed him to continue military service.

Craig's ingenuity and his insistent efforts to direct his own life, along with an expanding pension program for veterans with disabilities, shaped his experience of disability. It also shaped his relationship to government. Union soldiers could turn to the federal government; Confederate soldiers had to turn to their individual states. The pension system did reveal societal stigma and skepticism regarding mental disabilities and African American soldiers.

Yet the system, which expanded significantly from the Revolutionary War to the Civil War, provided vital support for many veterans and their families—support that ranged from prosthetics to employment assistance to money.

Referred to as disability pensions, and increasingly reliant on medical determinations, the pension system once again defined disability as incapacity to perform manual labor. This meant that people with disabilities who did labor for wages or other financial remuneration became increasingly disregarded as a contradiction in terms, for they didn't fit the preconception of someone with a disability. It also meant that the definition of disability, as it became increasingly regulated by law and the medical profession, became more gendered, raced, and class-based. Our African American veteran Robert Pinn, for example, may not have been able to perform some manual labor because of having only one arm, but he labored quite successfully as an attorney. Despite Pinn's personal success, African American veterans in general had less access to the pension system and individual advancement. Most men experienced the incapacity to perform manual labor as a masculine deficiency. If lucky, they came from or were able to elevate themselves to labor that was not manual, labor considered befitting of a middle- or upper-class man.

As noncombatants, women could not receive disability service pensions. Could they be disabled? Women's lives did not easily mesh with the definition of disability as an inability to labor. White women, particularly white women of middle- or upper-class status, were considered *incapable* of performing labor. Class- and race-based definitions of femininity presumed them unfit for labor. Race and gender paradoxically impaired and privileged such women. Working-class women, however, regardless of race or ethnicity, frequently engaged in rigorous manual labor: carrying heavy buckets of water up and down the steps of tenement housing or the narrow servant steps hidden in the back of luxury housing, planting and picking cotton, or daily milking cows. In the period after the Civil War, African American women sometimes were forced to perform wage work. They could be arrested for vagrancy if they did not engage in manual labor, while nearly all of society assumed that upper-class white women should never engage in manual labor. The increasing bureaucratic and social tendency to define disability as the incapacity to perform manual labor had radically different implications for different groups of people.

Despite sometimes being unable to perform manual labor, disabled veterans embodied a unique disability status. Veterans had, by definition, proved their masculinity in wartime. They were, many insisted, the valiantly and deservedly disabled. As one Union surgeon wrote in 1864, "Suffering is unpleasant; but, if one must suffer it is better to do so in a good cause: therefore I had rather have my leg blown off by a rebel shell, than crushed by a locomotive, or bitten off by a crocodile." Some men used their amputations to political advantage. Lucius Fairchild, for example, whose arm was amputated after being wounded in the Battle of Gettysburg, made much of his empty sleeve when he successfully ran for the position of Wisconsin governor (1866–1872). Disabled veterans Francis R. T. Nichols of Louisiana and James H. Berry of Arkansas used similar strategies while running successfully for their state's highest office.[14]

Wartime made disability heroic—but only for male veterans, and only for men with physical, and visibly exhibited, disabilities. Even heroic manhood, however, didn't guarantee social acceptance and financial security for disabled veterans. Despite the expansion of federal pension and support programs, disabled Civil War veterans struggled to find employment and family economic stability; Confederate veterans even more so than Union veterans. Wartime also drew lines between those who became disabled valiantly and those who were unable to claim the status of hero.

THE CONTRADICTIONS OF THE NEW ERA

From the Civil War of the 1860s until the early 1920s, the numbers and kinds of institutions for and about (and only sometimes by) people with disabilities expanded. By the time of the Civil War, the nation's citizens, and many of those who sought to be citizens, increasingly saw education as the means by which social reforms could happen, upward mobility could be achieved, and social integration could be either coerced or realized. This subsequently increased debates over who could appropriately and healthfully access higher education, and the race, class, gender, and ethnic appropriateness of education and educational contexts. Throughout all of this, people with disabilities sought to exercise their own educational, civic, and institutional leadership. Conversely, in contestations over who was fit to be present in the civic world, and who was not, people with disabilities often found themselves increasingly regulated. Those considered not fit for public life were variably shut away, gawked at, and exoticized.

Important in this story is urbanization, industrialization, and class disparities. Between 1870 and 1920, the number of Americans increased from ten million to fifty-four million, and a growing number resided in major cities. In the 1870s, the nation experienced economic crisis, the consolidation of labor unions, and political unrest. Expanding and crowded cities meant a greater need for schools, running water, sewage systems, transportation, and food distribution—but often those needs went unmet. Poor hygiene and crowding facilitated the spread of disease. The explosion of industries such as steel and textiles that were enabled by technology meant expanded employment opportunities, wealth for some, and poverty and pollution for others. Industrial technologies also brought an increase in industrial accidents.

What was to be the role of people with disabilities in these newly configured communities, if not in institutions? As Civil

War veterans returned home, as urban areas expanded and the number of industrial accidents increased, cities across the United States began to pass what have been referred to as "ugly laws." People with disabilities were to be made invisible. In 1867 San Francisco banned "any person who is diseased, maimed, mutilated, or in any way deformed so as to be an unsightly or disgusting object" from the "streets, highways, thoroughfares or public places of the city." Chicago and many other cities adopted similar bans. Portland prohibited "any crippled, maimed, or deformed person" from begging in public spaces. In 1911, Chicago updated its law to prohibit "exposure of diseased, mutilated, or deformed portions of the body."[15]

City officials and the proponents of ugly laws justified them on the basis of class. Crippled, unsightly beggars, they argued, had taken over the public spaces of American cities. Through the creation of anti-begging ordinances, city officials perhaps unwittingly drew distinctions between deserving people with disabilities (those with money) and the undeserving, ugly, unsightly, and disgusting people with disabilities (those without). The laws also penalized people for whom street begging or peddling was often the only means of making a living. Locales sought to eliminate "any crippled, maimed, or deformed person" from public reminder. Such laws reflected unease: industrialization and all the eventual Progressive Era efforts between the 1890s and the early 1920s to study, regulate, and improve society had neither eradicated bodily difference nor prevented misfortune. To the contrary, industrialization actively generated disability.

At the same time, the public seemed to have an expanding and insatiable curiosity about deviant bodies. Since as early as the 1840s, in traveling freak shows, in vaudeville, at P. T. Barnum's famous American Museum in New York and similar facilities, on riverboats, at county fairs, in circus side shows and World Fairs, the exhibition of human bodies considered both wondrous and freakish drew huge crowds always willing to hand over their cash. Exhibitors promoted armless wonders, legless wonders, conjoined twins, and humans considered unnaturally large and unnaturally small.

Lavinia Warren, one of the most privileged of those "exhibited," wrote of her life, "I belong to the public." Between 1862 and 1919, from age nineteen to seventy-eight, Warren traveled the globe, appearing at some of the most glamorous as well as some of the roughest public venues. She and her younger sister, Minnie, were dwarfs: two of eight children born to white, well-established, average-size parents in rural Massachusetts. After joining efforts with P. T. Barnum, and then marrying Barnum's already-famous star performer Charles Stratton, known as General Tom Thumb, Lavinia became even more famous as Mrs. Tom Thumb. After Stratton's 1883 death, Lavinia married an Italian dwarf, Count Primo Magri. Lavinia stubbornly clung to respectable self-presentation, insisting herself "an average middle-class new England woman of her day, conventional in all but size." Those she met, however, often wanted to pet and hold her. "It seemed impossible," she wrote in her 1906 autobiography, "to make people understand at first that I was not a child; that, being a woman, I had the womanly instinct of shrinking from a form of familiarity which in the case of a child of my size would have been as natural as it was permissible."[16] The public desire to pet and hold Warren, the perception of her as an innocent and child-like, made profits possible. At the same time, her size was her only means to the material comfort in which she lived. Her race, gender, and class rendered her a relatively safe and nonthreatening object for public viewing.

In comparison, exhibitors presented people of color as particularly exotic, embodied and savage missing links between humans and animals. The way they were shown, often with little clothing, was eerily similar to that on the slave block. Exhibitors made money from the titillating and perhaps slightly naughty nature, sometimes justified in the name of science, in which they displayed the bodies of people of color.

Fascination with the supposedly deviant bodies and minds of people of color went beyond the commercial sphere and also pervaded medical ideology. Medical experts did not consider John Patterson's physicality deviant, but they certainly considered his mind to be deviant and sought to remove him from the public sphere. In November 1867, Patterson entered the Alabama Insane Hospital as a patient. Hospital Superintendent Peter Bryce admitted the forty-five-year-old laborer, emancipated from slavery less than five years previous, with a diagnosis of acute mania. Bryce's notes indicated that Patterson had been insane for twelve years. The cause of Patterson's mental disturbance, Bryce reported further, was freedom—which, of course, had only come a few years prior due to emancipation and the Civil War.[17]

Superintendent Peter Bryce's diagnostic skills reflected racial understandings of insanity shared particularly by Southern slavery apologists and medical practitioners since before the controversial 1840 census. J. F. Miller, for example, superintendent of the segregated Goldsboro (North Carolina) Hospital for the Colored Insane, argued that emancipation had alarming deleterious consequences. Both insanity and tuberculosis, he warned in 1896, had been "rare diseases among the negroes of the South prior to emancipation." Indeed, conditions of enslavement were ideally "conducive to physical health and mental repose." Slavery protected vulnerable African Americans from "their promiscuous sexual indulgence and the baneful influences of the liquor saloon." Emancipation resulted in the removal of "the restraining influences which had been such conservators of healthfulness for mind and body." Bluntly, freedom led to insanity. The "influences and agencies which would not affect a race mentally stronger," combined with the innate weaknesses of the black body and mind, left African Americans succumbing to insanity in significant numbers.[18]

After the Civil War, segregated insane asylums developed quickly across much of the United States—simultaneous to and part of the trend by which schools for idiots, deaf, and blind people also developed. Many, but not all, were racially segregated. Southern state facilities included Central State Hospital (Virginia, 1870), Goldsboro Hospital for the Colored Insane (North Carolina, 1880), Mount Vernon Hospital for the Colored Insane (Alabama, 1902), Crownsville State Hospital (Maryland, 1911), Palmetto State Hospital (South Carolina, 1914), Lakin State Hospital for the Colored Insane (West Virginia, 1926), and Taft State Hospital (Oklahoma, 1933). An 1895 survey showed that asylums in Kentucky, Mississippi, Tennessee, Georgia, North Carolina, Arkansas, and Louisiana, and St. Elizabeth's Hospital in Washington, DC, segregated patients, even while they shared the same facility. [19]

While many medical professionals made racist claims about the mental and physical deficiencies of African Americans, they did not move to provide expanded care. Historian John Hughes found that staff doctors at the Alabama Insane Hospital in Tuscaloosa, the precursor to the Mount Vernon Hospital, clearly responded to black patients differently than white patients. Doctors took skimpy case histories of their African American patients and used different diagnostic labels than they did for white patients. Hospitals provided inferior living conditions, and black patients received their care from the least experienced physicians. Hughes argues that hospital records suggest that the inmates of the Alabama institution were malnourished—and that such malnourishment "actually increased mortality." As Hughes puts it, "blacks were admitted for a narrower range of conditions than whites and faced a greater chance of illness and death after admission."[20]

Freedom clearly did not result in insanity, but for newly freed slaves with some physical and mental disabilities the consequences of freedom could be complex. Newly freed slaves, many historians have noted, eagerly sought to find employment, reconstitute their families (if torn apart by slavery), and relocate to places of their own choosing. Mobility became the method by which emancipated peoples lived and acted out their freedom. As historian Jim Downs has noted, however, "freedom depended upon one's ability and potential to work." The Confiscation Acts passed during the war promised freedom to former slaves who crossed Union lines, but only in exchange for performing often grueling manual labor. While other former slaves eagerly moved away from the land of their former owners, equating mobility with freedom, some of the newly freed literally could not do so. If a physical disability resulted in limited mobility, living out freedom became very difficult. A postwar 1867 report to the Union secretary of war Edward Stanton noted that many "helpless" former slaves remained working on the plantations of their former owners—simply unable to leave, and working for food. "Scores of disabled slaves," in Downs's words, "remained enslaved." Hannah, of the Natchez district of Mississippi, for example, may have been emancipated, but the blind woman had no family to rely on. She remained in Natchez, unable to leave her former owner's home, and continued to work for him.[21]

For Hannah, the material realities of disability, racism, social isolation, and a federal government that did not move to defend her, were tragic. Equally tragic were the lives of formerly enslaved individuals supposedly made insane by freedom. Such analysis on the part of experts makes clear that social attitudes and power dynamics influenced definitions of insanity and appropriate behavior in the nineteenth century. It also should make us seriously question the means by which people were committed to insane hospitals as well as educational institutions, and the populations of people both interred and not interred—such as Hannah.

EDUCATING THE APPROPRIATE CITIZENRY
APPROPRIATELY

In 1873 Edward H. Clarke, a prominent professor at Harvard Medical School, warned the country of an issue that he felt should "excite the *gravest alarm,* and . . . demand the serious attention of the country": an important group of people had been "permanently disabled to a greater or lesser degree, or fatally injured, by these causes": respectable white women. A higher education, he warned, could and had "permanently disabled" such women. He gave the example of "Miss G," a fine young woman who had done well in college and her post-college life—but then died not long afterward, an autopsy showing no disease other than "commencing degeneration" of the brain. No woman, he warned, could simultaneously use "a good brain" and "a good reproductive system that should serve the race." It was simply too much for the female body.[22]

By the 1870s the common school movement, which sought to establish tax-funded public schools, had greatly expanded educational opportunities across the United States. Its proponents argued that a successful democracy required an educated citizenry. While schooling was still limited by race, gender, and class, more Americans had access to basic literacy than ever before. By the 1870s, women (generally white women) increasingly taught in the public schools. While educational reformer Catharine Beecher had argued that women were uniquely suited for educating children due to their innate maternal qualities, female teachers, conveniently, could also be paid less than male teachers. As educational opportunities expanded, a small but growing number of colleges and universities began to welcome white women and African Americans, both male and female (such as the disabled Civil War veteran Thomas Perrine), into their classrooms and libraries.

When Agatha Tiegel (1873–1959) graduated from DC's National Deaf-Mute College in 1893 (renamed Gallaudet College in 1894), the young white woman engaged in direct conversation with Edward Clarke—as well as many others closer to home. In 1887, the institution that was to become Gallaudet, the premier educational institution for deaf Americans, had allowed female students to enroll as a two-year experiment. While a seven-year-old growing up in Pittsburgh, Tiegel had become deaf, and blind in one eye, due to spinal meningitis. She first attended public schools, then Western Pennsylvania School for the Deaf in 1886, and then Gallaudet. She began coursework in the fall of 1888 as one of only eight women and the youngest student on campus. Gallaudet had no female dormitory accommodations (the women lived at the home of President Edward M. Gallaudet), women could not leave the school without chaperone, and the faculty had ruled that women could not join the extracurricular literary societies because of the "obvious impropriety of association of the young ladies with the young men." Skepticism remained about women's presence. Would the women be able to handle the demands of the curriculum? Should women and men attend segregated classes, with separate curriculums, for women's own safety and benefit? In 1895 some male students, using the language of the sideshows at which they easily could have been attendees, characterized the women "freaks." Many years later Tiegel wrote, "I resented that there might be any question of the right, the God given right, of my sisters and myself to take our places in the sun."[23]

As the valedictorian of 1893 Tiegel, the first female to graduate from Gallaudet with a BA, delivered an address entitled "The Intellect of Woman." On Presentation Day, likely before an audience of congressional as well as university dignitaries, Tiegel proclaimed boldly that "there is no inferiority in [women's] intellectual capacity, but only neglect of use and tardiness of development." She argued that "restrictive circumstances" had held women "so far below her powers that we do not apprehend the full evil of these circumstances." Tiegel drew connections between the racism that undergirded slavery and the sexism that undergirded the lack of educational opportunities for women, for both claimed that deficient bodies rendered women and African Americans unfit for a full civic life. "To argue also," she went on, "that a woman is not fit to be trusted with her liberty on the score of her emotional nature, her poor powers of logic and judgement, is to copy the fallacies of the opponents of emancipation, who used as arguments those very faults in slaves that slavery had produced."[24] Tiegel had no African American students in her courses, for they were not permitted to be there. Indeed, Andrew Foster, the first African American to graduate from Gallaudet, did not do so until 1954.

The creation of Gallaudet reflected the continued expansion of institutions and residential schools for people with disabilities that had begun decades earlier. By the turn of the century, over 130 residential schools served deaf students, 31 served blind students, and approximately 14 schools had been established for those diagnosed as feeble-minded.[25] The majority of adults in institutions, however, still lived in asylums, prisons, and alms-houses—a radically different experience than that at the National Deaf-Mute College.

Life at residential schools for deaf students, and life for deaf people in general, changed dramatically in the years following the Civil War due to the rise of oralism. Oralism is the belief that deaf people can and should communicate without the use of sign language, relying exclusively on lip reading and oral speech. In the early years of deaf education in the United States, teachers taught and used sign language (called manual education). Sign language, they argued, "liberated deaf people from their confinement" and enabled them to receive Christianity. Deaf people became leaders in emerging deaf social communities facilitated by educational institutions. The post–Civil War generation of educational theorists, however, led by Alexander Graham Bell, argued that sign language served as an "instrument of . . . imprisonment." Sign language, many proclaimed, made deaf people outsiders: "The gesturer is, and always will remain, a foreigner," never a true American. While European Americans forbade the use of indigenous languages at Native boarding schools, and while national hysteria about rising immigration spread, oralist educators increasingly forbade the use of sign language at deaf boarding schools. The stigmatization of deafness increased. By 1899 nearly 40 percent of deaf students were taught without sign language; by World War I that number had increased to 80 percent. The number of deaf adults hired as principals and teachers plummeted. Gallaudet College refused to even train deaf people as teachers.[26]

After her 1893 graduation from Gallaudet, running counter once again to national trends, Agatha Tiegel accepted a teaching position at the Minnesota School for the Deaf (sometimes called the Faribault School for the Deaf). After six years of teaching she married Olof Hanson. Born in Sweden, Hanson had received his education at both the Minnesota School for the Deaf and Gallaudet. He became a successful architect, Episcopal minister, and president of the National Association of the Deaf (1910–1913). The couple, who eventually had three daughters, lived for most of their married life in Seattle. As president of the NAD, Olof Hanson resisted the exclusive reliance on oralism in deaf education, once claiming that "fully 90 percent of the deaf entertain these views, and among them are many educated by the oral method."[27] While Agatha's views on oralism are not known, it is likely that she agreed with her husband.

Agatha Tiegel Hanson benefited greatly from the rise of women's and deaf education, despite oralism. Via her education she experienced upward class mobility, she met her husband, and she moved into a vibrant deaf community that she apparently loved.

She continued her lifelong love of poetry, even publishing her own poems. In one of her most famous poems, "Inner Music," she wrote of deafness as an "imperfection," but an imperfection that enabled "diviner harmony" and "peacefulness" that would otherwise have been lost "amid earth's din."[28]

Educator James William Sowell similarly resisted oralist trends in deaf education. Deaf since early infancy, Sowell attended the Alabama School for the Deaf, graduated from Gallaudet in 1900, and earned a master's degree in literature from Johns Hopkins University. Despite a successful teaching career, Sowell later lost his positions at the Nebraska School for the Deaf when it became purely oralist. In a poem entitled "The Oralist," he charged: "Oralist, whose traffic is a little child's despair . . . Oralist, O oralist, turn your head aside, Know you not the pitying Christ for sins like yours has died?"[29] Sowell considered oralism a sin. Despite his condemnation it would remain the dominant form of deaf education until approximately the 1970s. American Sign Language, however, remained alive and vibrant due to the sometimes covert, sometimes overt insistence and resistance of deaf people.

The period from the Civil War until the 1890s is one in which disability became increasingly institutionalized. The solidification of the federal government that developed in this period, along with emerging technologies and urbanization, aided the creation of institutions and the development of policies pertaining to people considered disabled. As the United States and its citizens debated the human capacity for education, they also explored and disagreed over which peoples should have access to various forms of education. In government policies and programs, in local laws, in entertainment, in educational institutions, and in asylums and other institutions that simply warehoused disabled people, the management of disability became increasingly built into national structures. The population of asylums expanded, sometimes resulting in horrific experiences. At the same time, educational institutions led and staffed by people with disabilities expanded, creating rich spaces of disability culture, although they generally remained racially exclusive. Some institutions enriched lives, others caused devastation, and some did both.

SIX

THREE GENERATIONS OF IMBECILES ARE ENOUGH

The Progressive Era, 1890–1927

In his 1923 State of the Union Address, President Calvin Coolidge proclaimed, "America must be kept American. For this purpose, it is necessary to continue a policy of restricted immigration."[1] Coolidge was not alone. The mass immigration of southern and eastern Europeans who provided the cheap labor that fueled the nation's industrial and economic expansion now generated fears about a deteriorating national body, as did the mass migration of African Americans out of the rural South and into the urban North. Since the early twentieth century, a growing wave of concern about the changing nature of the nation's citizens had overwhelmed the United States, its politics, and its culture. People with disabilities fought against increasingly stringent and harsh laws and cultural attitudes, but despite their efforts the definition of "undesirable" became ever more wide, fluid, and racially/ethnically based. Physical "defects," both scientists and the casual observer increasingly assumed, went hand in hand with mental and moral "defects." This resulted in the forced sterilization of more than sixty-five thousand Americans by the 1960s, and in the most restrictive immigration laws in US history (that, among other things, excluded people with disabilities). The ideal

American citizen was defined in increasingly narrow and increasingly specific physical terms.

Many in power—including politicians, educators, religious leaders, and jurists—sought to explain and address the growing social concerns caused by industrialization and urbanization. They used Gregor Mendel's scientific work on plant genetics and the newly developed Binet-Simon intelligence test to argue that criminality, feeble-mindedness, sexual perversions, and immorality, as well as leadership, responsibility, and proper expressions of gender, were hereditary traits (just as blue eyes were hereditary traits). Conveniently, this argument blamed the huge economic disparities between the small numbers of the rich and the large numbers of the poor on the deficiencies of poor people. While then and still widely discredited by many scientists, the gospel of eugenics was embraced wholeheartedly by many—including biologist Charles Davenport and then Harry Laughlin. Eugenics is the belief that the way to improve society is through better human breeding practices so that only those with "positive" hereditary traits reproduce. In law, in popular culture, in science, and even at local county fairs, eugenics was pervasive in the United States in the late nineteenth and early twentieth centuries.

The arguments of Chief Justice Harry Olson of the municipal court of Chicago, who decided the fate of many individuals considered defective, are reflective of popular eugenicists. He warned in 1911 that the success of the United States depended on limiting its undesirable elements—degenerate immigrants being only one of the many undesirable categories. In his 1922 foreword to Harry Laughlin's treatise on the state of eugenics in the United States, Olson warned that "the success of democracy depends on the quality of its individual elements . . . [If] there is a constant and progressive racial degeneracy, it is only a question of time when popular self-government will be impossible, and will be succeeded by chaos, and finally a dictatorship."[2]

Given such weighty political importance, judicial officials, physicians, psychiatrists, and others who contributed to and managed insane asylums took their resulting responsibilities seriously. In 1899 Dr. Henry Clay Sharp of the Indiana Reformatory, for example, instituted a sterilization program in order to prevent the spread of hereditary defects among US residents. As he warned in 1909, "There is no longer any questioning of the fact that the degenerate class is increasing out of all proportion to the increase of the general population." According to Sharp, the "degenerate class" included "most of the insane, the epileptic, the imbecile, the idiotic, the sexual perverts; many of the confirmed inebriates, prostitutes, tramps and criminals, as well as the habitual pauper found in our county poor asylums; also many of the children in our orphan homes."[3] With the degenerative population that large, action was necessary.

Laughlin had and would become widely recognized and effective as a leading proponent of restrictive immigration and forced-sterilization laws. The two strategies, he believed, together would ensure "the destiny of the American nation." For the nation to succeed, he maintained, it must limit its already dangerously expanding pool of intellectually, physically, and morally defective citizens. Restrictive immigration laws, he would argue over and over again in print as well as before Congress, would "forbid the addition through immigration to our human breeding stock of persons of a lower natural hereditary constitution than that which constitutes the desired standard." Forced-sterilization laws, accompanied by encouragement for those considered desirable for bearing children, would likewise limit the numbers of "socially inadequate, both within and not in custodial institutions," and thus inhibit "the birth rate among degenerates."[4] Laughlin became recognized as a leading scientist in both the United States and Germany. His model sterilization law became internationally renowned, eventually taken up by Adolf Hitler in his own bid for a national racial purity.

AN AMERICAN AMERICA

Beginning with the Immigration Act of 1882 and continuing up until the highly restrictive Immigration Act of 1924, immigration law increasingly restricted potential immigrants deemed defective—morally, physically, or intellectually—or even potentially defective. The 1882 law prohibited entry to any "lunatic, idiot, or any person unable to take care of himself or herself without becoming a public charge." Immigration officials determined "public charge" at their own discretion. In 1891 the phrase "unable to take care of himself or herself" was replaced by the far wider and more fluid "*likely* to become a public charge." In 1903 Congress specified those with epilepsy and in 1907 added "imbeciles" and "feeble-minded persons." As one Ellis Island official wrote, feeble-mindedness conveniently served as a "sort of waste basket for many forms and degrees of weak-mindedness." By 1907 immigration officials demanded a medical certificate from immigrants judged "mentally or physically defective, such mental or physical defect being of a nature which *may affect* the ability of such alien to earn a living." In 1917 immigration officials received instructions to reject all immigrants with "any mental abnormality whatever . . . which justifies the statement that the alien is mentally defective."[5]

At Ellis Island, during the peak years of US immigration from 1870 to 1924, more than twenty-six million people entered the United States, driven by the lack of political, economic, and social opportunities in their home countries, and expanding opportunities, or at least the potential for them, in America. Potential immigrants, already limited by immigration laws that excluded nearly all Africans, Asians, and South Americans, went through a vigorous inspection process. The physical path through Ellis Island included a set of steep steps, several sharp turns, and, usually, dense crowding. Immigration agents prided themselves on their ability to make "snapshot diagnoses," as each day a "handful of officials inspected between 2,000 and 5,000 people." One official later wrote, "Defects, derangements and symptoms of disease which would not be disclosed by a so-called 'careful physical examination,' are often easily recognizable in watching a person twenty-five feet away."[6] If suspect, officials marked the potential immigrant with a chalked letter, usually on their back. Those who were chalk-marked endured further examination. The accompanying illustration shows these various marks. Money served as the first signifier of potential defectiveness, for first-class passengers experienced far less scrutiny—a visual examination, for example, to detect the eye disease trachoma, rather than a painful eversion of the eyelids by inspectors.

The "defects, derangements and symptoms of disease" proudly discernible by immigration inspectors also included the facial expressions, "oddity of dress," "talkativeness, witticism, facetiousness," and "unnatural actions, mannerisms, and other eccentricities" that they believed to be indicators of sexual perversion. As scholar Jennifer Terry has argued, "American physicians habitually characterized homosexuality as emanating from elements and forces outside the native-born white population." Immigrants feared to be possible sex perverts were pulled aside for further inspection and could be asked questions such as: "Are

Bodily markings used by inspectors at Ellis Island

B= back	C= conjunctivitis	E = eyes
F = face	FT = feet	G = goiter
H = heart	K = hernia	L = lameness
N = neck	P = physical or lungs	PG = pregnant
SC = scalp	SI = sent to special inquiry board	S = senility
CT = trachoma	X = possible mental illness	X with circle = definite mental illness

Source: Rhonda McClure, "More Than Passenger Lists: The Other Records at Ellis Island," Ancestry.com, March 2006.

you married? Do you want to marry? Do you care for the opposite sex? Have you had acquaintances of the opposite sex?" American physicians generally considered the desire for sexual contact with others of the same sex to be proof of an inheritable form of insanity, and an embodiment contrary to the able-bodied citizen sought by immigration officials.[7] In this case, able-bodiedness included maritally restricted heterosexuality.

Race also mattered. At Angel Island in San Francisco Bay, where the immigrants were Asian and not European, the examinations were lengthier and deportation rates higher (at least five times that of Ellis Island). As far back as the Page Law of 1875, which had made Chinese immigration very difficult, US congressional reports had determined that "there is not sufficient brain capacity in the Chinese to furnish motive power for self-government." Their bodies were, in essence, too disabled for democracy. At the southern border, Mexicans who passed the border experienced little surveillance. Prior to 1924, most public officers, employers, and social commentators who paid attention to these immigrants considered them "uniquely able-bodied" for physical labor: ideally made for the harsh labor of farm work or food processing, as long as that was where they stayed, but not for democratic participation or more elite employment.[8]

At Ellis Island, Dr. Allan McLaughlin of the US Public Health Service warned immigration officials to "ever be on the alert for deception." The defective immigrant, he warned, would attempt purposeful and shrewd shams in order to enter the United States: "The nonchalant individual with an overcoat on his arm is probably concealing an artificial arm; the child strapped to its mother's back, and who appears old enough to walk alone, may be unable to walk because of infantile paralysis . . . and a bad case of trachoma may show no external evidence and be detected only upon everting the eyelid."[9]

Charles Proteus Steinmetz sailed into New York harbor in 1889. He and a friend, Oscar Asmussen, arrived in New York as two of the ship's six hundred steerage, or third-class, passengers. Steinmetz, however, barely made it through immigration. Within just a decade he would become an internationally leading inventor, scientist, engineer, and researcher. His adopted hometown of Schenectady, New York, still remembers him as president of the city council, president of the Board of Education, and a philanthropist who bought all local orphans a Christmas present every year.[10]

In 1889, however, Steinmetz was viewed disparagingly as a Jewish hunchbacked man of short stature, four foot three inches tall. Born to an educated family in the German-speaking city that is now Wroclaw, Poland, he spoke little English and likewise had almost no money. Steinmetz apparently rarely discussed what happened as he went through the immigration process, but immigration officials initially denied him entrance due to his disability and the resulting likelihood that he would become a public charge—the routine practice of the time. His friend Asmussen protested loudly, however, proclaiming Steinmetz's intellectual brilliance and stating (falsely) that a thick wad of money in his possession belonged to Steinmetz. Immigration officials relented and Steinmetz entered the country. It's likely at this point, while immigration officials scoffed at him due to his disability, that Steinmetz legally claimed Proteus as his middle name. Proteus, a nickname given him by his professors in Germany, referred to a wise Greek sea god with a hunched back. The name conferred wisdom, not the ableism he experienced at the border. Today Steinmetz remains most widely remembered as a leading engineer at General Electric and a pioneer developer of electric cars, though friends best remembered him for his delicious meatloaf.[12]

Steinmetz could have been excluded because he fell within the later-developed "poor physique" category. In use by 1905, the Immigration Services defined individuals of "poor physique" as those "who have frail frame, flat chest, and are generally deficient in muscular development," or "undersized—markedly of short stature—dwarf." As historian Margot Canaday has shown, immigration officials also used the "poor physique" category to reject individuals suspected of sexual perversion (homosexuality), having bodies with ambiguous sexual organs, or simply being undiscernibly distinctly male or female.[12]

Many thousands of immigrants, however, did not have the assistance of someone like Asmussen in navigating through immigration, or did not chance upon a lax inspector who gave them a pass, and were deported as "defectives" and "undesirables." In 1905 Domenico Rocco Vozzo, a thirty-five-year-old Italian immigrant, was rejected while entering the United States for the second time. Earlier he had spent two years in the States earning money and then returned to Italy. He sought to do the same again, but immigration officials determined him as having a "debility" and likely to become a public charge. Vozzo apparently had "a curiously shaped head, and his skin looks rather white, almost bleached, and his ears are quite thin." Those determining Vozzo's case used his photo as proof that he was not "a desirable acquisition" and deported him. Donabet Mousekian, an Armenian Turk, lacked male sexual organs—sometimes referred to by immigration officials as "lack of sexual development." He had made a living as a photographer, was a skilled weaver and dyer of rugs, and could cook well. Aside from that he had relatives in the United States who promised support. None of which swayed officials. "I am not ill," he said in his appeal, "have no contagious disease; my eyes, feet, hands and ears are sound; only I am deprived of male organs; this is not a fault because it has come from God and my mother: what can I do? It won't do any harm to my working." Immigration officials determined Mousekian likely to become a public charge and "weak, emaciated, and really repulsive in appearance"—sexually defective.[13]

Israel Bosak was similarly deported in 1906 for "poor physique." The tailor had lost his successful shop in anti-Jewish pogroms in Russia, had some cash, and had relatives who promised to help him establish a business. His unspecified and unexplained "poor physique," however, meant deportation. In 1913, thirty-year-old deaf blacksmith Moische Fischmann arrived at Ellis Island presumably with high hopes. Already in the country were his brother and sister, both well employed and ready to help him. At the gauntlet of the Public Health Service physician on duty, however, Fischmann was determined to have a physical defect and his case referred to the Board of Special Inquiry. There his siblings attested to their fiscal stability in great detail. Three cousins also promised to help support Fischmann while he sought work, and one of them carried with him a letter from his own employer guaranteeing the skilled blacksmith a job. The board, however, unanimously voted to deport the deaf man back to Russia. His "certified condition," it concluded, "is such that he would have considerable difficulty in acquiring or retaining employment." Under further appeal, which was rare, Fischmann's attorney from the Hebrew Immigrant Sheltering and Aid Society warned of the hostile conditions that Russian Jews faced. A second employer promised Fischmann a job and $12 a week. Despite these arguments, and the two job offers, the commissioner insisted that "there can be little doubt that the applicant's certified condition will seriously interfere with his earning capacity." Fischmann was deported. Given the ease with which both Bosak and Fischmann were identified as Jewish, it is possible that their Jewishness, coupled with deafness and "poor physique," became part of the formula that rendered them unfit.[14]

The LPC clause, as the "likely to become a public charge" clause has become known, clearly assumed that bodies considered defective rendered them unable to perform wage-earning labor. One immigration official saw no problem with his assumption that the "immigrant of poor physique is not able to perform rough labor, and even if he were able, employers of labor would not hire him." As historian Douglas Baynton wisely points out, for immigration officials "the belief that an immigrant was unfit to work justified exclusion, but so did the belief that an immigrant was *likely to encounter discrimination* because of a disability."[15] It also meant that if monetary assistance was needed due to a disability, such a need disqualified potential immigrants for US citizenship—quite clearly stating that such citizens already here were far from the ideal.

The issue, however, was not a straightforward economic matter, despite reliance on the LPC clause. Many immigrants rejected for their defective bodies had supported themselves quite well in their home countries. Others, like Moische Fischmann, had jobs awaiting them or relatives offering to support them. The economic rationale of the LPC clause could serve, and often did serve, as a false cover story. Ableism and a desire for a specific form of American bodies motivated the deportation of many potential immigrants.

When Patrick Eagan was refused entry into the United States in 1909, immigration officials noted that he "looks to be able-bodied," and had "always accomplished the full task of an able-bodied laborer." That was not enough. Eagan's penis was considered small by immigration officials (who examined such things) and they then rejected Eagan on the basis that immigrants "effeminately developed" were "undesirable in any community." Despite Eagan's solid wage-work history, officials insisted that future wage work was highly unlikely. As historian Margot Canaday explains, "immigration officials associated defective genitalia with perversion, and further viewed perversion as a likely cause of economic dependency."[16] In these immigration policies, able-bodiedness included normative genitalia.

In subtle ways, and sometimes not so subtle ways, the LPC clause also was embedded in class, ethnic, race, sexual, and gender assumptions. The LPC clause required that immigrant women have bodies interpreted as able to perform physical labor for wages, this despite the fact that many women in the United States did not work for wages at this time and were not expected to do so. The LPC clause set gendered requirements of appropriate womanhood that, depending on class, ethnicity or race, domestic-born women did not have to meet. Indeed, the LPC clause defined immigrant women as ineligible for the benefits of native-born womanhood.

The legal structures and the physical gates at US border locales became sites where ideals about the bodies of American citizens were enforced and reinforced. US lawmakers, scientists, and policymakers established which bodily, mental, and moral characteristics (perceived or real) were acceptable parts of the body politic—and which would disable the body politic. When Coolidge proclaimed that "America must be kept American," he had a very specific American body in mind.[19]

INSTITUTIONS AND THE REPRODUCTION
OF THE AMERICAN IDEAL

Alice Smith was not what many had in mind as the ideal American. In May of 1912 the New Jersey Board of Examiners of Feeble-Minded (Including Idiots, Imbeciles and Morons), Epileptics, Criminals and Other Defectives—yes, that really was the bureaucratic name—met to discuss Smith. The four men on the board unanimously determined that "procreation by her is inadvisable," and based on a 1911 New Jersey law, ordered that the almost twenty-eight-year-old white woman be sterilized. The New Jersey law, signed by then-governor Woodrow Wilson, had authorized sterilization of those individuals deemed "defective."[20]

Smith and her four surviving siblings had each been legally committed, at varying times, to the New Jersey State Village for Epileptics, in Skillman, New Jersey. At the initiation of the State Board of Children's Guardians, Alice had been committed in 1902 by the Court of Common Pleas of Essex County just twelve days short of her eighteenth birthday—likely because such an action was legally easier to achieve before she reached the age of majority. Smith and many of her family members had epilepsy. In 1912 she had not had a seizure for over five years.

Because Smith's case eventually reached the New Jersey Supreme Court, and because eugenicists relied upon very detailed case histories and genealogical data, more is known about Smith than many others in similar situations. Most of the data, however, is filtered through eugenicist interpretations and little of Smith's direct voice emerges.

It is clear that Smith's father, George, was a Civil War veteran who once worked as an engineer (though what that actually meant is not clear). Alice's mother, Susan Ann, was twelve years younger than her husband. Between 1880 and 1900 the family's social status had gone steadily downhill. For a brief period after 1900 the couple lived at the New Jersey Soldiers Home for Disabled Soldiers, Sailors, Marines, and Their Wives and Widows in Vineland, but the couple was kicked out because of Susan's epilepsy. Where their children lived during that period, and the nature of George's disability, is not clear. The couple had seven children, beginning in the 1870s, five of whom survived childhood.

In 1900 the Smith family lived in the back of a house, bordering an alley, in a largely black neighborhood of Bloomfield, New Jersey. The family generally lived on the $20 per month pension that George received as a disabled veteran of the Civil War, though George worked for a brief period as a railway flagman. Three children had already died: a son had drowned at seven years of age; a daughter died in infancy; and another son died after falling from a second-story window at four years of age. In 1900 Doretta (or Dora) was approximately twenty-seven, George Jr. twenty-three, Emma Jane eighteen, Alice sixteen, and Russell thirteen. Both Emma and Alice had given birth to daughters in the local almshouse, and the baby girls were removed from their unmarried mothers (though when Emma gave birth is not clear). By 1912 all five siblings lived at the State Village for Epileptics.

Eugenic investigators from the Village then described mother Susan Smith as "mentally deficient to a fairly marked degree," with many feeble-minded relatives, and an epileptic who'd had seizures since the age of fourteen. Alice's father George Smith was "mentally deficient . . . [with] an ugly disposition and an ugly temper," "commonly known as 'half-witted.'"[21]

Smith's sexuality and pregnancy at a relatively young age, interpreted as proof of her moral and intellectual feeble-mindedness, is hard to interpret. The case files, created by eugenic investigators working out of the Village, noted that Alice became pregnant after she and a neighboring African American man had "indulged in sexual intercourse" in a vacant lot one night. Alice said she had been raped. Later she said that she did not remember what had happened. Village officials "suspected" her "of being a masturbator" and claimed that she exhibited "the hypersexuality which is common in defectiveness." Possibly even worse, as far as the case report indicated, "This patient did not possess the normal aversions of a white girl to a colored man, who was perhaps nice to her." Elsewhere the case file indicated that Alice's father, George, frequently "in fits of anger," "would turn his daughters out of his house, and they would seek refuge among the negroes about the neighborhood." Alice lived among African Americans, and clearly had relied upon her black neighbors to avoid her father's violence. The case file indicated that a "colored man whose name is said to have been Washington" fathered her child. A thirty-two-year-old widowed black man named Charles Washington boarded several houses down the street during the year Alice became pregnant; perhaps he was the father. The true nature of the relationship is near impossible to discern; as is Alice's home situation. Historian Molly Ladd-Taylor has pointed out that "a disproportionate number" of women in legal situations similar to Alice's "were probable victims of incest or sexual abuse." Alice's case file simply concluded that if released unsterilized, "no doubt when at large she would soon fall victim to another unscrupulous man . . . and she would therefore be a social danger, as she would be the cause of a new generation of epileptics and imbeciles."[22] Smith's disabling transgressions were racial, sexual, and class based.

Research into Alice's family—her "pedigree"—was extensive. Informants included her nuclear family, aunts and uncles, great aunts and uncles, cousins and their spouses, second cousins, the local overseer of the poor, local police officers and reporters, and matron of the local Children's Home. No stone was left unturned in uncovering the sexual, medical, moral, and death histories of each and every person in Smith's extended family. The result was a four-generation pedigree chart that detailed the moral and physical defectiveness of the entire Smith clan. Such studies were commonly done, and used to determine which individuals should be sterilized and/or segregated within institutions.

The conclusion of the experts of the State Village for Epileptics, and that of eugenics advocate Harry Laughlin, was that Alice Smith was "congenitally defective, and [had] also inherited the epileptic tendency from her parents." To allow her to return home would be "a crime against society." Furthermore, "it would be indeed most wasteful to the nation and State to allow this defective to wander about, as it would entail perpetuation of her kind, and other evils due to this lack of proper care and segregation." Sterilization was thus the solution—to improve Alice Smith's life, and for the greater good of society.[21]

Beginning in Indiana in 1907, more than thirty states passed forced-sterilization laws. Their content varied, as did how, if, and to what extent they were put into practice. The model law developed by Harry Laughlin defined "socially inadequate classes" of people very broadly: "(1) Feebleminded; (2) Insane, (including the psychopathic); (3) Criminalistic (including the delinquent and wayward); (4) Epileptic; (5) Inebriate (including drug habitués); (6) Diseased (including the tuberculous, the syphilitic, the leprous, and others with chronic, infectious and legally segregable

Forced sterilization by state, 1907–1937

State	Date	No. sterilized
Indiana	1907	2,424
Washington	1909	685
California	1909	20,108
Connecticut	1909	557
Nevada	1911	0
Iowa	1911	1,910
New Jersey	1911	0
New York	1912	42
Oregon	1917	2,341
North Dakota	1913	1,049
Kansas	1913	3,032
Michigan	1913	3,786
Wisconsin	1913	1,823
Nebraska	1915	902
South Dakota	1917	789
New Hampshire	1917	679
Alabama	1919	224
Montana	1923	256
Delaware	1923	945
Virginia	1924	8,300
Idaho	1925	38
Utah	1925	772
Minnesota	1925	2,350
Maine	1925	326
Mississippi	1928	683
West Virginia	1929	98
Arizona	1929	30
Vermont	1931	253
Oklahoma	1931	556
South Carolina	1935	277
Georgia	1937	3,284

Source: Paul A. Lombardo, *Three Generations, No Imbeciles: Eugenics, the Supreme Court, and Buck v. Bell* (Baltimore, MD: Johns Hopkins University Press, 2008), 294.

diseases); (7) Blind (including those with seriously impaired vision); (8) Deaf (including those with seriously impaired hearing); (9) Deformed (including the crippled); and (10) Dependent (including orphans, ne'er-do-wells, the homeless, tramps and paupers)." All state sterilization laws passed prior to 1921, and many after, applied to individuals diagnosed as sexual perverts. Because definitions of insanity included same-sex contact, the laws sometimes doubly impacted gays, lesbians, and bisexuals. And while sterilization laws were never sex-specific, more women than men were sterilized (despite the greater ease of sterilizing men).[22]

Proponents of sterilization argued that it was a patriotic cause, and a better solution than long-term institutionalization. For the health of the nation the electoral body had to be protected against degenerative elements. Politicians, those in the judicial system, educators, and medical experts increasingly conflated political and economic strength with bodily and mental health. In a time of growing class disparities, contested racial and gender power relationships, and large-scale immigration, democracy had to be protected. For Dr. H. C. Sharp of the Indiana Reformatory, that meant the sterilization of "degenerates": which, he told the American Prison Association in 1909, included "most of the insane, the epileptic, the imbecile, the idiotic, the sexual perverts; many of the confirmed inebriates, prostitutes, tramps and criminals, as well as the habitual paupers found in our county poor asylums; also many of the children in our orphan homes." Civic undesirability was slippery and broad; and the definitions of disability, degeneracy, and immorality vague and permeable. Sharp assured his reading and listening audience, however, in ironically patriotic language, that sterilizations (and he performed them without anesthesia) in no way "impaired" the "pursuit of life, liberty, and happiness."[23]

Perhaps because of the permeability of disability and degeneracy, related concerns spread regarded maintaining able-bodied and able-minded women. Opponents of women's education such

as Edward Clarke had warned in the 1870s that a college education had the potential to permanently damage and disable
women. As the movement for female suffrage expanded, and as
women's employment and educational opportunities expanded,
so did social concern about the consequences for the female body
and greater society. This concern generally did not apply to all
women—but focused on white middle- and upper-class women
who sought expanded civic engagement.

The desire to maintain the female body needed for a healthy
nation is exemplified by William Lee Howard, a prominent physician and author of parental advice books at the turn of the
century. In 1909 he warned of rising physical and mental degeneration among women. According to Howard, "the female possessed of masculine ideas of independence," who proclaimed "her
sole right to decide questions of war or religion," and "that disgusting anti-social being, the female sexual pervert," embodied
"different degrees of the same class—degenerates." In essence,
women who sexually desired other women, women who lived
as gender nonconformists, and the mother "quick with children
who spends her mornings at the club, discussing 'social statistics,'" embodied different but related forms of a gender disability
caused by a degenerating body and mind. The true tragedy, Howard argued, was that if such a woman had children, "she is then
a menace to civilization . . . the mother of physical and mental
monstrosities who exist as a class of true degenerates." The poor
children would have no good future, for their "weak, plastic, developing cells of the brain are twisted, distorted, and a perverted
psychic growth promoted."[24] It was not enough to isolate the
Alice Smiths of the nation; they had to be sterilized.

Alice Smith's court-appointed attorney argued against her
sterilization in a case that reached the New Jersey Supreme
Court in 1913. The court agreed and pointed out that the surgery, salpingectomy, was dangerous. Those affected by the
law, the court noted, were poor and institutionalized in public

facilities. The law thus violated the Fourteenth Amendment's equal protection clause, because it was not applied to all. Alice Smith would not be sterilized. The court did not take up the more complicated legal question of whether or not sterilization statutes were constitutional.

In 1927 the US Supreme Court decided the issue in *Buck v. Bell*. In his majority opinion, Justice Oliver Wendell Holmes argued that "more than once" the nation's "best citizens" had given their lives for "the public welfare." "It would be strange," he went on, "if it could not call upon those who already sap the strength of the State for these lesser sacrifices . . . in order to prevent our being swamped with incompetence. It is better for all the world if, instead of waiting to execute degenerate offspring for crime or to let them starve for their imbecility, society can prevent those who are manifestly unfit from continuing their kind." Holmes concluded that in the family of plaintiff Carrie Buck, her mother, and her daughter, "Three generations of imbeciles are enough." The Court decided that sterilization statutes calling for sterilization of the institutionalized did not violate the Fourteenth Amendment's equal protection clause. The Supreme Court decision of *Buck v. Bell* has yet to be overturned.[25]

Alice Smith remained at the State Village for Epileptics until at least 1930, when she was listed in the federal census. Whether or not she was eventually sterilized, and whether or not she was released or died while institutionalized at the Village, is unknown. One wonders what her later life was like.

Carrie Buck, however, the subject of the *Buck v. Bell* Supreme Court decision, was sterilized and then released from the Virginia State Colony for Epileptics and Feeble-minded. Like Alice Smith, she was a young, poor, white girl who bore a child outside of marriage. She then entered the court system, her child was removed from her, and she was institutionalized. After Buck's sterilization and release she married and remained so for twenty-five years until her husband's death.

In the Progressive Era, a period of active governmental and social reform between the 1890s and 1920s, institutions for people considered either insane or feeble-minded transitioned from places where education and assimilation were sought to places that were simply custodial. More institutions embraced an organizational and ideological framework called "the colony plan." Dr. William Spratling, medical superintendent of the Craig Colony for Epileptics at Sonyea, New York (which many considered an ideal model), described the ideal colony as a beehive: "The innumerable hives picturesquely scattered through sweet smelling fields, or dotting the clover covered ground beneath fragrantly blooming apple trees, stand, in colony life, for contented and happy homes; the ceaseless hum of the wings of the busy little toilers stands for the activity of head and heart and hand of the common inhabitants of the colony, each striving for the common good; while the inevitable drones of the hives find their prototype in the lame, the unteachable and the mentally blind among the colonists, who are driven to seek refuge in such a home."[26]

Spratling's ideal architectural plans included an administrative building at the center from which paths radiated to various cottages. "Cottage" is a misleading term, for these spaces could house as many as fifty people. Such colonies embodied, as historian Lawrence Goodheart pointed out, an arrangement by which a "superior group rul[es] enclaves of inferior peoples." It is no historical accident that such language developed at the height of US colonialism abroad, such as that in the Philippines, and in the same period in which *Plessy v. Ferguson* (1896) ruled that separate was equal and that segregation served the public good.[27] In an era of US imperialism abroad, the supposedly inferior peoples at home, epileptics and the feeble-minded, remained segregated within their own geographical places, literally called a colony, and removed from larger society.

Money could provide one with a more comfortable facility, but money and social position did not remove the stigma from epilepsy, institutionalization, or insanity. Jean Clemens, the daughter of Mark Twain (Samuel Clemens), began experiencing blackouts at the age of fifteen. Seizures began later and doctors diagnosed her with epilepsy. Family resources meant that Jean never entered the court system. Instead she made the decision in her mid-twenties to enter Hillbourne Farms, a "private health resort" for individuals with epilepsy, in Katonah, New York. The decision was one made out of desperation and a lack of other options, encouraged by her doctor. In her diary she noted, "It was desperately hard to leave Father and Clara [her sister] in order to come out to a totally strange place. I tried my hardest not to cry before them, but as the time of departure began to approach I found it growing more and more difficult to restrain myself." During her fifteen-month stay Jean was aware, with some bitterness, of how difficult family life had been: "While I know that neither of them would admit being glad to have me away & therefore relieved of the presence of an ill person, I am sure that they must feel so . . . I am sure [father] is fond of me but I don't believe that he any more than Clara, really misses me."[28] While Jean was never threatened with sterilization by doctors, the courts, or her family, her family made clear their strong belief that she should never marry or bear children. And once institutionalized, she was deeply dependent on and controlled by doctors' orders and her father's money.

Institutionalization could be individually devastating, but often it also served larger ideological purposes. The warehousing of those considered deviant in one way or another, combined with the threat of sterilization, policed behaviors and literally controlled the reproduction of social norms. In these cases, the rhetoric of disability, benevolence, and care (both of the individual and of the nation) combined with and sometimes masked broader impulses of social control.

The Hiawatha Asylum for Insane Indians is an example that is both devastatingly singular and commonplace. Hiawatha

operated from 1903 to 1933. It may have begun with humanitarian goals, but even that is questionable. Because tribal peoples
were under federal authorities, state institutions had no legal obligation to accept indigenous peoples deemed insane. For South
Dakota senator Richard Pettigrew, it was a prime opportunity to
bring in money and jobs to Canton, South Dakota. Between its
founding and closure in 1933, more than three hundred indigenous people from at least fifty-three different tribes were sent to
Hiawatha. It was one of only two federal insane asylums. While
the majority of people were from the Great Plains and Midwest
nations of the Lakota Sioux, the Dakota Sioux, the Chippewa
and Menominee, some individuals arrived in Canton to find that
no one spoke the language of their home.

Commitment to the Hiawatha asylum involved virtually no
legal safeguards. Reservation superintendents, white agents of
the Bureau of Indian Affairs (BIA), could confine someone to
Hiawatha, and often included boarding school superintendents
in their decision making. Parents who opposed sending their children to boarding schools, individuals who resisted assimilation,
those who argued with BIA agents, those too rowdy or bother-
some, or those who steadfastly practiced indigenous religions,
could be and often were committed to Hiawatha. Standards of
insanity, normality, and health literally foreign to indigenous nations were imposed upon them, sometimes quite violently.

Dr. Harry Hummer, the second director of Hiawatha, believed that levels of "insanity among the Indians" were rising.
The arrival of civilized peoples and practices in North America,
he believed, were simply too much for those immersed in Native
cultures to handle. He also argued that "full-bloods" were more
likely to be insane than those with some European heritage. It
angered him that Hiawatha residents were "suspicious" of him,
stating that they were "much more reticent" than white insane
peoples. "Reticence, suspiciousness, superstitions" combined
with "the fact that oftentimes our only medium of conversation is

the sign language, which with us is very crude," he complained, made diagnosis difficult.[29]

Contemporary indigenous activist and elder Pemina Yellow Bird records that Hummer forbade Native dances and music, even to mourn the dead. Hiawatha staff commonly cut inmates' hair or shaved it off entirely. Boarding school officials also adopted this practice. Not only did it diminish possibilities of lice and make bathing easier, but it was, in Pemina Yellow Bird's words, "a form of spiritual murder." "In many Native belief systems," she says, "our hair is alive, and has a spirit and power of its own. We do not like others to even touch our hair, let alone shave it off." The forced cutting of hair also happened at boarding schools, another form of institutionalization. Zitkala-Sa, of the Yankton Sioux nation, chronicled having her hair cut at her first day of boarding school in roughly the same time period. She had tried to run away, and was tied to a chair: "I cried aloud, shaking my head all the while until I felt the cold blades of the scissors against my neck, and heard them gnaw off one of my thick braids. Then I lost my spirit."[30]

Family members and tribal representatives had filed complaints about Hiawatha with the BIA since its beginning, indicating among other things that they tried to maintain contact with their loved ones institutionalized at the facility. Employees had filed complaints against Hummer since his arrival, alleging sexual and monetary misconduct. In 1929 Dr. Samuel Silk arrived in Canton to inspect conditions at the federally funded facility (though this was certainly not the first such inspection). At the end of his six-day stay, he compiled a lengthy, highly critical report. The asylum, he said, was "a place of padlocks and chamber pots" with "intolerable conditions" throughout. Only the "poorest kind of medical care" was provided, and conditions were "very much below the standard of a modern prison." Straitjackets, metal wristlets, and ankle chains routinely confined people. Few ever went home; most died at Hiawatha and at least 131 are buried in a cemetery within sight of the asylum windows. For those inmates who came from tribal nations who valued being buried near one's ancestors, or with taboos against dwelling close to burial sites, being confined to a building that overlooked the cemetery, far from home, must have been horrific. One local resident remembered nighttime "wailing" coming from the asylum; likely it was not simply wailing, but the honoring and mourning of the dead with death songs.[31]

After Silk's condemnation of conditions at the facility in 1929, and again in 1933, the federal government closed the Hiawatha Asylum for Insane Indians. Silk's final report promoted Secretary of the Interior Harold Ickes to charge that the Canton institution remained open only "as a result of the greed and selfish inhumanity of certain interests there" and that conditions remained "sickening and intolerable," "filthy, inhuman, and revolting."[33]

Despite its brutalities, the Hiawatha experience was not unique, in that even within horrific institutions of terror human beings created community. As historian Susan Burch has shown, people institutionalized at Hiawatha cared for one another to the best of their abilities. They helped one another maintain contact with outside family members, and they sustained tribal relationships when at all possible.[35]

At the closing of Hiawatha in December 1933, sixteen patients were deemed lacking "insufficient mental derangement" for further institutionalization. They returned home, wherever that was. Sixty-nine people, apparently considered sufficiently mentally deranged, were transported to St. Elizabeth's Hospital in Washington, DC, the only other federal insane asylum—and one already segregated between whites and African Americans. It was also where Dr. Harry Hummer, Hiawatha's superintendent, had begun his career. Few former Hiawatha residents ever left St. Elizabeth's.[34]

At St. Elizabeth's, the former Hiawatha inmates encountered a staff already arguing about and building treatment regiments around the belief that African Americans lacked mental and physical capacity to handle contemporary and civilized life. In other words, they encountered institutionalized ideologies that already linked being not-white with disability. As Historian Martin Summers smartly notes, medical experts both in the United States and throughout European colonies in Africa thought that those of African descent had "underdeveloped nervous systems, and the more they came into contact with civilization the greater their propensity to become mentally disturbed." This was not simply an extension of the post–Civil War argument that freedom wrought insanity among former slaves, but part of the larger intellectual framework that justified colonialism abroad and domestically. It supported a segregated social order based on racial hierarchies. As Dr. John E. Lind put it in 1917, Africans as well as African Americans, no matter what pretext of sophistication they embraced, had a "savage heart beneath the civilized exterior."[35] The sixty-nine indigenous people who went by train from Canton, South Dakota, to Washington, DC, may have made a considerable geographic move, but they remained bound within the same ideological framework of subjugation.

Today a golf course lies on the grounds of the former Hiawatha Asylum for Insane Indians in Canton, South Dakota. What had been the unmarked cemetery is near the fifth tee. Because of the activism of Lakota journalist Harold Ironshield, activism that has been continued by others since his death, a memorial listing the names of those known to be buried in the Hiawatha cemetery now sits nearby. Like the cemeteries of many current and former insane asylums, only recently, if ever, have those buried been remembered by name. Its history is both unique and hauntingly commonplace.

The federal government provided even more reason for indigenous nations to fear its supposed caretaking efforts by undertaking a federal campaign against trachoma in the 1920s. Trachoma, a highly infectious eye disease also common among immigrant communities, affected nearly one in four Native Americans, and in some tribal nations and boarding schools the rate was as high as one out of every two people. Left untreated, the sometimes painful disease could result in blindness. In 1924 the federal Office of Indian Affairs initiated an anti-trachoma campaign. Instead of the more benign approach of improving sanitation conditions and providing health education, or the widely used strategy of prescribing medications such as silver nitrate, OIA officials endorsed an invasive and debated surgery called tarsectomy. This involved using forceps to turn the eyelids inside out in order to scrape off the infected corneal tissue. Among members of tribal nations as wide-ranging as those in Oklahoma, South Dakota, Michigan, Wisconsin, Montana, and California, over 22,773 tarsectomies were performed between 1925 and 1927.[36]

Among other problems, however, tarsectomy often did not work. It remained a controversial medical procedure that was quickly discredited, long before its use was abandoned, and tarsectomized patients "frequently experienced severe complications, which could include an untreatable recurrence of trachoma, entropion, scarring, or blindness." As historian Todd Benson has written, "OIA doctors had caused even more suffering for American Indian patients." Despite cautions and efforts to conduct small test cases, OIA doctors had gone ahead with their surgical efforts. They then blamed indigenous communities for the medical failures. As one OIA trachoma specialist wrote, "The Indian is a born skeptic anyhow, and must be handled by those familiar with his temperamental vagaries."[37] White racism thus resulted in both painful and ineffective surgical procedures—and in increasing blindness in an already marginalized population.

TECHNOLOGY, INDUSTRIALIZATION, AND AN "ARMY OF CRIPPLES"

When President Benjamin Harrison issued his first address to Congress in 1889, and as the nation wrestled with whether to assist or simply ignore disabled Civil War veterans, he warned of the undesirable consequences of industrialization. Railroad workers, he proclaimed, were subject "to a peril of life and limb as great as that of a soldier in time of war." Railroads were creating an "army of cripples." In 1910, Samuel Gompers of the American Federation of Labor (a man about as dissimilar to Harrison as could be) proclaimed that "'compensation for the victims of injury' stood 'above all' other issues in terms of its legislative significance; no other issue was 'of half the importance.'"[38] Industrialization was supposed to usher in both wealth and leisure, but it was disabling American workers in incredibly large numbers. Progressive Era reformers sought to soften the disabling blows of industrialization via protective labor legislation—and they used visuals of the disabled bodies of American workers to reveal the horrors of capitalism unchecked—but it is hard to exaggerate the impact of mines, steel plants, railroad yards, textile factories, lead poisoning, fast assembly lines, and repetitive motion on the bodies of working-class men, women, and children. And industrial accidents that resulted in a laborer's diminished income capacity, or a lack of income, meant that entire families suffered.

Thomas Johnston, perhaps, was lucky. The young black man employed at a Pittsburgh mill had both his arms broken by falling steel laths. His arms healed but "permanently took crooked and weak for any kind of mill work." He lost significant income while recovering but had the good fortune to then gain employment as a private cook, earning approximately the same as he had before.[39]

Samuel Jones's experience was more common. A dinkey, a small locomotive, ran over his foot and "crushed it so badly that he had to lose his leg below the knee." The Homestead Steel Works, his employer, gave him $150 and a watchman's job, but his earnings were cut by almost 40 percent. Crystal Eastman, a labor lawyer, journalist, and contemporary of Jones, estimated that approximately 43 percent of the survivors of industrial accidents had to make do with a diminished income.[40]

Too many men and women found themselves in situations similar to Andrew Antonik, a European immigrant who also worked at Homestead. He staffed the "skull-cracker," a heavy iron weight dropped from a height in order to break up scrap pieces of steel. One night in April 1907 Antonik failed to dodge the heavy flying steel scraps. He had worked a twenty-four-hour shift the day before. As Eastman reported, "His leg was crushed and had to be taken off below the knee." In October he had healed enough to appear at the company office with an interpreter (assumedly he didn't speak English). He had been given $150 "and the promise of an artificial leg and light work as soon as he should be able to get round." A year after his accident, Eastman found Antonik in the backyard of his boarding house. The artificial leg and the promised job had never materialized. He had sent $50 to his wife and five children in Europe, and was now out of money. Eastman estimated that approximately 13 percent of laborers who survived accidents were never again able to find work.[41]

Both temporary and permanently disabling work accidents were shockingly routine. In her investigations of Pennsylvania steel mills, Eastman found one mother who could not even remember how or when her sixteen-year-old son had lost two fingers in the mill, because it was so unremarkable. One retired steel worker insisted to her, "I never got hurt any to speak of." After persistent questions, "he recalled that he had once fractured his skull, that a few years later he had lost half of a finger, and that only three years ago he was laid up for nine weeks with a crushed foot."[42]

Investigators found similar statistics in every industrial field. An 1890 estimate was that 42 percent of Colorado railroad workers were injured on the job every year. Chinese immigrant laborers building the transcontinental railroads regularly lost their fingers and hands to both hammers and explosions. In 1907 protective labor legislation proposed by Robert "Fighting Bob" LaFollette, the progressive senator from Wisconsin, limited trainmen to *only* sixteen hours of labor per day, and telegraphers to nine hours. Complete accident numbers are difficult to attain. In 1907 death on the rails, for both passengers and employees, was nearly twelve thousand a year, and the number of serious injuries presumed to be several times larger.[43]

Workplace accidents, and disability caused by workplace poisons, seemed omnipresent. Textile mill operatives lost fingers, hands, and arms due to elevator shafts and other rapidly moving machinery. Female factory operatives were subject to "horrific injuries to their scalps by having their hair caught in power-operated shafts." Male and female cigar makers earned their own injury title, "cigarmaker's neurosis," caused by repetitive motion and a cramped working position—"characterized by severe pain in the shoulder, arm, and head . . . [and] might lose muscle control in their hands." Boilermakers, shipbuilders, and train engineers often lost hearing due to their noisy surroundings. Clock and watch painters, most of them female, experienced the paralysis and mental debility caused by lead poisoning as well as throat and mouth cancer.[44]

While industrialization had rapidly expanded the number of disabled US wage workers, adaptive technologies changed little until the onset of World War I. As nearly always, the return of heroic but disabled war veterans prompted technological change, improvements in prosthetics and other adaptive technologies, increased employment possibilities, and additional public attention. As one commentator wrote in 1918, the "peace-time cripple" had to "face an unkindly and prejudiced community because of a slightly physical difference." The "returned crippled soldier," however, had "force[d] the community to immediate action."[45]

At the end of World War I, the Committee on Vocational Training for Disabled Soldiers sought to provide recommendations for disabled soldiers but found that they had no idea about the lives of "peace-time" cripples: thus, the Cleveland Cripple Survey. The social service agencies of Cleveland "thought that

they surely knew all the cripples in their city," but were aston-
ished to find that more than 65 percent had been previously
unidentified—"the adult cripples," researchers discovered with
amazement, "are not the dependents" they had anticipated. The
Cleveland investigators had begun their research with an assumption that all people with disabilities were incapable of financial
self-support. The results astounded them, for they had been completely mistaken. For example, among armless men they found
a beggar, a successful street peddler, and a District Court judge
who had taken his bar examination by "holding a pencil between
his teeth." "The lives of unknown cripples are much more normal
than had been supposed," one researcher observed. This article
concluded, however, by drawing a line between "the successful"
cripples and "the begging type of cripples."[46] Class mattered.

In the aftermath of World War I, rehabilitation experts urged
disabled veterans to become successful cripples. Rehabilitation
industries, vocational programs, and civil rights talk for people
with disabilities expanded prolifically, but were not always extended to nonveterans. People increasingly distinguished between
good disabled people and bad disabled people, good citizens and
bad citizens; the largest distinguishing factor being whether or
not one earned a living. At the US General Hospital in Fort Sheri-
dan, Illinois, returning servicemen were told that "The Creed of
the Disabled Soldier" was: "Once more to be useful—to see pity
on the eyes of my friends replaced with commendation—to work,
produce, provide, and to feel that I have a place in the world—
seeking no favours and giving none—a MAN among MEN in
spite of this physical handicap."[47] A poster of the Red Cross Institute for Crippled and Disabled Men insisted that one-armed veterans could find future employment as ship-workers or welders, if
only they would accept vocational training.[48] A manly cripple, a
successful cripple, and a grateful disabled veteran could find and
attain success if only they would cheerfully seek it.

The reality, however, was not that easy. Disabled white women and people of color encountered substantial employment discrimination and social resistance, and they had much less success attaining the status of a *successful cripple*. And disabled veterans found that despite Red Cross posters proclaiming to employers that "the disabled man profitably employed is no longer handicapped," employers often denied them employment.[49]

President Calvin Coolidge ended his 1923 State of the Union address by calling for "good will and charity, confidence and peace." The nation, he proclaimed, had "taken her place in the world as a Republic—free, independent, powerful." The best thing its citizens could do, "the best service that can be rendered to humanity," Coolidge challenged Congress and the nation, was to provide "the assurance that this place will be maintained."

The question of how best to maintain the nation has dominated all eras of US history. In the Progressive Era, perhaps more than in any other, however, that meant surveillance and containment of bodies considered deviant or degenerative. Policies were put in place to carefully monitor the bodies of those entering the United States and sterilize the deviant bodies of those already within the nation's gates. Sexuality, class, race, gender, and ethnicity forcibly intersected with notions of disability and quality citizenship.

The educational, industrial, and institutional developments of the Progressive Era had contradictory consequences for people with disabilities. The rapid expansion of industry brought employment and wealth to many, and its accompanying technological changes revolutionized adaptive equipment used by people with disabilities who could afford them, but it also wrought devastation on the bodies and minds of many American laborers. The rapid expansion of institutions had similar contradictory results. For some, particularly blind and deaf people, institutionalization created rich communities, sources of political organizing, and individual empowerment. For others, particularly those considered to have cognitive or mental disabilities, institutionalization often meant isolation and abuse. The wonder is that in nearly all circumstances, people with disabilities generated, to the best of their abilities, community. Like nearly all other Americans, people with disabilities sought the "good will and charity, confidence and peace" of which Coolidge spoke."[50]

SEVEN

WE DON'T WANT TIN CUPS

Laying the Groundwork, 1927–1968

Just two years after the Supreme Court ruling of *Buck v. Bell* legalized, for the good of the nation, compulsory sterilization of the unfit, the US economy collapsed. Beginning with a 1929 stock market crash and continuing through the development of Franklin Roosevelt's New Deal and World War II, the majority of Americans struggled with economic devastation. Despite the economic wreckage and the personal and familial destruction it wrought, the activism of people with disabilities and the federal policy changes generated in response to the Great Depression created new opportunities for people with disabilities.

When nineteen-year-old Miss H. P. wrote First Lady Eleanor Roosevelt from Cleveland, Ohio, in 1934, however, she saw few opportunities. She had left school at sixteen in order to help her mother. Her father, disabled by diabetes since 1928, was "not himself anymore." He had "too many worrys [*sic*] . . . is always grouchy and scolding at us children." Her seventeen-year-old sister had never been able to walk, had never attended school, and had "to be carried to bed at night and lifted up from bed in the morning." As the older sister explained, "all she does is sit in a chair all day long." The local "Relef Office" had not helped the family with seven children, so Miss H. P. sought the First Lady's help, for "there is never peace and happiness in our home." The disability of father and daughter, coupled with the nation's economic woes, left the household with virtually no economic or emotional resources.[1]

In Holland, Texas, the family household of eighteen-year-old E. C. was in similar straits in 1941. Four years earlier, then just fourteen years old, the young man's left leg had been caught in the wheel of a field planter while he helped his tenant-farmer father. The mules had not stopped. His mangled leg was now stiff, sore, and drained fluid constantly; he had no muscle control over his foot. The family had spent all its money on hospital bills. He wrote to Mrs. Roosevelt about his steadfast desire to "get an education" and make his "life worthwhile to serve my home and my country." How, he asked, could he do that?[2]

These two young adults, both affected by disability, made preliminary activist moves by writing Eleanor Roosevelt—clearly given hope by the attention that both Eleanor and President Franklin Roosevelt had paid to issues of poverty, disability, and disadvantage. Throughout the country, slowly, inconsistently, but increasingly, other individuals lived out their own forms of activism.

In the spring of 1935, for example, a group of largely white, physically disabled New Yorkers spent several weeks protesting at the city's Emergency Relief Bureau. With slogans such as "We Don't Want Tin Cups. We Want Jobs," and "We Are Lame But We Can Work," the group expressed their anger and disgust at city and federal policies that automatically rejected all people with disabilities from work relief programs—categorizing all people with disabilities as "unemployable." The group, which came to be known as the League of the Physically Handicapped, handed out fliers that read, "The Handicapped still are discriminated against by Private Industry. It is because of this discrimination that we *demand* the government recognize its obligation to make adequate provisions for handicapped people in the Works

Relief Program." As the league's president Sylvia Flexer Bassoff wrote to Harry Hopkins, head of the Works Progress Association, she wanted "not sympathy—but a concrete plan to end discrimination . . . on WPA projects."[3]

Similarly, in the late 1940s Henry Williams and fellow African American veterans of World War II organized a series of "wheel-ins" and "body pickets" in front of the Cleveland mayor's office. They sought quality and racially equitable rehabilitation centers and housing for disabled veterans. Williams reflected later, "Though broken in body, I was fighting . . . to stamp out those same principles that we fought against during the war. Basically, sir, I was fighting for the civil rights of every disabled citizen."[4]

Like many other individuals and groups in the period from the beginning of the Great Depression in 1929 through the late 1960s, Henry Williams and the League of the Physically Handicapped embraced the language, the ideology, and the laws of rights and citizenship in order to advance the claims of people with disabilities. They also inched toward the argument that all people with disabilities—whatever the kind or cause of those disabilities—shared experiences of stigma and discrimination. Cross-disability organizations and alliances began, though haltingly and inconsistently, to draw connections between disability, race, and sex discrimination. Throughout the Depression and extending into the Cold War period, people with disabilities and their allies laid important groundwork that later disability rights activists would build on.

CREATING COMMUNITY, DESPITE ALL

The organized Deaf cultural community had grown increasingly stronger throughout the early twentieth century.[5] Centered around a common linguistic identity, that of users of American Sign Language, deaf clubs flourished. Dramas, poetry, picnics, religious services, and athletic programs created community. Building on these strengths, the National Fraternal Society of the Deaf (founded in 1901) and the National Association of the Deaf (founded in 1880) actively confronted insurance discrimination, job discrimination, driving restrictions, lack of vocational training, and other issues the Deaf community identified as vital. Though both organizations were initially predominantly white and exclusionary, they became important centers of deaf activism.[6]

Sarah Uhlberg later reminisced to her son about how she savored the community she found at New York City's Lexington School for the Deaf in the early 1920s, where she lived during the weekdays. "When the lights were turned out," she told him, "we went to the bathroom, where a light was always on, and we talked till our eyes refused to stay open. We loved to talk to one another in our language. We lived for sign, and the ability to communicate with one another was like the water of life, our oasis of language and meaning, in the midst of the huge expanse of desert silence and incomprehension that was the greater hearing world." Every Friday evening she left this linguistic oasis and rode the subway to her family home, sitting beside her father while they sat without communicating—for he knew no sign language.[7]

The Depression hit the deaf community hard. One study found that 44 percent of deaf workers who had been employed prior to the Depression had lost their jobs by 1935; compared to an overall national unemployment rate of 20 percent. By 1938 the DiMarco household of Dubuque, Iowa, had experienced unemployment for over eight years. Bernard DiMarco and his wife, who then had a three-year-old daughter named Shirley, had met at a deaf club picnic in Rockford, Illinois. Both adults expressed frustration at the discrimination they faced while finding and keeping employment. Mrs. DiMarco told an interviewer of the Works Project Administration that employers "don't seem interested in a deaf man [and] won't listen to us. I've been in the Candy Factory & Halls trying to get on also and they won't talk [and] just shake their head as if I were a freak. I wish I could make them understand we have to live like others . . . But it's awfully hard on us deaf—as they don't seem to care for a deaf person when they can get one who can hear." She hoped that something good would come for deaf people from the WPA interview: "I am glad to help you in any way we can & the deaf in General if it will interest anyone in them. God knows we need it." She asked the interviewer, "Do you suppose we ought to stay on here in Dubuque or try to get away[?]. I don't know whether we'd be any better off somewhere else or not. If only I knew where there was a steady job."[8]

Louis Uhlberg was a fortunate man during the Depression. He worked as a printer at a New York newspaper for over forty years. Though money was tight, and though he sometimes feared the loss of his job, he remained employed, courted, married, and had two children in the midst of the national economic crisis. His son Myron, then a young boy, remembered passing a man, old and dirty, sitting on a curb, who had whispered to Myron that he was hungry. The father asked his hearing son what the older man had said, and then gave the older man some apples and a loaf of bread. Louis instructed his son, "Tell him I'm sorry . . . but tell him things are bound to get better." The father and son then continued their walk home.[9] Uhlberg undoubtedly knew of the difficulties he would face if he were to lose his job.

Like other people with disabilities who sought employment through the Work Projects Administration and state or local work relief programs, deaf people found themselves categorically classified as "unemployable"—regardless of prior employment, vocational training, the conditions of their bodies, or educational background. As part of the New Deal developed by President Roosevelt as a solution to the economic problems of the Great Depression, the Work Projects Administration employed millions of unemployed Americans in the construction of public buildings and roads, literacy projects, cultural programs of art and music, as well as social services. WPA programs, however, as with nearly all other work relief programs, refused to hire people with disabilities. Just as the League of the Physically Handicapped had done, the National Association of the Deaf battled this. While exceptions were not made for most people with disabilities, in 1938 deaf workers became "employable" per WPA regulations. By 1939, however, policies shifted and deaf workers once again became "unemployable."[10]

Most Deaf organizations and workers did not reject the categorization of people with disabilities as "unemployable," but insisted that deaf people were not disabled people. Since the organization of the first institutions for and of deaf people in the United States, they had emphasized their separateness as a linguistic community, their normality, and their full citizenship potential. Already marginalized they sought to distinguish themselves from those they considered *the truly disabled*. Some feared that hearing individuals within a larger disability community would seek to dominate if they made cross-disability alliances. Some deaf leaders, as historian Susan Burch has written, "thought they could reject the stigma of disability" by "rejecting overtures from disabled activists."[11] Deaf leaders thus rejected alliances with disabled activists such as the League of the Physically Handicapped who challenged the employment discrimination within New Deal employment programs.

For deaf African Americans, if they were familiar with this argument it must have seemed like privileged folly. Like white deaf Americans, deaf African Americans used the relationships and institutional resources of schools to foster community. The NFSD, the NAD, and southern state associations remained white by policy. Many western and northern schools for deaf people were integrated, but southern schools resoundingly were not. Most had substandard facilities due to substandard state or local funding. Trained white teachers rarely went to black schools; black teachers generally had little training in deaf education because of segregation in deaf schools. Because of this the students and staff at many African American deaf schools created their own unique sign language dialects, different from the standardized American Sign Language and sometimes even from that of neighboring state schools for African American deaf students.[12] Such linguistic developments were of necessity, but contributed to and continued racial segregation.

Southern legislatures tended to place African American deaf and blind students together: for example, the North Carolina State School for the Colored Deaf and Blind; Texas's Institute for Deaf, Dumb and Blind Colored Youth; the Alabama School for the Negro Deaf and Blind; or the Virginia State School for Colored Deaf and Blind. When deafblind activist Helen Keller testified before Congress about the importance of expanding the Social Security Act in 1944, she emphasized discriminatory state funding and the ways in which racism and ableism intersected to limit opportunities. "In my travels up and down the continent," she testified, "I have visited their shabby school buildings and witnessed their pathetic struggles against want. I have been shocked by the meagerness of their education, lack of proper medical care and the discrimination which limits their employment chances." It was a disgrace, she went on, "that in this great wealthy land such injustice should exist to men and women of a different race—and blind at that! It is imperative that colored people without sight be granted financial aid worthy of their human dignity and courage in the face of fearful obstacles."[13]

The economic inequalities of race in the United States meant that poor medical care sometimes created disability—and the Depression exacerbated those inequalities. Henrietta Evers, the youngest of eight children born to a poor African American farming family in Georgia in 1929, contracted polio at the age of four. In an era when news of polio spread fast and sent fear throughout entire communities, Evers remembered hearing of a white girl in the same county who had also acquired polio but who had the privilege of hospital care. Evers received care from a country doctor of questionable repute. "My leg had drawn up, it was bending at the knee and I couldn't bend it out. So, what he [the doctor] did, he just takes it, and pulls the leg out, and breaks all the tendons and all the ligaments. It did hurt! Oh, my did it hurt. You could hear me holler all over Georgia. I remember—I will never forget." A family friend in Philadelphia took Evers in, all of her family hoping she could find better medical care. In Philadelphia, Evers received rehabilitation treatment, surgery, and better care, but the damage done by an inadequate doctor remained.[14]

The changing history of disability—its intersection with class, race, and rights activism—is particularly evident in the lives of polio survivors. Polio hit the United States very late in the nineteenth century. The 1916 epidemic, the first large epidemic, included an estimated twenty-seven thousand cases and six thousand deaths. Polio, also called infantile paralysis and poliomyelitis, is a virus that attacks the central nervous system. Now eradicated in the United States, polio once resulted in widespread fears and quarantines. Those who survived polio sometimes acquired significant physical disability, largely but not exclusively among children. Children aged five to nine were hit the hardest. When news spread of polio's arrival in a community, playgrounds emptied as parents attempted to protect their children. During the 1916 epidemic both Pennsylvania state officials and Paterson, New Jersey, civic officials blocked the roads in an attempt to deny entry to fleeing New Yorkers—the region hit with the highest number of cases.[15]

For children, polio often meant removal from their family household. For Henrietta Evers, polio meant moving to the home of a family friend in Philadelphia in order to escape the limited opportunities available to a disabled African American child in rural Georgia. For rural Minnesotan Richard Maus, a white farm boy, polio meant admittance to the Gillette State Hospital for Crippled Children in St. Paul, Minnesota, at the age of six months, in 1939. During his 314-day stay, his parents could see him only through the glass wall of the ward. Before he was fifteen, Maus had been "admitted to Gillette seven times, spent 938 days in the hospital, and underwent sixteen operations."[16] Maintaining family ties and emotional support in this context was tremendously difficult.

For children with polio such as Maus, the hospital or rehabilitation facility thus became a community of necessity that was determined by place. Often ostracized by others when they were home—both from fear of the disease and from discomfort with disability—children with polio built important emotional networks during their hospitalization in wards of four to twenty children or adolescents. Spitball battles, surreptitious wheelchair races, parties, flirting, and nighttime pillow fights were common. Arvid Schwartz remembered he and his friends making so much noise at night that the boys would "catch hell" from the nurses. "But really," he went on, "what could they do to us?" In a marvelous twist on the old-boy network, historian and scholar Sucheng Chan made important professional connections once she became an adult based on the relationship she had built decades earlier with her childhood friend Janet Frandendese, both of them polio survivors, as they spent hours riding back and forth to school on the bus for kids with physical disabilities.[17]

One of the most famous polio-rehabilitation centers is the Roosevelt Warm Springs Institute for Rehabilitation in Warm Springs, Georgia. Franklin Delano Roosevelt founded Warm Springs in 1926 and spent significant time there between first visiting the thermal springs in 1924 and his death at his nearby cottage in 1945. For FDR, who became governor of New York in 1928 and president in 1932, Warm Springs was a physical and emotional retreat. Roosevelt had contracted polio in 1921 and was paralyzed from the waist down. While many knew of his past with polio, he, the media, and those around him colluded in hiding the extent of his disability. At Warm Springs, Roosevelt felt comfortable acknowledging and revealing his disability. There he made no effort to hide his wheelchair, his paralyzed legs, and his reliance on personal assistants.[18]

In 1938 Roosevelt and others affiliated with Warm Springs founded the National Foundation for Infantile Paralysis. The NFIP, which later became known as the March of Dimes, raised substantial funds for polio prevention and treatment research, including the treatments advocated by Sister Elizabeth Kenny and the development of polio vaccines. It also provided braces, wheelchairs, iron lungs, and other assistive devices to those unable to purchase them on their own.[19]

Partially designed by Roosevelt, the facilities at Warm Springs were an early example of architectural accessibility—built on what is now called universal design principles and easily accessible to Roosevelt and other wheelchair users. The thermal hot springs eased bodies, but most important was the rich community enabled by Warm Springs. At Warm Springs no one stared. At Warm Springs wheelchairs and assistive devices were the routine. Lifelong friends and lovers emerged, as did lifelong professional and economic ties.

The ideology, experiences, and institutions of polio were racialized, however. Warm Springs was a retreat, but a retreat for "an elite group of the disabled." African Americans served as waiters and cleaning staff at Warm Springs but were not welcome as users of the health facilities or employed as doctors, nurses, or administrators. Indeed, through the early twentieth century, medical and rehabilitation personnel throughout the country had justified the exclusion of African Americans from their institutions by erroneously insisting that blacks, and sometimes also Asian Americans, were not susceptible to polio. Black civil rights leaders first drew attention to segregation at Warm Springs during Roosevelt's 1936 reelection campaign. Civil rights leaders praised the 1944 March of Dimes funding of a nonsegregated polio clinic during a fierce epidemic in North Carolina but wondered "why they can't do the same thing year round." The March of Dimes funded a polio center at the Tuskegee Institute in 1939, and Warm Springs desegregated in 1945 (at the personal insistence of Eleanor Roosevelt).[20]

Yet race continued to shape experiences of polio and disability. Wilma Rudolph, the 1960 multiple Olympic gold medal winner, remembered having to ride a segregated bus more than fifty miles to be treated for her polio when she was a child in Tennessee. In May 1954, the very month that the Supreme Court issued its decision in *Brown v. Board of Education,* black children had to leave their schools and stand in lines outside white public schools in order to receive the polio vaccine developed by Jonas Salk. The restrooms and water fountains inside, of course, were forbidden to those children. In 1964, when white and black college students arrived in Mississippi as Freedom Riders, one young middle-class white man, fresh from New England, was appalled to meet a polio survivor who made her livelihood by picking cotton while on her knees—unable to stand as other cotton pickers did. And that same year, as state patrolmen forced others to beat civil rights activist and Mississippi sharecropper Fannie Lou Hamer with a tire jack after she had dared to attend a voter-registration workshop, she sought to protect the left side of her body, where she still felt the effects of the polio she had had as a six year old.[21] The intersection of disability and race could make economic and political survival extremely difficult.

Surviving polio also, however, often provoked activism. Many of the educational reforms that provided better education for children with disabilities came about at the insistence of the parents of polio survivors. Access to higher education came about due to the stubbornness and confidence of the young adults who had survived polio as children and wanted full lives as adults with disabilities. For example, in 1958, when Anne Emerman, the future director of the New York Mayor's Office for People with Disabilities, said that she wanted to attend college, a social worker told the white wheelchair user that such dreams were delusional. "This idea is a fantasy," Emerman had been warned, "and fantasies can lead to mental illness."[22] Emerman went anyway. More equitable access to all aspects of civic life mattered to people with disabilities. They did not want to be shunned.

In the 1940s New Jersey housewife Laura Blossfield was sadly accustomed to her isolation. Like many other parents of children considered mentally retarded, her life had become "a social island." But she also knew that she was not alone. In October 1946 she placed a notice in her local paper, seeking out parents in similar circumstances. "Each parent," she hoped, "can ultimately help his own child by doing something to help all children similarly affected . . . Therefore, I suggest an organization for all parents of mentally retarded children[, one that] may well prove to be the first chapter in a nationwide organization." She and two others soon formed the New Jersey Parents Group for Retarded Children.[23]

Doctors routinely encouraged parents to institutionalize their children with mental retardation in the postwar period, and at their encouragement many parents never mentioned or acknowledged such children again. Physicians and psychologists warned parents that the immense needs of such a child would ruin marriages and destroy the lives of other children in the household. Many parents followed this advice. The famed child psychoanalyst Erik Erickson and his wife, Joan, institutionalized their child after he was born, telling their other children that he had died at birth.[24]

Despite this incredible social pressure, and the dire predictions of medical professionals, some parents began to organize and advocate on behalf of their children and their families—rejecting the social stigma associated with cognitive disabilities.[25] Parents, in essence, came out of the closet and brought national attention to the lack of appropriate educational options, living options, and family support. In 1950 author Pearl Buck, the only female ever to receive the Pulitzer Prize and the Nobel Prize, published *The Child Who Never Grew,* about her daughter Carol. Buck presented Carol not as shameful but as an innocent and joyful child. Similarly, in 1953 television and movie star and evangelical Christian Dale Evans published *Angel Unaware*—about her cognitively disabled daughter Robin, who had died at two years of age. Robin, she said, was not a punishment: instead, she was a gift from God, sent to "strengthen us spiritually and to draw us closer together in the knowledge and love and fellowship of God." Eugenicist claims that cognitive disabilities represented defective family genes were even more publicly challenged when the Kennedy family embraced the cause of mental retardation and (at least some of them) acknowledged Rosemarie Kennedy, the cognitively disabled sister of President Kennedy. In 1962 Eunice Shriver Kennedy, another Kennedy sister, wrote in *The Saturday Evening Post,* "Mental retardation can happen in any family. It *has* happened in the families of the poor and the rich, of governors, senators, Nobel prizewinners, doctors, lawyers, writers, men of genius, presidents of corporations—the president of the United States."[26]

Parent groups in many states, most often energized and staffed by volunteer mothers, eventually merged to form the National Association for Retarded Children in 1952. By 1964 their membership exceeded one hundred thousand people—nearly all of them parents. Minnesota mothers, like many mothers across the nation, became professional and astute lobbyists: they befriended the female secretaries of the male legislators as they sought sway, and in 1963 took legislative wives on a tour of state hospitals. In 1974 the organization changed its name to become the National Association for Retarded Citizens, attempting to reject the assumption that people with cognitive disabilities were perpetual children. In 1992 the national organization became simply The Arc, in an effort to recognize the organizational leadership and involvement of those individuals with developmental and intellectual disabilities as well as to rid itself of the term "mental retardation."[27]

Parent advocate groups changed the institutional and educational landscapes of people with cognitive disabilities, as did a number of sensationalized media exposés. Stories that brought to light the horrific conditions at institutions for people with disabilities were not new. Dorothea Dix had used a similar strategy in the 1840s and 1850s. Journalist Nellie Bly had kicked off her career by deceiving her way into the infamous insane asylum of Blackwell's Island and then writing about it in *Ten Days in a Madhouse* (1888).

In the mid- to late 1940s, activists—many of them accidental activists—shone a spotlight on the horrific conditions, squalidness, and brutality within American institutions for people with psychiatric and intellectual disabilities. The onset of World War II had stripped such institutions of much of their staff. Many men went to war, and those who did not, as well as female employees, often found better-paying employment, with better working conditions, in wartime defense plants. At the same time, the federal government sought placements for the nearly twelve thousand World War II conscientious objectors assigned to public service. Nearly three thousand were assigned to state mental hospitals and training schools containing an array of people with cognitive and developmental disabilities.

As disability scholar Steven Taylor has characterized it, their work was hard: "Ten hour days were commonplace. As few as 1 to 3 men were in charge of as many as 350 patients, including those individuals with the most severe disabilities." The common use of physical restraints and brutality challenged "the humanitarian and pacifist beliefs" of many of the conscientious objectors. Shaken by their experiences and determined to bring about social change, the young men brought institutional conditions to the attention of local media, community leaders, academics, and prominent Americans in popular culture and politics. Their experiences were documented in a 1947 book, *Out of Sight, Out of Mind*, compiled by Frank Leon Wright; it was praised by Eleanor Roosevelt in her "My Day" newspaper column. With photographs and beautiful prose, it forced attention to the brutality, cruelty, neglect, and disdain that were the everyday experience of too many institutionalized Americans.[28]

Christmas in Purgatory (1966) became an even more successful exposé. Burton Blatt, a professor at Boston University, and his friend, photographer Fred Kaplan, visited four large New England state institutions for people with psychiatric and cognitive disabilities, after Senator Robert Kennedy's unexpected but highly publicized visit to two New York institutions in 1965. The pair secretly took pictures and published them as a photographic exposé. The stark black-and-white images of *Christmas in Purgatory* remain disturbing to this day: naked or half-dressed individuals in crowded and barren environments, the common use of physical restraints simply to relieve staff of care obligations, and the jarringly casual disregard for fellow human beings. Blatt hoped for reform, especially after being invited to address the Massachusetts legislature convened at one of the state schools.[29]

By 1979, however, Blatt had given up on reform. He bluntly concluded, "We must evacuate the institutions for the mentally retarded."[30] Blatt and others would expand the push for deinstitutionalization.

WORLD WAR II AND THE EXPERIENCE OF DISABILITY

During World War II, those on the home front expected to be asked to sacrifice. They grew their own food, ate meatless meals, did without silk, recycled tin, often moved into new fields of employment, sent letters and care packages to soldiers they loved, and mourned those who died. Industry and the federal government worked together to staff the ever-growing wartime industrial needs. The African American community, whose young men went off to war, questioned how they could be asked to give lives in sacrifice while being allowed only limited and segregated access to wartime industrial employment and civil rights. Able-bodied white women wondered the same.

World War II had profound impact on the disabled community as a whole. Even though wartime federal policies were ostensibly designed to meet labor needs, they sometimes had the ironic consequence of driving people with disabilities away from the workplace—regardless of race or sex. Simultaneously, however, other government and industrial policies encouraged the employment of people with disabilities in order to meet the wartime crisis demands. And like other wars before it, World War II expanded the ranks of Americans with disabilities.

In October 1942, as Germany began the assault on Stalingrad and US troops landed on Guadalcanal, Bay Crockett, of Pueblo, Colorado, sought help from President Roosevelt. Crockett, who had broken his back in 1918, used crutches, and could not walk for more than a block, supported his wife and child and had done so for quite a while. His success as a provider, which understandably made him proud, required a car. What could he do, he asked his president, when his work travel required more gas-rationing coupons than he had? Like many others with mobility disabilities, he feared losing his job as an unexpected result of World War II's tire and gasoline rationing. How could he, who could not walk to work, continue to support his wife and child? Could he and others in similar circumstances have extra gas allowance?[31]

Victor Lee of Los Altos, California, similarly asked, "What is to happen to the invalid under the tire rationing program?" Trains, buses, and streetcars, he knew, were not accessible. "It seems to me," he went on, "that in authentic cases of invalidism certified by a registered physician an exception might be made to permit the purchase of tires for cars owned by such persons. No great amount of new rubber would be involved in making life at least endurable for such people whose pleasures are at best few."[32]

After being sent back and forth between local and state appeal boards several times in her efforts to acquire new car tires, Julia O'Brien also wrote to FDR's office, with great frustration. She appealed to FDR because, as she put it, "you know what it means to have your wings clipped." Due to polio at age five, O'Brien was unable to walk. For over twenty-one years she had taught English and chaired the English Department at a local school, leading "a busy, active life." "This would not be possible," she wrote, "if I couldn't get around in a car." In fall 1942 her tires had already traveled over forty thousand miles. She feared that any day her tires would "blow" and that she would have "no redress." It infuriated her that during her appeals process each of her requests had been denied and a clerk had glibly given her "some platudinous remarks about the need for sacrifice in time of war."[33]

"Sacrifice," she proclaimed, "I think I know the meaning of the word! For twenty-eight years I have met the competition in my field and naturally had never asked nor received special consideration because of my lameness." In a later letter, after again being denied an additional tire ration, she wrote, "As I start the new school year, I rather envy the defense workers to whom the rationing boards are so rational. This is truly a man's world; and we women can be pardoned for saying, 'What a mess they are making of it!'"[34]

When employment was needed and encouraged, wartime rationing policies hindered people with disabilities from continuing in the employment that sustained their households and contributed to their communities. How many people were affected is unclear. Government employment programs, public and private relief agencies, and the general public—even when faced with direct contrary evidence—tended to assume that people with disabilities did not and could not work for wages. These policies that resulted in discouraging people with disabilities from employment existed simultaneously with federal and industrial efforts to bring people with disabilities into the wage workforce—again, built on the erroneous assumption that people with disabilities were not already working for wages.

During World War II, however, "when an exceptional demand for labor arose, there was a significant increase in the employment of disabled workers who compiled impressive records of productivity." As men and women left private employment for government and military service during the war, and as wartime industrial needs expanded exponentially, government agencies began to encourage the employment of people with disabilities. Government employment-agency placement of people with disabilities "rose from 28,000 in 1940 to 300,000 in 1945"; between 1940 and 1950, placements numbered almost 2 million.[35] Private agencies joined the effort as well.

As early as 1942, the Society for Crippled Children of Cleveland, Ohio (which later became Easter Seals), encouraged using "the physically disabled" as "an important source of labor supply for the all-out war effort." Its Cleveland Placement Bureau, the society went on, was already placing "eight out of every ten seriously handicapped men and women" in "useful jobs in industry." Before the bombing of Pearl Harbor, the society admitted, its employment placement programs had generally been considered "community services for the disabled." After Pearl Harbor, however, the efforts met the patriotic and wartime needs of the nation. Employment placement programs for people with disabilities had much larger meaning. "Handicapped men and women," the article explained, "must be prepared to take the places of those called for active military service. They must be trained to fill the many new jobs in the factories turning out the planes, tanks, and guns needed for Democracy and Freedom."[36] The nation needed its disabled citizens.

The Cleveland Placement Bureau touted the case of John Millard. Millard, it was explained, "had not been able to find a job in industry for eight years because no concern seemed interested in hiring a man with two artificial legs." A local employer hired Millard in an assembly line at the recommendation of the bureau. He proved such "an efficient workman" that "five other handicapped persons have been added to this department." For Millard, with a wife and six children, the job must have been both a relief and a thrill. Other success stories included "a girl with a back deformity" who stood out as "one of the outstanding workers in a large factory producing signal equipment for the Navy." A man "with both hands deformed since birth" tested metals for Army transport trucks, and "a boy on crutches" drafted plane plans.[37]

For many people with disabilities, wartime employment provided great pride, national service in the midst of a national crisis, and a solid and reliable income. May Curtis, a deaf alumnus of Gallaudet College, worked both on the fuselages of B-29s and as a typist for the Pentagon. When interviewed by contemporary blind activist and poet Kathi Wolf, she proclaimed, "It's not in the history books, but I'm the deaf Rosie!"[38]

The many Rosie the Riveters, as the women working in industrial plants were known, and all of those who worked in wartime industry, deserved to be proud of their wartime service. Wartime industrial work was dangerous, resulting in injuries, disability, and death. As historian Andrew Kersten has shown, "during the first few years of the Second World War, it was safer for Americans to be on the battlefront than it was for them to work on the home front in the arsenal of democracy." Industrial accidents were not new, and in the nineteenth century the US industrial accident rate beat that of other industrial countries, but as war hit and industry sped up, accident rates rose even further.[39] Worker carelessness often received the blame, and newly disabled citizens did not bask in the heroic adulation reserved for disabled veterans. More historical research needs to be done, but it is likely that when employees with disabilities had accidents they and their disabilities received the blame.

Just as previous wars had furthered public discussion about the employment, assistance needs, gender roles, and rights of disabled citizens, so did World War II. After World War I, Congress had passed legislation providing vocational training for disabled veterans. In 1920 the Smith-Fess Act established similar vocational training programs for disabled civilians. The Barden-LaFollette Act of 1943 expanded these efforts substantially, providing manual vocational training, higher-education opportunities, and physical rehabilitation services.[40]

Underlying the creation of such programs, and postwar educational and employment policies in general, were debates about the role of government and citizenship rights. Were people with disabilities entitled to employment? Was disability a question of charity? Could employers restrict employees based on disability, race, and sex? What obligation did the nation have toward creating and guaranteeing its citizens equal access to education, housing, and/or employment? In 1944 Great Britain adopted a quota policy, in which employers with more than twenty employees were required to have a workforce of which at least 3 percent were people with disabilities. This idea was never broached seriously in the United States. In the early 1940s, when some in Congress attempted to pass legislation prohibiting employment discrimination against people with disabilities, the idea was quickly shot down.[41]

Paul Strachan and the American Federation of the Physically Handicapped (AFPH), a cross-disability activist organization, pushed the argument that people with disabilities had civil rights that included access to employment, education, and all of society. From today's perspective, and at first glance, it is easy to dismiss Strachan's views as simplistic. He tends to be remembered as the father of the National Employ the Physically Handicapped Week, signed into existence by President Truman in 1945.

Strachan, however, understood disability as a rights issue—not one of social welfare or the individual. Rather than focusing on individuals and their emotional and physical "adjustment" to disability (which the emerging rehabilitation profession did), he urged policies and programs that focused on social structures and the ways in which they excluded people with disabilities. Disability, he argued, was a class and labor issue. Economic security—either through employment or a reliable pension program for those unable to work—was vital. For example, he urged that people with disabilities be given low-cost loans for educational and housing purposes, just as veterans had received, so that they might live independently. He urged an employment quota program, a form of affirmative action for people with disabilities, as Britain had adopted.[42]

In 1940 Strachan used his experiences as a labor organizer to found the American Federation of the Physically Handicapped (AFPH), the first national cross-disability activist organization. Though active in the Deaf community (and despite the opposition of some in Deaf activist organizations), Strachan insisted that the AFPH embrace people with a variety of disabilities—"the blind, deaf, hard-of-hearing, those with cardiac conditions, those with tuberculosis, arthritics, epileptics, those with poliomyelitis, those with cerebral palsy, amputees, and diabetics." "WHY, oh WHY," Strachan asked, "is it that there still exists this unreasoning, unjust prejudice against millions of Handicapped people? Why cannot Industry, and the public, generally, realize that we, too, aspire to the comforts, the feeling of security that comes from fair recognition of our rights, as citizens, and our needs, as Handicapped?" As historian Audra Jennings characterizes it, "the AFPH saw unemployment and economic insecurity brought on by discrimination hiring practices and a piecemeal, disorganized federal-state disability program as the core problems faced by people with disabilities." Much of its funding came from labor unions, which knew that disability was an issue for US workers. The organization also urged building accessibility policies, and better prevention of disability through better worker safety and public health. Just as importantly, its members enjoyed each other's company at picnics, sporting events, card parties, and even in marriages. By 1946 the AFHP had groups in eighty-nine cities.[43]

Strachan's campaigns exemplify the ways in which disability and labor activism intersected in the post–World War II period. Strachan, the AFPH, the Department of Labor, and organized labor worked together to advocate federal disability policies that stressed secure wage employment as the best means to guarantee quality of life for people with disabilities and their families. They argued against medical rehabilitation and needs-based charity services that focused exclusively on altering the individual, rather than altering social and employer attitudes. They also argued that the Department of Labor understood employment issues and the job market far better than the Federal Security Administration.

In this political context, organized labor and disability activists worked together to bring about federal government programs pertaining to those with disabilities, including the National Employment of the Physically Handicapped Week, centered in the Department of Labor. Instead, the Federal Security Administration oversaw the Office of Vocational Rehabilitation. It had no formal job placement program and a relatively low employment success rate, was accused of rejecting those considered *too disabled*, and the myriad tests it used to determine eligibility ("from psychiatric evaluations to venereal disease scans to collections of life histories") left many to consider it charity.[44] Union monies, lobbying, and individuals supported Strachan and the AFPH. So did much of the Department of Labor and activist veterans. Indeed, increasingly they used the language of rights, discrimination, prejudice, and citizenship to argue that wage employment was a right—and key to securing the lives of people with disabilities.

For example, in 1946 Major General Graves B. Erskine, formerly commander of the US Marines at Iwo Jima, and by then employed at the Department of Labor, and Secretary of Labor Leslie

Schwellenbach, joined cause with Strachan. Erskine pointed out that 83 percent of industries had employed people with disabilities during the war, with "a smaller labor turnover among these workers, less absenteeism, and equal or higher production rates." Now, those disabled "from the war and those from war industry" were being forgotten, and "there is a very noticeable tendency to slight the disabled worker in favor of the worker with no disability." Not only that, he went on, but during June of that year, the current rehabilitation employment services had placed only one out of every twenty-one disabled veterans in secure employment. Schwellenbach called attention to the 250,000 unemployed disabled veterans. "Many of these men," he said, "are the bravest of the brave. That they should suffer from discrimination or selfishness on the part of the employers is the rankest injustice. Labor, industry, and every private citizen must be made aware of the sorry facts and figures."[45]

In 1952 Strachan resigned from the President's Committee that sponsored the National Employment of the Physically Handicapped Week. He'd had enough. The committee, he wrote in frustration, "was filling up . . . with a lot of 'do-gooders, social welfare workers, and the like,' most of whom, we, the Handicapped, know, from bitter experience, 'WILL DO ANYTHING IN THE WORLD FOR THE HANDICAPPED, EXCEPT, *GET OFF OUR BACKS!*'" Despite the continued efforts of the AFPH and organized labor, a medical-based approach to disability continued to dominate federal policies and programs. The FSA and then later the Department of Health, Education, and Welfare had control of disability services—not the Department of Labor.[46]

Another group promoting a departure from understanding disability as a personal and physical tragedy in the period following World War II was the Blind Veterans Association. Approximately fourteen hundred servicemen were blinded during the war, either due to combat, disease, or accident. The BVA was founded in 1945, largely by blind veterans who had shared experiences of hospitalization and rehabilitation programs. Like the AFPH, the organization advocated for better rehabilitation and employment programs, involvement and the leadership of blind people in such programs, and better physical accessibility. Russell Williams, one of the BVA founders, went on to establish one of the most rigorous mobility and independent-living training programs for blind people to that date. While in general blind veterans "had fewer interactions with blind people and more sighted friends than did the civil blind of their generation," and often rejected use of a white cane in favor of the arm of their sighted wives, the BVA and the rehabilitation program organized by Williams at the Hines, Illinois, Veterans Administration hospital encouraged mobility independence, use of a white cane, and employment.[47] Like the AFPH, the BVA used the language of discrimination and rights.

The BVA encouraged the solidarity of *all* blind veterans, and this made it unique. The largest veterans' organizations of the period—such as the American Legion, the Veterans of Foreign Wars, and the Disabled American Veterans—either excluded African American members or encouraged separate racially segregated chapters. In direct contrast, the Blind Veterans Association explicitly welcomed both black and Jewish veterans and spoke against racism and anti-Semitism. And when African American veteran Isaac Woodard was brutally attacked and blinded by white police officers as he headed home through South Carolina, still wearing his military uniform after being discharged with medals, the BVA raised funds on his behalf.

Historians David Gerber and Robert Jefferson both argue that by wrestling with their own internal ableism as they went through rehabilitation and reintegration into community life, by rejecting the stigma often connected to disability, black and white blind veterans in the BVA came to understand the connection between race and disability. As Jefferson puts it, "They understood race and disability to be social markers used to justify social and political inequality between groups, rather than as markers of personal tragedy and insult." While simplified, the 1951 novel *Lights Out* (situated at Old Farms Convalescent Hospital in Connecticut, where most of the BVA founders had gathered) tells the story of this learning experience. Later made into a film, the story is based on the experiences of blinded veteran Larry Niven. Niven was forced to confront his own prejudices after realizing that a fellow blinded GI, Joe Morgan, whom he had embraced as a friend, was an African American. Simultaneously wrestling with his ableist despair over losing his sight, and his racist rejection of a fellow veteran, Niven eventually renews his friendship with Morgan and together the men learn to live successfully with their blindness.[48]

In the decades immediately following World War II, the ideology and language of rights, discrimination, and citizenship increasingly dominated discussions of disability. In disability organizations, in religious institutions, in labor unions, and with respect to the issues of racial and gender equality, people with disabilities increasingly rejected the idea that they had either to adapt to or withdraw from society. Instead, they argued, ableist ideologies that viewed people with disabilities as inherently undesirable and deficient, and that underlay social policy, employment practices, architecture, cultural attitudes, and education, needed to change. Prejudice and discrimination was not acceptable.[49]

Disability activists also inched toward two important and new ideological positions that would make organizing and activism far more effective. Slowly and haltingly, activists began to argue that people with disabilities shared common experiences of stigma and discrimination, across a wide spectrum of disability. Some began to claim that creating hierarchies among disabilities may have benefited a few, those who could claim that they were not the *truly disabled* and thus should not be discriminated against or ostracized, but justified and reinforced ableist ideology generally.

Activists also began to explore the relationship between ableism, sexism, and racism. As the Blind Veterans Association began to learn, rejecting hierarchy based on one form of physical difference (like disability) while embracing hierarchy based on another form of physical difference (such as race) left one ideologically (and perhaps ethically) inconsistent and made organizing less effective. Both of these lessons, however, were hard to learn. Racism, sexism, classism, heterosexism, and ableism were hard to unlearn—and continued to hinder cross-disability organizing.

These intellectual and organizational moves set the stage for the disability rights movement that developed over the next several decades.

EIGHT

I GUESS I'M AN ACTIVIST. I THINK IT'S JUST CARING

Rights and Rights Denied, 1968–

In the summer of 1970, Robert Payne went to jail with three of his buddies—all four of them disabled coal miners and members of the Disabled Miners and Widows of Southern West Virginia. Payne had been found guilty of contempt of court while leading a wildcat strike involving as many as forty thousand coal miners across West Virginia, Kentucky, Ohio, Tennessee, and Indiana. Later he said of his fourteen days in prison, "It didn't scare me and I'm still not scared, because I'm fighting for a cause." He and his fellow disabled miners, he proclaimed proudly, "don't intend to be mistreated or discriminated against."[1]

Described in the local newspaper as a "soft-spoken Negro," Payne went to work in the mines as a member of the United Mine Workers of America when he was fifteen years old. "I believe in the union," he said. "I was born a union man 'cause my daddy was a union man." In 1967 he had been burned seriously in a mine explosion and was unable to mine any longer; and like so many other coal miners, so many that it was unremarked upon, he had lost several fingers. He and his wife, Dorothy, had three children. Payne, who also had a reputation as a dynamic preacher, lived with his family in a "modest but comfortable frame house" just sixteen steps away from Route 10, in the unincorporated small town of Itmann, near Beckley, West Virginia. The Itmann mine had been opened in 1918 by the Pocahontas Fuel Company and was one of the most productive in West Virginia in the 1950s and 1960s.[2]

Coal mining in West Virginia, like elsewhere in the United States, was incredibly hazardous. During World War I, more miners died in southern West Virginia than did US soldiers in Europe. While finding reliable disability statistics is difficult, the rate of serious injury among miners was at least eight times higher than the death rate. On top of that, exposure to coal dust caused black lung disease; coal miners were not fooled by the reassurances of company doctors who told them that coal dust promoted health. When UMWA president John L. Lewis negotiated the industry-financed and union-controlled Welfare and Retirement Fund that included disability benefits and health care in the 1950s, the measure had the potential to change lives. It did transform lives—particularly for the estimated fifty thousand disabled coal miners who were "bedridden or housebound" in 1945, and the thousands who came after them, like Robert Payne.[3]

Under the corrupt leadership of W. A. "Tony" Boyle in the early 1960s, the assets of the UMWA fund fell and the fund's trustees eliminated benefits to some disabled miners and widows. By 1964, 17.7 percent of the fund's beneficiaries had lost their benefits. In 1967 Payne and others formed the Disabled Miners and Widows of Southern West Virginia in protest and began to file lawsuits against the UMWA fund and West Virginia's workers' compensation system. Receiving little assistance or response from the UMWA, they organized rallies and rolling wildcat strikes in the summer of 1967. As one disabled miner put it, "Boys, we've been forced to beg for the crumbs off the table that we built."[4] From the sparse evidence available, it appears

that members of the Disabled Miners and Widows were disproportionately African American and female.

Then a perfect storm of events focused national attention on
West Virginia. In 1968 seventy-eight miners died at a mine explosion in Farmington, West Virginia; nineteen of the bodies were
never recovered. Galvanized by the disaster, regional doctors
frustrated by the mining companies' long medical coverup and
denial of black lung disease began to bring information about
black lung directly to the miners, in union halls, small-town living rooms, wherever they could. The Black Lung Association
(BLA), a group of miners, medical practitioners, and mining
family members, organized on behalf of a black lung compensation bill. As the UMWA and mine managers wavered, in 1969
the BLA held massive rallies in Charleston and shut down mines
across the state. Around this time, Joseph "Jock" Yablonski ran
against Boyle for the presidency of the UMWA, seeking democ-
ratization of the union and an end to corruption. Miners were
horrified when Yablonski and his wife and daughter were shot
in their beds on New Year's Eve 1969, and even more horrified
when the courts determined that Boyle had hired the shooters.

Angered, saddened, and demanding change, miners attending Yablonski's funeral founded Miners for Democracy. This
group, together with the Disabled Miners and Widows and the
Black Lung Association, led the effort to reform the UMWA. In
1972 Arnold Miller, a miner disabled by black lung disease and
an activist in the black lung insurgency, was named president of
the union.

The story of Robert Payne and the Disabled Miners and Widows is a story of class, labor, race, and place; it is also the story
of the social reform movement that culminated in President Lyn-
don B. Johnson's Great Society; and it is the story of mining-
community women who sought political and economic changes
in order to protect themselves and their loved ones. It is also a

story of disability. As Payne put it, "My union has turned its back on the rank and file miner and those men crippled underground."[5]

The reform efforts of disabled miners propelled other miners to activism. During the five-week strike of 1970, while more than twenty-five thousand workers adhered to the picket lines, UMWA "henchmen physically abused the disabled miners and their wives." A plot to murder Payne and other DMWA members was uncovered. During the strike, "working miners were appalled at the sight of UMWA officials crashing through picket lines of wheelchair bound miners and old women." Jack Smith was among those protesting union policies during this period. Both of his legs had been crushed when a mine roof caved in. It took eighteen years for him to receive workers' compensation. Able-bodied miners joined the strike, knowing their risk of being injured in an industrial accident or developing lung disease as a result of a nearly daily intake of coal dust.[6]

Like people with disabilities before them, Payne, Smith, and other members of the Disabled Miners and Widows proclaimed themselves worthy citizens. Using terms such as "rights" and "discrimination," and employing the protest methods of the anti-war and racial freedom movements, people with disabilities increasingly, in the late twentieth century, demanded the opportunities and protections of full citizenship. These demands came from both activists and advocacy organizations and ordinary citizens. People with disabilities wanted a better life—and felt themselves deserving of it.

The disability rights movement was energized by, overlapping with, and similar to other civil rights movements across the nation, as people with disabilities experienced the 1960s and 1970s as a time of excitement, organizational strength, and identity exploration. Like feminists, African Americans, and gay and lesbian activists, people with disabilities insisted that their bodies did not render them defective. Indeed, their bodies could even be sources of political, sexual, and artistic strength.

BECOMING ACTIVIST CITIZENS

In August of 1990, less than one month after the passage of the groundbreaking civil rights legislation the Americans with Disabilities Act, a local reporter from Frederick, Maryland, sat down to interview Clara Clow. Clow had moved to Frederick in 1956, with her then new husband, after attending Hunter College. Her early adult years were spent raising three children. She embraced feminism in the 1960s, but because she was busy parenting she remained "on the sidelines applauding and rooting."[7]

Clow became active in the public arena in the early 1970s. Having had polio at the age of two, she was long accustomed to using a wheelchair. When she heard of government hearings about possible discrimination against people with disabilities, she attended. The people who spoke at the hearing amazed her. "They so inspired me," she said. "I joined the movement immediately. The '70s were exciting for the disabled." In 1973 she began to fight locally for accessible public spaces and in 1976 she and her husband helped to organize the Disabled Citizens of Frederick County United. "Our main focus is architectural and attitudinal barriers," she explained. "In the beginning, people really did think we were outrageous. It's been kind of a long fight."[8]

"I guess I'm an activist," she concluded. "I think it's just caring."[9]

The activists of the disability rights movement that so inspired Clow sought to extend the full exercise of citizenship, democracy, and self-determination to people with disabilities. The movement focused on legal efforts to prohibit discrimination in employment and education, access to public spaces and public transportation, and on institutional transformations that better enabled the self-determination of those with disabilities. Like the movements for women's rights, lesbian, gay, bisexual, and transgender rights, the environment, and racial freedom, the disability rights movement began to coalesce into one movement in the late 1960s and 1970s, from previously disparate elements. Groups of disabled veterans, parents, blind people, deaf people, and other physically disabled persons had sought to shape their own lives in the decades leading up to the disability rights movement.[10]

Movement participants argued that disability was not simply a medical, biologically based condition. Indeed, the movement sometimes directly challenged medical authority to define "disability." Using the work of activists and intellectual theorists such as Erving Goffman, Jacobus tenBroek, and Irving Kenneth Zola, advocates argued that disability is a social condition of discrimination and unmerited stigma, which needlessly harms and restricts the lives of those with disabilities and results in economic disparities, social isolation, and oppression.

Just as the civil rights movement critiqued hierarchy based on racial differences, and just as the feminist movement critiqued hierarchy based on sex and gender differences, the disability rights movement critiqued hierarchy based on the physical, sensory, and mental differences of disability.

A vital element of the early activist wave that came to call itself the disability rights movement was the independent-living movement. Grounded in several decades of activism, the movement centered on the counterculture of the University of California, Berkeley, in the 1960s and 1970s. In 1962, the same academic year in which African American James Meredith matriculated at the University of Mississippi after suing for access and racial integration, a polio survivor named Edward Roberts sued UC Berkeley for access and integration. Roberts was no newcomer to discrimination, or to resistance. His high school principal had initially refused to let the young white man, who used a wheelchair and an iron lung, graduate, because he had not completed his gym requirement. The California Department of Rehabilitation had initially refused him financial aid for college, because it determined him unemployable. (Roberts became director of the California Department of Rehabilitation in 1975, in a lovely historical twist.) Eventually Roberts's suit was successful, but Berkeley required him to live in the school's infirmary rather than in a dormitory. Within a year other physically disabled students, energized by news of Roberts's admittance, joined him in the Berkeley infirmary. The third floor of the infirmary soon became the emotional and activist center of the "Rolling Quads," a disability pride and activist group with Roberts at its center, and the Disabled Students' Program (DSP), which provided support such as personal care attendants. The group sought barrier-free access to the community and to the university.[11]

Battling paternalistic assumptions about disability, Roberts and others across the nation developed independent-living centers organized on the principle of self-determination, consumer control, and deinstitutionalization. In the 1970s and 1980s independent-living activists sought the removal of both the architectural and transportation barriers that made civic participation almost impossible for people with disabilities. They worked toward and created institutional supports and accommodations that would enable people with disabilities to live independently, manage their own lives, and make their own decisions. Services ranged from wheelchair repair, attendant care services, peer counseling, legal assistance, adaptive equipment, and training in self-advocacy to providing safe community spaces in which people could openly discuss their families, their sex lives, clothing adaptations, and dreams.

Independent-living centers flourished. As Judy Huemann, eventual director of Berkeley's Center for Independent Living, explained, "When we go into most 'establishment' organizations, we hardly meet any disabled individuals; there are no peers that we can look up to."[12] Across the country, in cities such as Boston, New York, Chicago, and even in smaller urban centers like Green

Bay, Wisconsin, people with disabilities found peers from whom they could learn. Many with access to the movement found the resulting peer support and independence thrilling.

One reality of deinstitutionalization was that neither the federal government, states, or cities developed enough structures to provide sufficient support for those people who needed it in order to live on their own—even when doing so was far cheaper than institutional living. In the 1970s state-run psychiatric facilities began to release long-term residents to their home communities as a result of media exposés, lawsuits, activism, and legislation. From 1965 to 1980 the number of people institutionalized in public asylums fell by 60 percent: from 475,000 to 138,000. And, as historian Gerald Grob has noted, whereas "before 1965 many patients spend years, if not decades, in asylums, after 1970 length-of-stays began to be measured in days or weeks."[13]

The lucky, the privileged, and sometimes those with successful advocate families found support in independent-living centers, community-based mental health centers, or in community-based group homes. The remaining ended up homeless and living on the streets; and even more found themselves in jails and prisons. Incarceration has since become the dominant method of "care" and institutionalization for poor people perceived to have mental or psychiatric disabilities. A 2006 Bureau of Justice Statistics study reported that more than half of all prison and jail inmates had a mental health problem. In that same year, Human Rights Watch estimated that the number of prisoners considered to have mental health diagnoses was close to 1.25 million. As historian Michael Rembis notes, that is "twice the number of mad citizens incarcerated in state hospitals during the peak years of 'institutionalization' in the mid-1950s." The vast majority of those incarcerated are poor and people of color. Deinstitutionalization has not accomplished all that many hoped for it; nor has it been supported by the means necessary for it to succeed.[14]

THE ARCHITECTURAL BARRIERS ACT
AND THE REHABILITATION ACT

The government hearings that so inspired Clara Clow likely were held in the years between passage of the 1968 Architectural Barriers Act (ABA) and the Rehabilitation Act of 1973. Because of the ABA's weak enforcement measures, it has often been overlooked, but the activism that generated it and its argument that access was a rights issue are important. Many people with disabilities were denied access to public spaces. For example, when President Dwight Eisenhower bestowed the Handicapped American of the Year award on Hugo Deffner in 1957, he recognized Deffner's remarkable efforts to promote architectural accessibility in his hometown of Oklahoma City. Deffner wheeled himself forward to receive the award, but two Marines had to lift him onto the stage, which was not wheelchair accessible. The campaign continued in 1961 when, at the urging of the National Society for Crippled Children and Adults (now known as Easter Seals) and the President's Commission on Employment of the Handicapped (PCEH), one of the main regulatory bodies for the architectural trade issued building code standards that would ensure accessible facilities. The chairman of the PCEH characterized the measure as "the Declaration of Independence for the Handicapped." In 1968 Congress passed the Architectural Barriers Act, which stated that all future public buildings and those buildings significantly altered with federal funds needed to be accessible to all citizens. The legislation, however, had no enforcement arm. Nor did it apply to public transportation, housing, privately owned commercial spaces, or recreational facilities. The legislation did, however, set the stage for future activism. It also brought together, one more time, labor and disability organizations.[15]

The campaign for civil rights continued around the 1973 Rehabilitation Act. The intention to establish rehabilitation programs was not new; such programs had been first established in order to meet the needs of returning World War I veterans. The Rehabilitation Act, however, was driven by the needs of Vietnam veterans, but directly generated discussion of civil rights, largely because of the language of its Section 504, which would come to have the most significance for historians, activists, and the courts.

In the early 1970s, a small number of members of Congress began to argue that civil rights legislation prohibiting discrimination on the basis of race, sex, and religion should be extended to encompass people with disabilities. In January 1972 Senator Hubert Humphrey and Congressman Charles Vanik unsuccessfully introduced bills to amend the Civil Rights Act of 1964 to include disability. Building on this argument, congressional staffers drafting the Rehabilitation Act added language near its conclusion—Section 504—stating that people with disabilities should not "be denied the benefits of, or be subjected to discrimination under any program or activity receiving federal financial assistance." Throughout all of the congressional debates and public hearings, only one person commented on Section 504, a representative of the National Foundation for the Blind.[16] Few paid any attention to the measure's antidiscrimination language.

While Congress and President Richard Nixon argued about how much money should be dedicated to the Rehabilitation Act, people with disabilities quickly picked up on the potential of Section 504. Ironically, Nixon vetoed the bill first in October 1972, coincident with the yearly conference of the President's Committee on Employment of the Handicapped. Conference attendee Eunice Fiorito, a blind social worker from New York also active in Disabled in Action (a cross-disability activist group), remembered spending six hours demonstrating in the rain protesting the president's veto after leaving a banquet, while still in her formal dress.[17]

Activism also flourished at the state level. Texas debated whether state agencies discriminated "against the hiring of certain categories of handicapped persons." In West Virginia, "J.B." wrote to the "Question Line" of the *Charleston Daily Mail,* "Why does the Legislature tear down a bill to protect the handicapped? They have one for race, creed, color, sex, and age but none for the handicapped. Do they not think they are human or what?" In Lima, Ohio, a local group called the Able-Disabled Club pushed for the elimination of architectural barriers. Imogene Pritchard from Lima believed that the consequences could be huge: "So many kids with bedside teachers could go to school. This should automatically make jobs more accessible and a lot of the prejudice could be broken down, especially in the area of handicapped teachers." In Brooklyn, a student group called SO FED UP worked "to alleviate the architectural, educational and bureaucratic barriers." A Colorado activist testified to the state legislature, "People with handicaps don't all want rehabilitation. What they need is the opportunity to get their foot in the door and to be considered [for jobs]." In Montana activists formed the Montana Coalition of Handicapped Individuals (MCHI). In Maine, complaints about disability discrimination constituted 20 percent of employment discrimination, and a government official said that "a higher percentage of them are based on legitimate grounds than other discrimination complaints." And winning the prize for best acronym, a group in Florida declared itself on the ARPATH (World Association to Remove Prejudice against the Handicapped) to abolish barriers in public transportation.[18]

After being vetoed a second time by President Nixon due to financing disagreements, the "Rehab Act" eventually passed in September 1973. Its Section 504 and the 1975 Individuals with Disabilities Education Act (IDEA), which guaranteed a public education to children with disabilities, meant that the legal and cultural frameworks that shaped the daily lives of people with disabilities had changed dramatically. Estimates are that in 1970 US schools educated only one in five children with disabilities. Expanded legal rights gave shape to expanded expectations.[19]

The laws, however, were not enforced. Disability advocates initially tried to demand enforcement of Section 504 through the courts. James Cherry, eventual instigator of the lawsuit *Cherry v. Matthews,* which resulted in the development of enforcement regulations, began querying its enforcement almost immediately after its passage. Hospitalized at the National Institutes of Health from 1974 to 1976, he made so many phone calls garnering allies that nurses "asked me if I was making obscene phone calls." In July 1976 a federal judge ordered the Secretary of Health, Education, and Welfare to develop Section 504 regulations "with all deliberate speed."[20]

Increasingly frustrated with the federal failure to enforce federal law, in April 1977 disability activists staged demonstrations in Washington, DC, and at each of the ten Health, Education, and Welfare (HEW) offices around the country (HEW and HEW secretary Joseph Califano had responsibility for the law). In San Francisco, 120 protesters occupied the HEW building, and over half of those stayed for an entire twenty-five day sit-in. The protesters received support from allies both expected and unexpected. Former Berkeley student Ed Roberts, now director of the California Department of Rehabilitation, made an appearance at the protest and gave a public warning about the power of people with disabilities. "As a severely disabled individual and director of the largest state rehabilitation agency in the country, I know that HEW underestimates the strength and commitment of the civil rights movement among disabled people." He asked the press, "Are we going to perpetuate segregation in our society for one of the largest minority groups in the nation?"[21]

The Section 504 sit-in exemplifies the ways in which the disability rights movement intersected with and borrowed from the free speech, antiwar, feminist, and racial freedom movements. Many of its activists had first become activists elsewhere, and then learned of the ways in which disability discrimination and oppression paralleled that of others. The organizing skills of leaders such as Kitty Cone meant that the protesters found support from traditional disability organizations, such as United Cerebral Palsy and the Easter Seals, as well as churches and synagogues.

The Section 504 protests, however, also found unexpected allies—again, often due to the organizing skills of its leaders and their prior activism. Local and national labor unions provided protesters and statements of support. The Butterfly Brigade, a group of gay men who patrolled the streets in order to prevent anti-gay violence, smuggled walkie-talkies to the protesters after the phone lines to the HEW offices were cut. Chicano activists and a grassroots group of substance abusers and former felons named Delancey Street often brought food. The Black Panthers provided one hot meal a day. Disabled Black Panther member Brad Lomax was part of the protest, as was his friend and fellow Panther member Chuck Jackson—who provided attendant-care services for Lomax and many others during the protest. Corbett O'Toole, one of the 504 protesters, who'd been raised a Catholic in Massachusetts, remembered Black Panther support as particularly notable and transformative: "By far the most critical gift given us by our allies was the Black Panthers' commitment to feed each protester in the building one hot meal every day . . . I was a white girl from Boston who'd been carefully taught that all African American males were necessarily/of necessity my enemy. But I understood promises to support each other's struggles." For O'Toole, "The steadfastness of the Black Panthers to a loosely organized, mostly white group of people fighting for disability rights was moving and profound."[22]

The support provided to the Section 504 protesters proved essential. Nearly four weeks into the occupation of the San Francisco HEW building, and after increasing national media attention and pressure, HEW secretary Joseph Califano signed the enforcement regulations ensuring that programs receiving federal funding could not discriminate based on disability.

LIVING OUT DISABILITY RIGHTS

Across the nation, people with disabilities also sought an end to employment discrimination—and used the emerging civil rights legislation to do so. Sandra Blackham became one of the first to use New York's new human rights law to battle what she considered discrimination in the Madison County Sheriff's Office. A wife and mother of two, a college graduate, an accomplished skier, and disabled with one leg, Blackham had worked in the Sheriff's Office as a civil division deputy for many years. The newly arrived sheriff removed her from the position and denied her a new post. "If I were a male with two legs, I would have been civil deputy years ago," she had said to the sheriff. His reply: "That is true." Blackham noted that her disability had sometimes meant "rough times in my life, like when I was growing up and was a teenager and everybody was going to proms, but that's life." Now she sought her legally recognized rights: "This time I'm right . . . I know I'm right and I've just got to stand up for myself."[23]

In Denver, those testifying on behalf of a bill banning disability discrimination in housing and employment shared similar stories. Legislators heard of the discrimination disabled students from Colorado University faced. One man, a paraplegic, was denied housing. A blind student, despite ranking at the top of his class, could not find employment. Don Galloway of the Governor's Advisory Committee on the Handicapped testified that every day, his office received phone calls from "people who are being discriminated against," and that as many as three hundred thousand Colorado citizens with disabilities needed civil rights protection.[24]

Attorney John W. Leibold, testifying on behalf of the Ohio antidiscrimination bill he helped to write, said it wonderfully: "We're going to take disabled people out of the closet. They are no longer going to be shut-ins." Guaranteeing civil rights was the means to do so. The Ohio bill, which eventually passed, banned disability discrimination in housing, employment, credit, and insurance.[25]

Sometimes, however, Section 504 did not do enough. When Paul S. Miller graduated near the top of his class at Harvard Law School in 1986 he initially had over forty firms seeking his application. After interviewing Miller, who was four and a half feet tall, firms changed their minds. One member of a hiring committee told him, and could say legally, "Our clients would think we are running a freak circus if they saw you."[26] Miller later became a commissioner of the US Equal Employment Opportunity Commission and an international disability-rights expert.

Disability activists and their allies also sought to remove other employment barriers. In October 1988 historian Paul Longmore, for example, protested restrictive social security policies that, in his words, "made the American Dream inaccessible to many disabled citizens." As a polio survivor with extensive needs, Longmore required personal aids to assist with bathing, dressing, and eating, and equipment such as a ventilator and motorized wheelchair. After earning his PhD and publishing his first book, *The Invention of George Washington,* Longmore discovered that his publishing royalties (which, for an academic, are rarely enough to live on for a month) would likely render him ineligible for the social security benefits that made it possible for him to "work and live and, literally, to breathe." After borrowing a barbecue grill from a friend, Longmore and a crowd of supporters gathered in front of the Los Angeles Federal Building. Their signs read, "Jobs. Not Tin Cups" and "We Want to Work! Why Won't the Government Let Us?" Longmore placed a copy of *The Invention of George Washington,* the result of more than ten years of labor, on the barbecue grill and watched it burn. It was, he wrote later, "a moment of agony."[27] Though Congress changed social security policies in 1990, partly in response to Longmore's protest, it still was not enough. Ironically, just a few months before Longmore died in 2010, the then full professor at San Francisco State University learned that even the altered law meant that he would have to turn down a substantial and prestigious research fellowship he had been awarded by the US Department of Education.

Other people with disabilities focused on family issues, with less success. In 1988, for example, Tiffany Callo of San Jose, California, lost custody of her sons David and Jessie because California welfare officials determined that her cerebral palsy rendered her too disabled to care for them. Rather than provide the less expensive in-home support, the state placed her sons in much more expensive foster care. As Callo put it, "So what if it takes longer to change a diaper? That's where disabled parents do their bonding. It's quality time."[28] Callo lost custody of her sons, like many other parents with disabilities.

Parental custody issues remain important for parents with disabilities today. According to the University of Minnesota's Center for Advanced Studies in Child Welfare, almost two-thirds of US states continue to list "parental disability" as possible grounds for terminating parental rights, and parents with disabilities lose custody of their children at disproportionately high rates. This is despite research that overwhelmingly indicates that parents with disabilities are no more likely to mistreat their children than parents without disabilities.[29]

THE UNITED HANDICAPPED FEDERATION:
COMMUNITIES IN PROCESS

In September 1974, the United Handicapped Federation of the Twin Cities of Minneapolis and Saint Paul, Minnesota, announced its creation with a press release. It would, the UHF proudly proclaimed, "become a strong consumer advocate for its constituents in the major areas of transportation, housing, architectural barriers and employment." It would use "confrontation and pressure tactics" and "significant public actions" instead of lobbying in the "time-consuming and restrictive legislation process." Audrey Benson, the newly elected president of the UHF, reflected the organization's confident manner in her acceptance speech. "We will hold up our end," she declared. "We will act—force the issues into the open and gain control over the decisions that affect our lives. We will not stand still. Now is the time. This is the place. *And we are the people.*"[30]

As more people with disabilities became empowered by the actions of others with disabilities, as more and more began to think in terms of rights and citizenship, many disabled people began to consider seriously their own place in the American story—and who got to define that place. What this meant in daily life is perhaps best understood by examining one locale and one group. The story of the United Handicapped Federation exemplifies the growing expansiveness and excitement surrounding disability politics, culture, and life in the years after 1970. The United Handicapped Federation, despite its audacious name, was a local group. It was only one of many organizations of people with disabilities.

Sometime in the early 1970s the Catholic Interracial Council (CIC) sponsored an Action Leadership Techniques Seminar for people with disabilities. In the Twin Cities, the CIC had previously worked for the racial desegregation of local neighborhoods. As Audrey Benson described it, those attending the seminar "learned about [Saul] Alinsky principles and decided that we would organize as other minority groups have." Originally from North Dakota, Benson had cerebral palsy and had graduated from Jamestown's Crippled Children's School. After earning her social work degree from Moorhead (Minnesota) State University, the young white woman moved to Minneapolis. Michael Bjerkesett became the UHF's first executive director. While a college student Bjerkesett became paralyzed in a car accident. After finishing his degree he became a counselor in a hospital rehabilitation program. He left that position to help organize the UHF. The new organization brought together nineteen state organizations of and for people with disabilities.[31] Other early members included Marilyn Rogers, Frances Strong, Stephen Marcinel, Scott Rostron, and Ronnie Stone.

The UHF addressed a wide array of issues, reflecting both the shared experiences and the broad differences among people with disabilities. Its members were most active during the last half of the 1970s, as others across the nation sought to explore and expand the consequences of emerging civil rights legislation. Reflecting national trends with respect to accessible housing, in early 1975 the UHF became involved with what was first known as the United Handicapped Federation Apartment Associates—an early example of universal design. Bjerkesett considered the ninety-unit South Minneapolis apartment complex "probably one of the most progressive housing projects for the handicapped in the country" at the time. Also in early 1975, in a letter reminiscent of those advocating that the handicapped be exempt from gas rationing during World War II, Bjerkesett asked that the transportation needs of people with disabilities be taken into consideration if gas rationing or higher gas taxes went into effect due to the national energy crisis. It would, he wrote, have "possible discriminatory effects . . . on the handicapped driver," who had "no alternative forms of transportation."[32]

The UHF did not hesitate to point out the occasional political condescension directed at people with disabilities. In early 1975, when it looked as though the state legislature was going to pass legislation giving free license plates to paraplegics but allow insurance companies to deny health coverage to people with disabilities, the UHF pointed out the irony. "The bill dealing with license plates for paraplegics . . . is probably the most meaningless piece of legislation I have ever been acquainted with," wrote Bjerkesett, while, "the lack of insurance coverage will, often times, severely affect one's ability to become independent in the community and also has serious effects on one's ability to maintain gainful employment." Free license plates were not the goal of the UHF.[33]

Like many other groups across the nation, the UHF focused on the accessibility of public buildings and transportation. In 1975 the organization began making the case that the famed Minneapolis Orchestra Hall be made accessible as it went through a planned renovation. UHF leaders submitted a list of building barriers and asked to meet with the building's leaders. "Now is the time," Benson wrote, "for you to listen to those most affected by the problems of inaccessibility." Not getting the answer they wanted, the UHF protested repeatedly outside the building—collecting over nine hundred signatures of support at an event in July. The "handicapped," they pointed out, were being "denied Mozart." Building smart alliances, the UHF succeeded in getting resolutions of support from the Minneapolis City Council, the Minneapolis Mayor's Advisory Committee on the Handicapped, and the St. Paul Mayor's Advisory Committee on the Handicapped. Similarly, the UHF protested its members' lack of access to the Minneapolis skyways that connected buildings and made wintertime shopping easier. At a wintertime rally sponsored by the UHF, Benson asked, "Are we going to allow these people to keep sixteen and a half percent of the population oppressed? Are we going to remain invisible? Are we going to allow them to deny us the usability of Minneapolis?"[34]

Like activist groups in Denver, San Francisco, New York, and other cities across the nation, the UHF also sought access to public transportation. After several years of requests and then protests that shut down city streets, the UHF sued the Metropolitan Transit Commission of Minneapolis/St. Paul and its chairperson Doug Kelm. In an early 1976 press release, the UHF firmly positioned itself in the tradition of rights: "The right to travel and move about in this country is as fundamental as the right to life, liberty and the pursuit of happiness," the UHF proclaimed.

Despite Section 504 of the 1973 Rehabilitation Act, the MTC had recently purchased an additional 338 inaccessible buses. By so doing, Kelm was "denying the rights and freedoms guaranteed to the handicapped people by the US Constitution." By 1989 ADAPT, a national disability-rights organization, ranked the MTC as one of the ten worst large-city transit systems in the country.[35]

The Minnesota UHF reflected and intersected with national trends in many ways. In 1976 the UHF office first received TTY technology, which made telephones accessible for deaf people; the affordability and national availability of TTY was made possible by deaf activists. Like other national and regional disability-rights groups, the UHF found financial and institutional support from religious organizations (both Catholic and Lutheran) and unions. For example, in the middle of the transit lawsuit, a local of the Minnesota Teamsters Public Employees Union donated money for legal fees.[36]

Also like other disability activist organizations across the nation, the UHF increasingly sought to welcome and advocate for people with a wide range of disabilities—physical, sensory, cognitive, and psychiatric. In 1977 the AFL-CIO contacted the Twin Cities UHF and the Minnesota Association of Retarded Citizens (MARC) as part of a larger discussion about organizing disabled laborers in sheltered workshops. The concept of sheltered workshops—employing people with disabilities separately from other workers—dates to the nineteenth century. By the 1970s, sheltered workshops provided employment to people with disabilities—but at dismally low wages, basically exempt from labor law, with few benefits, and with virtually no possibility of advancement or additional training. Built into them was the assumption that people with disabilities could not survive in the outside world and needed a special, protected, environment. By the time it contacted the UHF, the AFL-CIO had successfully unionized workers at a sheltered workshop in Clinton, Iowa. In 1979 the National Labor Relations Board would rule that sheltered-workshop employees must be allowed the opportunity to unionize if they so desired. What became of the Minnesota effort is unclear, but it prompted discussions about welcoming those with cognitive disabilities into the disability activist community.[37]

Just as the Section 504 protesters in San Francisco and those across the country drew connections between racial, sex, and (sometimes) sexuality discrimination, and created alliances, so did those emerging disability activists in Minnesota. In the *Progress,* the UHF's newsletter, UHF member Scott Rostron wrote in a 1977 column, "Equality is coming to the handicapped communities slowly, as it has for the black, women, elderly, and other sub-cultures in America today . . . It is time that we move from the special needs category to the people category. From segregation to integration. Identify to ourselves and to others our true needs . . . The point is the handicapped, black and elderly all need as people . . . It is more than the rights of the handicapped, it is the rights of the people, equal people."[38]

In 1978 events highlighted the intersections between systems of oppression. After a UHF member was raped in her apartment, she utilized the resources of the UHF in reaching out to advocates and other rape victims, thus bringing the emerging feminist and disability rights movements together. In its attempt to learn more about people with disabilities and sexual assault, the UHF concluded that "sexual and physical assault of the handicapped is a real problem and probably bigger than anyone knows." Other victims shared their stories, and community law enforcement provided information about the sexual assault of blind, mobility impaired, and cognitively disabled women. UHF members learned that rape support services were generally inaccessible to women with disabilities: architectural barriers, inaccessible transportation, a lack of TTY and ASL interpreters, and few Braille resources

existed. An emerging coalition of police, feminist activists, disability activists, county attorneys, and social workers participat-
ing in a July 1979 conference uncovered some sixty cases of sexual
assault against local women with a wide variety of disabilities in
just the previous one-year period. As one community antiviolence
activist wrote to the UHF, there was a "lack of services and facilities for physically handicapped or disabled sexual assault victims.
The time has come for us to share our expertise in our respective
fields in order to develop accessible, effective services to disabled
sexual assault victims."[39]

The barriers were not merely physical. As conference activists pointed out, many assault victims "experienced the barrier
of community disbelief," "stereotypes that make it hard for the
average person to accept the fact or even imagine that handicapped people are raped and beaten." An additional barrier was
that 1970s Minnesota law, like that of many states, required that
victims bringing rape charges prove the use of "legal force" in resisting their assault. While there are many reasons that a woman
would not physically resist sexual assault, for some disabled rape
survivors, doing so was physically impossible. In such cases, even
if the assault was reported and the rapist caught, prosecutors had
to free the perpetrator. When the sexual assault law was finally
changed in 1982, the UHF was recognized as both a sponsor of
and impetus for the legislative amendment.[40]

The UHF disbanded in the mid-1990s. It had, however, accomplished a tremendous amount. In 1975 Minnesota citizen
Curtis Mohn had written to the *Minneapolis Star* protesting the
use of the word "cripple." To him, the word had connotations of
"uselessness, ugliness and helplessness." "I am," he insisted, "far
from that, as any other handicapped individual is. We are strong
of heart, mind and soul." Most importantly, he went on, "there
are over ten million physically handicapped people in the US. We
have strength; we have numbers; we have friends, relatives, and
concerned citizens on our side. We must use that strength."[41]

It is not known if Mohn affiliated with the UHF. It is clear, however, that through organizations such as the UHF, and because of organizations such as the UHF, people with disabilities used the strength they had. And likely, and perhaps unexpectedly, Minnesota citizens with disabilities discovered that they had far more strength than they thought they did, like many others across the nation. Through collective work, people with disabilities and their allies created community, asserted influence, claimed power, and shaped policy in such a way that enhanced both their lives and the lives of many others.

DISABILITY PRIDE

Disability activism, community, and empowerment grew as people with disabilities increasingly insisted on having a voice in shaping their own lives, the policies that affected them, and the institutions in which they lived, worked, and learned. In 1988 deaf students at Gallaudet University staged a successful protest that enabled a deaf person to serve as the university's president. For several days students engaged in civil disobedience in what has become known as the Deaf President Now (DPN) campaign—until Gallaudet's board of trustees named I. King Jordan the university's first deaf president.[42]

Disability culture flourished. Building on the works of earlier generations, poets, visual artists, novelists, playwrights, and scholars forced a redefinition of culture and created new spaces of welcome and community. In *The Disability Rag*, for example, one of only several disability activist and cultural magazines, those who created art found places of expression. Performance artists such as Neil Marcus, whose poem prefaces this book, questioned the medicalization of disability and challenged ableist assumptions. Deaf poets used American Sign Language and forced a redefinition of poetry. In the 1970s, 1980s, and 1990s

Paralympian competitors similarly pushed for a reconsideration of what it meant to be an athlete. Dance and theater troupes that included or were limited to people with disabilities prompted those in their audiences to ponder alternate ideas of beauty, sensuality, and movement. Marilyn Hamilton nearly single-handedly transformed wheelchair design when she founded Quickie, creating lightweight wheelchairs (rather than the sixty-pound megaliths originally made available to her after a hang-gliding accident) with personality that served the needs of athletes as well as ordinary consumers (or at least those who could afford them or had the requisite insurance coverage).[43]

The contemporaneous landmark court decisions that expanded civil rights for many population groups, the growing advocacy and discontent of people with disabilities and their allies, and a series of legislative victories expanded the scope and successes of the disability rights movement. The growing cross-disability community both made possible and was a result of the increasingly confident disability-rights movement and disability community. People with disabilities increasingly thought of themselves as having a shared experience and common goals—regardless of variations in their physical, mental, or cognitive disabilities, and regardless of their race, class, sexual, and gender differences.

The Americans with Disabilities Act (ADA) of 1990 is the best-known civil rights legislation for those with disabilities—impacting an estimated 43 million people at the time of its passage. The ADA built on the Architectural Barriers Act of 1968, the Rehabilitation Act of 1973, and the Individuals with Disabilities Education Act of 1975. It also built on the 1964 Civil Rights Act, which banned discrimination based on sex and race in employment and public places. Most importantly, the ADA built on centuries of activism on the part of people with disabilities, and centuries of public debate over rights, citizenship, and engagement in civic life.

When the ADA was first introduced in Congress in 1988, people with disabilities, advocates, and family members from all over the country shared their stories of discrimination, harassment, and inaccessibility. They also shared their dreams of what a truly accessible democracy could mean. Those with HIV/AIDS shared their stories of how homophobia and ableism often combined in fiercely destructive ways. The ADA's eventual passage required tremendous labor and sacrifice, from activists such as Justin Dart and Evan Kemp of the George H. W. Bush administration, as well as from street-level activists and protesters. The ADA prohibits employment, access, housing, and educational discrimination against people with disabilities.[44]

It would be easy to conclude *A Disability History of the United States* with a victorious and culminating celebration of the 1990 Americans with Disabilities Act. The story of the ADA can be told in many ways—as a story of disability, as a story of civil rights, as a story of activism. It would not exist without the activism of people with disabilities. Nor, however, would the ADA exist without the nation's long history of debate over the very notion of rights.

As federal law, the ADA has made and continues to make a tremendous difference in the daily lives of people with disabilities, their allies, and their families. The inclusion of people with disabilities into higher education, employment, popular culture, and all venues of public life has enriched society greatly. The reality of the ADA, however, is that like nearly all civil rights legislation, it has been consistently tested and eroded in the courts, and sometimes ignored in practice. In 2008 Congress passed the ADA Amendments Act, in an effort to redress decisions made by state courts and Supreme Court decisions that limited the ADA's breadth. What power the ADA has retained is only due to the constant vigilance and activism of disabled people and their allies— activism that the disability rights movement has made possible.

DISABILITY HISTORY AND THE ACT OF RECLAMATION

A Disability History of the United States began with the argument that disability history is at the core of the American story. My hope is that by looking at US history through the lens of disability, we discover an American past both radically transformed and profoundly familiar. The experience of people with disabilities is pivotal to US history, just as the concept of disability is at the core of American citizenship, contested explorations of rights, racial and gender hierarchies, concepts of sexual deviance, economic inequalities, and the process of industrialization. There is no question that the power to define bodies as disabled has given justification, throughout US history, for subjugation and oppression.

US disability history is not only the history of people with disabilities. Whether one's life is shaped by able-bodiedness and the economic and legal advantages that issue from that, or by the economic and legal implications of disability's long-stigmatized past, disability, both as lived reality and as concept, impacts us all.

United States disability history is a complicated and contradictory story, like the entirety of United States history. It is a story of land and bodies stolen. It is a story of rights and wrongs, of devastation and ruin, of defeat and stubborn persistence, of beauty and grace, of tragedy and sadness, of transformative ideals, and of the reinvention of self. It is, to borrow the words of white, disabled, queer writer and activist Eli Clare, "bold, brash stories about reclaiming our bodies and changing the world."[45]

US disability history has frequently been a story of stigma and of pride denied—particularly when ableism defines disability and people with disabilities as defective and inadequate, and when disability is used to create and justify hierarchies. Ableist ideologies make pride difficult for disabled people. And as Clare has written, "Pride is not an inessential thing. Without pride, disabled people are much more likely to accept unquestioningly the daily material condition of ableism: unemployment, poverty, segregated and substandard education, years spent locked up in nursing homes, violence perpetrated by caregivers, lack of access. Without pride, individual and collective resistance to oppression becomes nearly impossible. But disability pride is not an easy thing to come by. Disability has been soaked in shame, dressed in silence, rooted in isolation."[46] Such shame, silence, and isolation have been built into the institutions, the laws, the perceived and unperceived elements of US history. It permeates our lives.

The most important, repeated, and consequential part of the story of people with disabilities in the United States has been the effort to re-create and reclaim the body—the personal body, the "stolen body" (to once again borrow words from Eli Clare), the national body, and the civic body—as one's home. As Neil Marcus writes in the poem that begins this book, "In my life's journey / I am making myself / At home in my country."

The story of the US nation is a contested, sometimes vicious, sometimes gloriously marvelous story of creating a national home. People with disabilities have been and will continue to be an integral part of that story. It is my home, our home, and your home.

EPILOGUE

When I was four or five, every week for almost a year, apparently twice a week at the beginning, one of my parents drove me from a small town in a very rural part of Montana to the sophisticated metropolis of Great Falls. I remember this trip as a trek, but today my computer tells me that the journey was only around forty miles. My memories of this experience are vague, but overwhelmingly are those of feeling cared for and loved: time alone with a parent, a happy room with brightly colored toys, a cheerful lady who played games with me, and beanbags that I attempted to throw at a wooden target with circles cut into it. The delight of throwing beanbags is such a vivid part of the fuzzy memory that by doing so I must have been violating a rule at home that forbade throwing things inside buildings.

It was not until I had been doing disability history for several years that it dawned on me that my memories were of attending an Easter Seals facility for speech therapy. All along, of course, I knew that I had gone through speech therapy. I had never, however, considered myself an Easter Seals kid. Naively young, I slid in, and then slid out of the disability category—never being quite old enough even to know it.

I could not pronounce my *k, d,* and soft *g* sounds. "Kim" came out "Tim." For a little girl with short hair, who enjoyed playing outside and probably got dirty sometimes, being mistaken for a boy was a huge affront. The family story is that at one point, completely fed up with people who heard me say my name as "Tim," I almost quit talking to people. Apparently I have long been stubborn. In a rural county that had few social services and no kindergarten program, my parents turned to Easter Seals—which, around 1970, was primarily privately funded. Wherever the funding came from, my parents much appreciated the sliding fee scale.

Looking back, I'm grateful to Easter Seals—once known as the Society for Crippled Children. My gratefulness is for the respect with which they treated my parents and for the fact that, as interpreted through my four- or five-year-old brain, the entire experience was great fun. I got to throw things. That was incredibly empowering, helping me to feel at home in my voice and in my body. That should be the experience of us all.

ACKNOWLEDGMENTS

The creation of this book generated more debts than I can ever list or repay. Generations of scholars, activists, archivists, scrapbookers, and others, some well known and others not, laid the groundwork on which this book is built. People tolerated my out-of-the-blue phone calls, my repetitive e-mails, and my failures to comprehend. More than ever before, it is hard for me to disentangle the interwoven threads of the personal, the intellectual, and the professional. More than ever before, doing so is artificial. Forrest Brooks, Lisa Poupart, and David Voelker shared their wisdom. Daniel Blackie answered many e-mails. Harold and Arlene Ripple provide beautiful space on the Lake Superior shore. Katherine Ott provided hospitable lodging that helped to make research delightful. Jeff Brunner, formerly of the UWGB interlibrary loan, cheerfully accomplished the impossible. Becky Dale does her best to keep me on an even keel. Neil Marcus kindly let me use his poetry. Susan Burch, Andy Kersten, and Michael Rembis generously and adeptly commented on the entire manuscript. At Beacon Press, Gayatri Patnaik acted on her faith in me and this project. Joanna Green provided guidance, good cheer, smarts, time, and wisdom. This book is much better because of her. Both women have incredible patience.

People I know well and those new to me helped in tangible and intangible ways, all profound; with food, phone calls, poetry, love, chocolate, reassurance, care packages, hand holding, bibliographies, occasional snow-blowing, and encouragement. All make my life easier, more pleasant, and remind me of the ways in which Green Bay and the larger academic world consists of many marvelous people. I am thankful for Susan Burch, Eli Clare, Tim Dale, Jim Ferris, Dr. Tracy Gallagher, Linda Kerber, Andy Kersten, Cathy Kudlick, Paul Longmore, Kathie Nielsen, Ron Nielsen, Corbett O'Toole, Katherine Ott, Michael Rembis, Penny Richards, Walt Schalick, Caroline Sullivan, Maya Tuff, Morgan Tuff, Nathan Tuff, and Kris Vespia—so very, very thankful.

NOTES

INTRODUCTION

1. Linda K. Kerber, "Women and Individualism in American History," *Massachusetts Review* 30, no. 4 (Winter 1989): 600.
2. Jacobellis v. Ohio, 378 U.S. 184 (1964).

CHAPTER ONE

1. Tom Porter, *And Grandma Said . . . Iroquois Teachings as Passed Down through the Oral Tradition* (Philadelphia: Xlibris: 2008), 416; Oneida Dictionary, at "Oneida Language Tools," University of Wisconsin–Green Bay, accessed May 2011, http://www.uwgb.edu/oneida.
2. Carol Locust, "Wounding the Spirit: Discrimination and Tradition in American Indian Belief Systems," *Harvard Educational Review* 58, no. 3 (1988): 326. See also: Carol Locust, *American Indian Concepts of Health and Unwellness* (Tucson, AZ: Native American Research and Training Center, 1986); Robert M. Schacht, "Engaging Anthropology in Disability Studies: American Indian Issues," *Disability Studies Quarterly* 21, no. 3 (Summer 2001): 17–36.
3. Jennie R. Joe and D. L. Miller, *American Indian Perspectives on Disability* (Tucson, AZ: Native American Research and Training Center, 1987); Lavonna Lovern, "Native American Worldview and the Discourse on Disability," *Essays in Philosophy* 9, no. 1 (January 2008), available at http://commons.pacificu.edu/eip.
4. Joe and Miller, *American Indian Perspectives on Disability*; Jeanne L. Connors and Anne M. Donnellan, "Citizenship and Culture: The Role of Disabled People in Navajo Society," *Disability, Handicap, and Society* 8, no. 3 (1993): 265–80.
5. Locust, "Wounding the Spirit."
6. Joe and Miller, *American Indian Perspectives on Disability*; Connors and Donnellan, "Citizenship and Culture."
7. Carol Locust, *Hopi Indian Concepts of Unwellness and Handicaps* (Tucson, AZ: Native American Research and Training Center, 1987), 13.
8. Carol Locust, *Apache Indian Concepts of Unwellness and Handicaps* (Tucson, AZ: Native American Research and Training Center, 1987), 17, 24.
9. Ibid., 17.
10. Donna Grandbois, "Stigma of Mental Illness among American Indian and Alaska Native Nations: Historical and Contemporary Perspectives," *Issues in Mental Health Nursing* 26, no. 10 (2005): 1005–6.
11. Jeffrey E. Davis, *Hand Talk: Sign Language among American Indian Nations* (New York: Oxford University Press, 2010), 3.

12. Jeffrey E. Davis, "A Historical Linguistic Account of Sign Language among North American Indians," in *Multilingualism and Sign Languages: From the Great Plains to Australia*, ed. Ceil Lucas (Washington, DC: Gallaudet University Press, 2002): 3–35; Davis, *Hand Talk*, 19.
13. Locust, *Apache Indian Concepts*, 39.
14. Locust, *Hopi Indian Concepts*, 15.
15. Porter, *And Grandma Said*, 350.

CHAPTER TWO

1. Cornelius J. Jaenen, "Amerindian Views of French Culture in the Seventeenth Century," in *American Encounters: Natives and Newcomers from European Contact to Indian Removal: 1500–1850*, ed. Peter Mancall and James H. Merrell (New York: Routledge, 2000), 77.
2. John D. Bonvillian, Vicky L. Ingram, Brendan M. McCleary, "Observations on the Use of Manual Signs and Gestures in the Communicative Interactions between Native Americans and Spanish Explorers of North America: The Accounts of Bernal Díaz del Castillo and Álvar Núñez Cabeza de Vaca," *Sign Language Studies* 9, no. 2 (Winter 2009): 146, 149, 153; Jeffrey E. Davis, "A Historical Linguistic Account of Sign Language among North American Indians," in *Multilingualism and Sign Languages: From the Great Plains to Australia*, ed. Ceil Lucas (Washington, DC: Gallaudet University Press, 2002), 6. See also: Susan Wurtzburg and Lyle Campbell, "North American Indian Sign Language: Evidence of Its Existence before European Contact," *International Journal of American Linguistics* 61, no. 2 (April 1995): 153–67.
3. This dismissive attitude toward indigenous signed languages suggests that significant additional research needs to be done on pre-1700s signed language in Europe. It also raises the question of whether such languages existed in Asia and/or Africa.
4. Alfred W. Crosby, "Virgin Soil Epidemics as a Factor in the Aboriginal Depopulation in America," *William and Mary Quarterly* 33 (1976): 289–99; David S. Jones, "Virgin Soils Revisited," *William and Mary Quarterly* 60 (2003): 703–42. See also: Gerald Grob, *The Deadly Truth: A History of Disease in America* (Cambridge, MA: Harvard University Press, 2002).
5. Crosby, "Virgin Soil Epidemics," 290; Daniel K. Richter, *Facing East from Indian Country: A Native History of Early America* (Cambridge, MA: Harvard University Press, 2001), 121.
6. Crosby, "Virgin Soil Epidemics," 296.
7. Cristobal Silva, "Miraculous Plagues," *Early American Literature* 43, no. 2 (June 2008): 251–52.
8. William Cronon, *Changes in the Land: Indians, Colonists, and the Ecology of New England* (New York: Hill and Wang, 1983), 85; Jones, "Virgin Soils Revisited," 736.
9. Jones, "Virgin Soils Revisited," 737.
10. Richter, *Facing East from Indian Country*, 61; James M. Merrell, "The Indians' New World: The Catawba Experience," in *American Encounters: Natives and Newcomers from European Contact to Indian Removal: 1500–1850*, ed. Peter Mancall and James H. Merrell (New York: Routledge, 2000), 30. See also: Paul Kelton, "Avoiding the Smallpox Spirits: Colonial Epidemics and Southeastern Indian Survival," *Ethnohistory* 51, no. 1 (Winter 2004): 45–71; Nile Robert Thompson and C. Dale Sloat, "The Use of Oral Literature to Provide

Community Health Education on the Southern Northwest Coast," *American Indian Culture and Research Journal* 28, no. 3 (2004): 20.

11. Jaenen, "Amerindian Views of French Culture," 77.

12. Nathaniel B. Shurtleff, ed., *Records of the Colony of New Plymouth in New England* (Bowie, MD: Heritage Books, 1998); "The Massachusetts Body of Liberties" (1641), available via Hanover Historical Texts Project, Hanover College, http://history.hanover.edu; Parnel Wickham, "Conceptions of Idiocy in Colonial Massachusetts," *Journal of Social History* 35, no. 4 (2003): 939.

13. Wickham, "Conceptions of Idiocy," 940.

14. Parnel Wickham, "Idiocy and the Law in Colonial New England," *Mental Retardation* 39, no. 2 (2001): 107.

15. Wickham, "Idiocy and the Law," 104–13; Parnel Wickham, "Images of Idiocy in Puritan New England," *Mental Retardation* 39, no. 2 (2001): 147–51.

16. Wickham, "Images of Idiocy," 149.

17. Seth Malios, *Archaeological Excavations at 44JC568, The Reverend Richard Buck Site* (Richmond: Association for the Preservation of Virginia Antiquities, 1999), 12.

18. Parnel Wickham, "Idiocy in Virginia, 1616–1860," *Bulletin of the History of Medicine* 80, no. 4 (2006): 683; Malios, *Archaeological Excavations*. See also: Irene W. D. Hecht and Frederick Hecht, "Mara and Benomi Buck: Familial Mental Retardation in Colonial Jamestown," *Journal of the History of Medicine* (April 1973): 171–76; Richard Neugebauer, "Exploitation of the Insane in the New World: Benoni Buck, the First Reported Case of Mental Retardation in the American Colonies," *Archives of General Psychiatry* 44, no. 5 (1987): 481–83.

19. Roger Thompson, *Sex in Middlesex: Popular Mores in a Massachusetts County, 1649–1699* (Amherst: University of Massachusetts Press, 1986), 137–38.

20. Ibid., 138.

21. Lawrence B. Goodheart, "The Distinction between Witchcraft and Madness in Colonial Connecticut," *History of Psychiatry* 13 (2002): 436.

22. Gerald Grob, *The Mad Among Us: A History of the Care of America's Mentally Ill* (Cambridge, MA: Harvard University Press, 1995), 7, 15; Albert Deutsch, "Public Provision for the Mentally Ill in Colonial America," *Social Science Review* 10, no. 4 (December 1936): 614.

23. Grob, *The Mad Among Us*, 16.

24. Deutsch, "Public Provision," 611–13; Grob, *The Mad Among Us*, 17.

25. Mary Ann Jimenez, *Changing Faces of Madness: Early American Attitudes and Treatment of the Insane* (Hanover, NH: University Press of New England, 1987), 13; Carol Gay, "The Fettered Tongue: A Study of the Speech Defect Of Cotton Mather," *American Literature* 46, no. 4 (1975): 451–64.

26. Robert J. Steinfeld, "Subjectship, Citizenship, and the Long History of Immigration Regulation," *Law and History Review* 19, no. 3 (2001): 645–53.

27. Sara Evans, *Born for Liberty: A History of Women in America* (New York: Free Press, 1997), 32.

28. Valerie Pearl and Morris Pearl, "Governor John Winthrop on the Birth of the Antinomians' 'Monster': The Earliest Reports to Reach England and the Making of a Myth," *Proceedings of the Massachusetts Historical Society*, 3d ser., 102 (1990): 37.

29. Anne G. Myles, "From Monster to Martyr: Re-Presenting Mary Dyer," *Early American Literature* 36, no. 1 (2001): 4.

CHAPTER THREE

1. Mary Ann Jimenez, *Changing Faces of Madness: Early American Attitudes and Treatment of the Insane* (Hanover, NH: University Press of New England, 1987), 32.
2. Philip M. Ferguson, "The Legacy of the Almshouse," in *Mental Retardation in America*, ed. Steven Noll and James W. Trent (New York: New York University Press, 2004), 46; Ruth Wallis Herndon, *Unwelcome Americans: Living on the Margin in Early New England* (Philadelphia: University of Pennsylvania Press, 2001), 8.
3. Adams Papers, Diary of John Adams, January 16, 1770, Massachusetts Historical Society; Nancy Rubin Stewart, *The Muse of the Revolution: The Secret Pen of Mercy Otis Warren and the Founding of a Nation* (Boston: Beacon Press, 2008), 41; John R. Waters Jr., *The Otis Family in Provincial and Revolutionary Massachusetts* (Chapel Hill: Institute for Early American History and Culture, University of North Carolina Press, 1968), 178.
4. Stewart, *The Muse of the Revolution*, 42–44; William Tudor, *The Life of James Otis, of Massachusetts* (Boston: Wells and Lilly, 1823), 475–85; Waters, *The Otis Family*, 178–81.
5. James Otis (Sr.) to James Otis Jr., August 1, 1772 (Barnstable), Otis-Gay Family Papers Collection, Columbia University, Rare Book and Manuscript Library.
6. Wickham, "Idiocy in Virginia," 688; Mark Couvillon, "Patrick Henry's Virginia: Three Homes of an American Patriot," *Virginia Cavalcade* 50, no. 4 (2001): 158–67. Different resources give different dates for Sarah Shelton Henry's death: either 1775 or 1776.
7. Wickham, "Idiocy in Virginia," 687.
8. Philip D. Morgan, "'Who died an expence to this town': Poor Relief in Eighteenth-Century Rhode Island," in *Down and Out in Early America*, ed. Billy G. Smith (University Park: Pennsylvania State University Press, 2004), 139.
9. Karin Wulf, "Gender and the Political Economy of Poor Relief in Colonial Philadelphia," in *Down and Out in Early America*, ed. Billy G. Smith (University Park: Pennsylvania State University Press, 2003), 163–212.
10. Jimenez, *Changing Faces of Madness*, 37.
11. Ibid., 41.
12. Albert Deutsch, *The Mentally Ill in America: A History of Their Care and Treatment from Colonial Times,* 2nd ed. (New York: Columbia University Press, 1967), 52.
13. Deutsch, *The Mentally Ill*, 52; Wickham, "Idiocy in Virginia," 688–89.
14. Deutsch, *The Mentally Ill*, 52, 59–61.
15. John Wesley, *Primitive Physic: An Easy and Natural Method of Curing Most Diseases* (Bristol, England: William Pine, 1773), 77.
16. Alfred W. Crosby, "Virgin Soil Epidemics as a Factor in the Aboriginal Depopulation in America," *William and Mary Quarterly* 33 (1976), 290; Nile Robert Thompson and C. Dale Sloat, "The Use of Oral Literature to Provide Community Health Education on the Southern Northwest Coast," *American Indian Culture and Research Journal* 28, no. 3 (2004): 20.
17. Alfred W. Crosby, "Ecological Imperialism: The Overseas Migration of Western Europeans as a Biological Phenomenon," in *American Encounters: Natives and Newcomers from European Contact to Indian Removal: 1500–1850*, ed. Peter Mancall and James H. Merrell (New York: Routledge, 2000), 62.

18. David W. Galenson, *Traders, Planters, and Slaves: Market Behavior in Early English America* (Cambridge, England: Cambridge University Press, 1986), 112–13.
19. Hugh Thomas, *The Slave Trade: The Story of the Atlantic Slave Trade: 1440–1870* (New York: Simon and Schuster, 1997), 376, 378.
20. Ibid., 386.
21. Ibid., 311.
22. *Foreign Slave Trade: Abstract of the Information Recently Laid on the Table of the House of Commons on the Subject of the Slave Trade* (London, 1821): 84–85.
23. George Francis Dow, *Slave Ships and Slaving* (1927; repr. New York: Dover, 1970), xxxv.
24. John Greenleaf Whittier, "The Slave Ships," 1834.
25. Galenson, *Traders, Planters, and Slaves*, 76–80; Thomas, *The Slave Trade*, 438–39.
26. James Oliver Horton and Louise E. Horton, *In Hope of Liberty: Culture, Community, and Protest among Northern Free Blacks, 1700–1860* (Oxford: Oxford University Press, 1979), 12; Darold D. Wax, "Preferences for Slaves in Colonial America," *Journal of Negro History* 58, no. 4 (October 1973): 382.

CHAPTER FOUR

1. David J. Rothman, *Discovery of the Asylum: Social Order and Disorder in the New Republic* (Boston: Little, Brown, 1971).
2. Dawn Keetley and John Pettegrew, eds., *Public Women, Public Words: A Documentary History of American Feminism,* vol. 1 (Madison, WI: Madison House, 1997), 48.
3. Douglas Baynton, "Disability and the Justification of Inequality in American History," in *The New Disability History: American Perspectives,* ed. Paul K. Longmore and Lauri Umansky (New York: New York University Press, 2001), 43–44.
4. Daniel Blackie, "Disabled Revolutionary War Veterans and the Construction of Disability in the Early United States, c. 1776–1840" (PhD diss., University of Helsinki, 2010), 1–2, 36.
5. Ibid., 42, 49, 56; James E. Potter, "'He . . . regretted having to die that way': Firearms Accidents in the Frontier Army, 1806–1891," *Nebraska History* 78, no. 4 (1997): 175–86.
6. Blackie, "Disabled Revolutionary War Veterans," 60–61.
7. Ibid., 69–71.
8. Ibid., chapter 4.
9. Ruth Wallis Herndon, *Unwelcome Americans: Living on the Margin in Early New England* (Philadelphia: University of Pennsylvania Press, 2001), 170–73.
10. For a smart and extended analysis of this, see Baynton, "Disability and the Justification of Inequality," 33–57.
11. Thomas Jefferson, *Jefferson's Notes on the State of Virginia; With the Appendixes—Complete* (Baltimore, MD: printed by W. Pechin, 1800), 143.
12. Harriet A. Washington, *Medical Apartheid: The Dark History of Medical Experimentation on Black Americans from Colonial Times to the Present* (New York: Doubleday, 2006), 35–36; Dea Boster, "Unfit for Bondage: Disability and African American Slavery in the United States, 1800–1860" (PhD diss., University of Michigan, 2010). While limited scholarship exists on slavery and disability, Boster's dissertation is a marvelous beginning and sets a high bar for future scholarship.

13. Baynton, "Disability and the Justification of Inequality," 39–40.
14. Boster, "Unfit for Bondage," 70, 75–76.
15. Ibid., 86, 90, 101.
16. Ibid., 56–57; Olive Gilbert and Sojourner Truth, *Narrative of Sojourner Truth: A Northern Slave, Emancipated from Bodily Servitude by the State of New York in 1828* (Boston: privately printed, 1850), 39; *Norfolk (VA) Herald*, October 25, 1798, accessed via "The Geography of Slavery in Virginia," Virginia Center for Digital History, University of Virginia, www.virginia.edu.
17. *Virginia Gazette*, August 11, 1774, accessed via "The Geography of Slavery," Virginia Center for Digital History, University of Virginia, www.virginia.edu.
18. Boster, "Unfit for Bondage," 56–57.
19. For a strong analysis of soundness, see Sharla M. Fett, *Working Cures: Healing, Health, and Power on Southern Slave Plantations* (Chapel Hill: University of North Carolina Press, 2003), chapter 1; Fett, *Working Cures*, 23; Boster, "Unfit for Bondage," 92–93.
20. Dea H. Boster, "An 'Epeleptick' Bondswoman: Fits, Slavery, and Power in the Antebellum South," *Bulletin of the History of Medicine* 83, no. 2 (Summer 2009): 271–301; Ellen Samuels, "'A Complication of Complaints': Untangling Disability, Race, and Gender in William and Ellen Craft's Running a Thousand Miles for Freedom," *MELUS: Multi-Ethnic Literatures of the United States* 31, no. 3 (Fall 2006): 15–47. Samuel's marvelous essay chronicles not an instance of malingering, but a case in which William and Ellen Craft used disability as a ploy in order to escape from slavery.
21. Boster, "Unfit for Bondage," 111, 122.
22. Marie Jenkins Schwartz, *Birthing a Slave: Motherhood and Medicine in the Antebellum South* (Cambridge, MA: Harvard University Press, 2006), 212–14; Ellen Samuels, "Examining Millie and Christine McKoy: Where Enslavement and Enfreakment Meet," *Signs* 37, no. 1 (Autumn 2011): 53–81.
23. Washington, *Medical Apartheid*, 61–67.
24. Kirby Ann Randolph, "Central Lunatic Asylum for the Colored Insane: A History of African Americans with Mental Disabilities, 1844–1885" (PhD diss., University of Pennsylvania, 2003); Frederick Douglass, *Life and Times of Frederick Douglass, Written by Himself* (1892), electronic edition available at "Documenting the American South," University of North Carolina, Chapel Hill, http://docsouth.unc.edu, 137–38; Frederick Douglass, *Narrative of the Life of Frederick Douglass* (Oxford: Oxford University Press, 1999), 56.
25. Gerald Grob, "Edward Jarvis and the Federal Census," *Bulletin of the History of Medicine* 50, no. 1 (1976): 4–27; Albert Deutsch, "The First US Census of the Insane (1840) and Its Uses as Pro-Slavery Propaganda," *Bulletin of the History of Medicine* 15 (1944): 469–82; Patricia Cline Cohen, *A Calculating People: The Spread of Numeracy in Early America* (Chicago: University of Chicago Press, 1982), chapter 6. I'm using Cohen's statistics.
26. "Reflections on the Census of 1840," *Southern Literary Messenger* (Richmond, VA) 9 (1843): 345, 350.
27. Grob, "Edward Jarvis"; Deutsch, "The First US Census of the Insane"; Cohen, *A Calculating People.*
28. Alfred W. Crosby, "Virgin Soil Epidemics as a Factor in the Aboriginal Depopulation in America," *William and Mary Quarterly* 33 (1976): 290–91.
29. Edward D. Castillo, "Blood Came from their Mouths: Tongva and Chumash Responses to the Pandemic of 1801," in *Medicine Ways: Disease, Health, and Survival among Native Americans*, ed. Clifford E. Trafzer and Diane Weiner (Walnut Creek, CA: AltaMira, 2001): 16–31.

30. Helpful in my formulation of this argument was Philip M. Ferguson, *Abandoned to Their Fate: Social Policy and Practice toward Severely Retarded People in America, 1820–1920* (Philadelphia: Temple University Press, 1994).
31. Lois Bragg, ed., *Deaf World: A Historical Reader and Primary Sourcebook* (New York: New York University Press, 2001), 6; Harlan Lane, *A Deaf Artist in Early America: The Worlds of John Brewster Jr.* (Boston: Beacon Press, 2004); Harlan Lane, *When the Mind Hears: A History of the Deaf* (New York: Vintage Books, 1984).
32. Samuel Gridley Howe, *On the Causes of Idiocy* (1848; New York: Arno Press, 1972), 1–2. For more on this trend, see: James W. Trent Jr., *Inventing the Feeble Mind: A History of Mental Retardation in the United States* (Los Angeles: University of California Press, 1995); Ferguson, *Abandoned to Their Fate*; Peter L. Tyor and Leland V. Bell, *Caring for the Retarded in America: A History* (Westport, CT: Greenwood, 1984); Lawrence B. Goodheart, "Rethinking Mental Retardation: Education and Eugenics in Connecticut, 1818–1917," *Journal of the History of Medicine & Allied Sciences* 59, no. 1 (2004): 90–111.
33. Ernest Freeberg, *The Education of Laura Bridgman* (Cambridge, MA: Harvard University Press, 2001); Elisabeth Gitter, *The Imprisoned Guest: Samuel Howe and Laura Bridgman, the Original Deaf-Blind Girl* (New York: Farrar, Straus and Giroux, 2001); Kim E. Nielsen, "The Southern Ties of Helen Keller," *Journal of Southern History* 73, no. 4 (November 2007): 783–806; Kim E. Nielsen, *The Radical Lives of Helen Keller* (New York: New York University Press, 2004); Kim E. Nielsen, *Beyond the Miracle Worker: The Remarkable Life of Anne Sullivan Macy and Her Extraordinary Friendship with Helen Keller* (Boston: Beacon Press, 2009); Harlan Lane, *A Deaf Artist in Early America: The Worlds of John Brewster Jr.* (Boston: Beacon Press, 2004); Phyllis Klein Valentine, "A Nineteenth-Century Experiment in Education of the Handicapped: The American Asylum for the Deaf and Dumb," *New England Quarterly* 64, no. 3 (1991): 355–75; Hannah Joyner, "This Unnatural and Fratricidal Strife: A Family's Negotiation of the Civil War, Deafness, and Independence," in *The New Disability History*, ed. Paul K. Longmore and Lauri Umansky (New York: New York University Press, 2001), 83–106; Hannah Joyner, *From Pity to Pride: Growing Up Deaf in the Old South* (Washington, DC: Gallaudet University Press, 2004).
34. Mary Ann Jimenez, *Changing Faces of Madness: Early American Attitudes and Treatment of the Insane* (Hanover, NH: University Press of New England, 1987), 81.
35. Shawn Smallman, "Spirit Beings, Mental Illness, and Murder: Fur Traders and the Windigo in Canada's Boreal Forest, 1774–1935," *Ethnohistory* 57, no. 4 (Fall 2010): 580.
36. Jimenez, *Changing Faces of Madness*, 103, and see examples 101–2.
37. Ibid., 106–7; Laurel Thatcher Ulrich, "Derangement in the Family: The Story of Mary Sewall, 1824–1825," *Dublin Seminar for New England Folklife Annual Proceedings* 15 (1990): 168–84.
38. Dorothea L. Dix, "Memorial to the Legislature of Massachusetts, 1843," in *The History of Mental Retardation: Collected Papers,* vol. 1, ed. Marvin Rosen, Gerald Clark, and Marvin Kivitz (Baltimore, MD: University Park Press, 1976), 17; Benjamin Reiss, "Letters from Asylumia: The *Opal* and the Cultural Work of the Lunatic Asylum, 1851–1860," *American Literary History* 16, no. 1 (2004): 1–28; Lawrence B. Goodheart, "The Concept of Insanity: Women Patients at the Hartford Retreat for the Insane, 1824–1865," *Connecticut History* 36, no. 1 (1995): 31–47; Gerald Grob, "Class, Ethnicity, and Race in American Mental Hospitals, 1830–1875," *Journal of the History of*

Medicine & Allied Sciences 28, no. 3 (July 1973): 207–29; Peter MacCandless, "Curative Asylum, Custodial Hospital: The South Carolina Lunatic Asylum and the State Hospital, 1828–1920," in *The Confinement of the Insane: International Perspectives, 1800–1965,* ed. Roy Porter and David Wright (Cambridge: Cambridge University Press), 173–92; Lawrence B. Goodheart, "From Cure to Custodianship of the Insane Poor in Nineteenth-Century Connecticut," *Journal of the History of Medicine and Allied Sciences* 65 (2010): 106–30; Lawrence B. Goodheart, *Mad Yankees: The Hartford Retreat for the Insane and Nineteenth-Century Psychiatry* (Amherst: University of Massachusetts Press, 2003); Shomer S. Zwelling, *Quest For a Cure: The Public Hospital In Williamsburg, Virginia, 1773–1885* (Williamsburg, VA: Colonial Williamsburg Foundation, 1985); Ellen Dwyer, *Homes for the Mad: Life inside Two Nineteenth-Century Asylums* (New Brunswick, NJ: Rutgers University Press, 1987); Nancy Tomes, *The Art of Asylum-Keeping: Thomas Story Kirkbride and the Origins of American Psychiatry* (Philadelphia: University of Pennsylvania Press, 1994); Benjamin Reiss, *Theaters of Madness: Insane Asylums and Nineteenth-Century American Culture* (Chicago: University of Chicago Press, 2008); Katherine K. Ziff, David O. Thomas, and Patricia M. Beamish, "Asylum and Community: The Athens Lunatic Asylum in Nineteenth-Century Ohio," *History of Psychiatry* 19 (2008): 409–32.

39. Penny Richards, "'Besides Her Sat Her Idiot Child': Families and Development Disability in Mid-Nineteenth-Century America," in *Mental Retardation in America: A Historical Reader,* ed. Steven Noll and James W. Trent Jr. (New York: New York University Press, 2004), 65–68.

40. Samuel Gridley Howe, "Report Made to the Legislature of Massachusetts," 1848.

41. Richards, "'Besides Her Sat Her Idiot Child,'" 65.

42. Carl T. Steen, "The Home for the Insane, Deaf, Dumb, and Blind of the Cherokee Nation," *Chronicles of Oklahoma* 21 (1943): 402–19; Rev. W. A. Duncan, Works Progress Administration, Indian Pioneer History Project for Oklahoma, University of Oklahoma, Western History Collections, http://libraries.ou.edu, accessed August 5, 2011.

43. Steen, "The Home for the Insane," 418.

44. Mary L. Day, *Incidents in the Life of a Blind Girl* (Baltimore, MD: James Young, 1859), 163, 175. Day also wrote a second and later volume of autobiography: *The World as I Have Found It* (Baltimore, MD: James Watts, 1878). For an analysis, see: Mary Klages, *Woeful Afflictions: Disability and Sentimentality in Victorian America* (Philadelphia: University of Pennsylvania Press, 1999), 146–63.

45. Christopher L. Tomlins, "A Mysterious Power: Industrial Accidents and the Legal Construction of Employment Relations in Massachusetts, 1800–1850," *Law and History Review* 6, no. 2 (Fall 1988): 375–438.

46. Robert J. Steinfeld, "Subjectship, Citizenship, and the Long History of Immigration Regulation," *Law and History Review* 19, no. 3 (2001); William J. Bromwell, *History of Immigration to the United States: Exhibiting the Number, Sex, Age, Occupation, and Country of Birth of Passengers Arriving from Foreign Countries by Sea from 1819 to 1855* (New York: August J. Kelley, 1855), 199, 201.

47. Kay Schriner and Lisa A. Ochs, "Creating the Disabled Citizen: How Massachusetts Disenfranchised People under Guardianship," *Ohio State Law Journal* 62 (2001): 481–533.

48. Ibid.

49. George L. Marshal Jr., "The Newburgh Conspiracy: How General Washington and His Spectacles Saved the Republic," *Early American Review* (Fall 1997), available at http://www.earlyamerica.com.

CHAPTER FIVE

1. Thomas A. Perrine, "A Sinister Manuscript," undated, William Oland Bourne Papers, Box 2, Folder 4, Manuscript Division, Library of Congress, Washington, DC.
2. Thomas A. Perrine was promoted to sergeant April 2, 1863; lost his arm at Chancellorsville, May 3, 1863; discharged on surgical certificate August 7, 1863; and died July 21, 1890. Per the website of the 140th Pennsylvania Volunteer Infantry Reenactors, http://www.140pvi.us. Louisa May Alcott, *Hospital Sketches*, ed. Alice Fahs (Boston: Bedford/St. Martin's, 2004), 73.
3. Fred Pelka, ed., *The Civil War Letters of Colonel Charles F. Johnson: Invalid Corps* (Amherst: University of Massachusetts Press, 2004), 224.
4. Undated letter of Albert T. Shurtleff, William Oland Bourne Papers, Box 5, Folder 6, Manuscript Division, Library of Congress, Washington, DC; John Bryson, June 11, 1867, William Oland Bourne Papers, Box 5, Folder 2, Manuscript Division, Library of Congress, Washington, DC.; B. D. Palmer, undated letter, William Oland Bourne Papers, Box 5, Folder 2, Manuscript Division, Library of Congress, Washington, DC; Laurann Figg and Jane Farrell-Beck, "Amputation in the Civil War: Physical and Social Dimensions," *Journal of the History of Medicine & Allied Sciences* 48, no. 4 (1993): 474; Jeffrey W. Mc-Clurke, *Take Care of the Living: Reconstructing Confederate Veteran Families in Virginia* (Charlottesville: University of Virginia Press, 2009), 104, 109.
5. Robert A. Pinn, undated letter, William Oland Bourne Papers, Box 2, Folder 2, Manuscript Division, Library of Congress, Washington, DC; William B. Neff, *Bench and Bar of Northern Ohio* (Cleveland, OH: Historical Publishing, 1921), 131.
6. Pelka, *The Civil War Letters,* 27, 28.
7. Ibid., 14.
8. Donald R. Shaffer, "'I do not suppose that Uncle Sam looks at the skin': African Americans and the Civil War Pension System, 1865–1934," *Civil War History* 46, no. 2 (June 2000): 132–47.
9. Peter Blanck and Chen Song, "'Never Forget What They Did Here': Civil War Pensions for Gettysburg Union Army Veterans and Disability in Nineteenth-Century America," *William and Mary Law Review* 44 (February 2003): 907–1520. See also: Peter Blanck, "'The Right to Live in the World': Disability Yesterday, Today, and Tomorrow," *Texas Journal on Civil Liberties and Civil Rights* (Spring 2008): 367–401; Larry M. Logue and Peter Blanck, *Race, Ethnicity, and Disability: Veterans and Benefits in Post–Civil War America* (New York: Cambridge University Press, 2010).
10. McClurke, *Take Care of the Living,* 124, 138.
11. Ibid., 119, 130, 138; Pelka, *The Civil War Letters,* 2.
12. Larry M. Logue and Peter Blanck, "The Civil War," in *Encyclopedia of American Disability History,* ed. Susan Burch, vol. 1 (New York: Facts on File, 2009), 181–83; Jennifer Davis McDaid, "'How a One-Legged Rebel Lives': Confederate Veterans and Artificial Limbs in Virginia," in *Artificial Parts, Practical Lives: Modern Histories of Prosthetics,* ed. Katherine Ott, David Serlin, and Stephen Mihm (New York: New York University Press, 2002), 136; Geoffrey

C. Ward, Ric Burns, and Ken Burns, *The Civil War: An Illustrated History* (New York: Knopf, 1990), 206; Figg and Farrell-Beck, "Amputation in the Civil War," 463; McClurke, *Take Care of the Living,* chap. 6.

13. McDaid, "'How a One-Legged Rebel Lives,'" 136; Figg and Farrell-Beck, "Amputation in the Civil War," 460; Pelka, *The Civil War Letters,* 23.

14. Figg and Farrell-Beck, "Amputation in the Civil War," 471–72, 474.

15. Susan M. Schweik, *The Ugly Laws: Disability in Public* (New York: New York University Press, 2009), 291, 293. See also: Adrienne Phelps Coco, "Diseased, Maimed, and Mutilated: Categorizations of Disability and an Ugly Law in Late Nineteenth-Century Chicago," *Journal of Social History* 44, no. 1 (Fall 2010): 23–37.

16. Lauri Umansky, "Lavinia Warren," in *Encyclopedia of American Disability History,* ed. Susan Burch, vol. 3 (New York: Facts on File, 2009), 950–52. For more on freak shows, see: Robert Bogdan, *Freak Show: Presenting Human Oddities for Amusement and Profit* (Chicago: University of Chicago Press, 1988); Rosemarie Garland Thomson, ed., *Freakery: Cultural Spectacles of the Extraordinary Body* (New York: New York University Press, 1998).

17. John Paterson is a pseudonym. John S. Hughes, "Labeling and Treating Black Mental Illness in Alabama, 1861–1910," *Journal of Southern History* 58, no. 3 (August 1993): 435–60.

18. J. F. Miller, "The Effects of Emancipation upon the Mental and Physical Health of the Negro of the South" *North Carolina Medical Journal* 38 (1896): 285–94.

19. Vanessa Jackson, "Separate and Unequal: The Legacy of Racially Segregated Psychiatric Hospitals," cited with author's permission; Hughes, "Labeling and Treating Black Mental Illness," 441.

20. Hughes, "Labeling and Treating Black Mental Illness," 445–54, 456.

21. Jim Downs, "The Continuation of Slavery: The Experience of Disabled Slaves during Emancipation," *Disability Studies Quarterly* 28, no. 3 (2008).

22. Edward H. Clarke, *Sex in Education; or, A Fair Chance for the Girls* (Boston: J. R. Osgood, 1873), 103.

23. Katherine Jankowski, "'Til All Barriers Crumble and Fall: Agatha Tiegel's Presentation Day Speech in April 1893," in *Deaf World: A Historical Reader and Primary Sourcebook,* ed. Lois Bragg (New York: New York University Press, 2001), 286, 289. For more on Tiegel see: O. Robinson, "Agatha Tiegel Hanson," in *Encyclopedia of American Disability History,* ed. Susan Burch, vol. 2 (New York: Facts on File, 2009): 423–24.

24. Ibid.

25. Lindsey Patterson, "Residential Schools," in *Encyclopedia of American Disability History,* ed. Susan Burch, vol. 3 (New York: Facts on File, 2009): 778–80.

26. Douglas Baynton, *Forbidden Signs: American Culture and the Campaign against Sign Language* (Chicago: University of Chicago Press, 1996), 26, 28–29.

27. Baynton, *Forbidden Signs,* 77. For more on Hanson, see: John Vickrey Van Cleve and Barry A. Crouch, *A Place of Their Own: Creating the Deaf Community in America* (Washington, DC: Gallaudet University Press, 1989), 132–35; Robert Buchanan, *Illusions of Equality: Deaf Americans in School and Factory, 1850–1950* (Washington, DC: Gallaudet University Press, 2002), 37–51.

28. Agatha Tiegel Hanson, "Inner Music," in *American Annals of the Deaf,* vol. 48, ed. Edward Allen Fay (Washington, DC: 1903), 207.

29. John Lee Clark, ed., *Deaf American Poetry: An Anthology* (Washington, DC: Gallaudet University Press, 2009), 86–88.

CHAPTER SIX

1. Calvin Coolidge, "1923 State of the Union Address," in State of the Union Address (1790–2001) by United States Presidents, available from Project Gutenberg, www.gutenberg.org.

2. Harry Laughlin, *Eugenical Sterilization in the United States* (Chicago: Psychopathic Laboratory of the Municipal Court of Chicago, 1922).

3. Jennifer Terry, *An American Obsession: Science, Medicine, and Homosexuality in Modern Society* (Chicago: University of Chicago Press, 1999), 82.

4. Laughlin, *Eugenical Sterilization,* 451–52. Laughlin built on the work of Charles Davenport, *Heredity in Relation to Eugenics* (New York: Henry Holt, 1911). See also: Harry Bruinius, *Better for All the World: The Secret History of Forced Sterilization and America's Quest for Racial Purity* (New York: Alfred Knopf, 2006) and Paul A. Lombardo, *Three Generations, No Imbeciles: Eugenics, the Supreme Court, and Buck v. Bell* (Baltimore, MD: Johns Hopkins University Press, 2008).

5. Jay Dolmage, "Disabled upon Arrival: The Rhetorical Construction of Disability and Race at Ellis Island," *Cultural Critique* 77 (Winter 2011): 45; Douglas Baynton, "Defectives in the Land: Disability and American Immigration Policy, 1882–1924," *Journal of American Ethnic History* 24, no. 3 (2005): 33, 35; Douglas C. Baynton, "'The Undesirability of Admitting Deaf Mutes': US Immigration Policy and Deaf Immigrants, 1882–1924," *Sign Language Studies* 6, no. 4 (Summer 2006): 393.

6. Dolmage, "Disabled upon Arrival"; Alan M. Kraut, *Silent Travelers: Germs, Genes, and the "Immigrant Menace"* (New York: Basic Books, 1994), chap. 3; Victor Safford, *Immigration Problems: Personal Experiences of an Official* (New York: Dodd, Mead, 1925), 245.

7. Margot Canaday, *The Straight State: Sexuality and Citizenship in Twentieth-Century America* (Princeton, NJ: Princeton University Press, 2009), 32; Terry, *An American Obsession,* 96.

8. Howard Markel and Alexandra Minna Stern, "Which Face? Whose Nation?: Immigration, Public Health, and the Construction of Disease at America's Ports and Borders, 1891–1928," *American Behavioral Scientist* 42 (1999): 1322; Dolmage, "Disabled upon Arrival," 40; Natalia Molina, "Medicalizing the Mexican: Immigration, Race, and Disability in the Early-Twentieth-Century United States," *Radical History Review* 94 (Winter 2006): 24; Emily Abel, "From Exclusion to Expulsion: Mexicans and Tuberculosis Control in Los Angeles, 1914–1940," *Bulletin of the History of Medicine* 77 (2003): 823–49.

9. Allan McLaughlin, "How Immigrants Are Inspected," *Popular Science Monthly* 66 (February 1905): 357–61. For more on trachoma, see: Howard Markel, "'The Eyes Have It': Trachoma, the Perception of Disease, the United States Public Health Service, and the American Jewish Immigration Experience, 1897–1924," *Bulletin of the History of Medicine* 74, no. 3 (2000): 525–60.

10. Ronald R. Kline, *Steinmetz: Engineer and Socialist* (Baltimore, MD: Johns Hopkins University Press, 1992).

11. McAlister Coleman, *Pioneers of Freedom* (New York: Vanguard Press, 1929), 265; John Winthrop Hammond, *Charles Proteus Steinmetz: A Biography* (New York: Century and Company, 1924), 8–9.

12. Baynton, "Defectives in the Land," 35; Canaday, *The Straight State,* chap. 1.

13. Baynton, "Defectives in the Land," 36–39; Canaday, *The Straight State,* 34–35.

14. Baynton, "Defectives in the Land," 36–39; Baynton, "The Undesirability of Admitting Deaf Mutes," 391–392; Sarah Abrevaya Stein, "Deaf American

Jewish Culture in Historical Perspective," *American Jewish History* 95, no. 3 (September 2009): 277–305.

15. Baynton, "Defectives in the Land," 34–35. Emphasis in original.

16. Canaday, *The Straight State,* 34, 36.

17. Calvin Coolidge, "1923 State of the Union Address."

18. Laughlin, *Eugenical Sterilization,* 164; The State, Alice Smith, Prosecutor vs. The Board of Examiners of Feeble-Minded (Including Idiots, Imbeciles and Morons) Epileptics, Criminals and Other Defectives, Defendants (1913), University of Wisconsin–Madison, General Library System.

19. Laughlin, *Eugenical Sterilization,* 293, 300; 1900 Census.

20. Laughlin, *Eugenical Sterilization,* 293, 294, 296, 300; Molly Ladd-Taylor, "Eugenic Sterilization in Minnesota," *Minnesota History* (Summer 2005): 243. The linkage between young women's sexual activities and feeble-mindedness was a common one. See, for example, Steven Noll, "Care and Control of the Feeble-Minded: Florida Farm Colony, 1920–1945," *Florida Historical Quarterly* 69, no. 1 (July 1990): 57–80; Molly Ladd-Taylor, "Eugenic Sterilization in Minnesota"; Michael A. Rembis, *Defining Deviance: Sex, Science, and Delinquent Girls, 1890–1960* (Chicago: University of Illinois Press, 2011).

21. Laughlin, *Eugenical Sterilization,* 294.

22. Terry, *An American Obsession,* 82; Laughlin, *Eugenical Sterilization,* 446–47.

23. Jonathan Katz, ed., *Gay American History: Lesbians and Gay Men in the USA* (New York: Harper Colophon, 1976), 143.

24. George Chauncey, "From Sexual Inversion to Homosexuality: The Changing Medical Conceptualization of Female 'Deviance,'" in *Passion and Power: Sexuality in History,* ed. Kathy Peiss and Christina Simmons, with Robert A. Padgug (Philadelphia: Temple University Press, 1992): 105; Douglas Baynton, "Disability and the Justification of Inequality in American History," in *The New Disability History: American Perspectives,* ed. Paul K. Longmore and Lauri Umansky (New York: New York University Press, 2001).

25. Buck v. Bell, 274 US 200 (1927); Lombardo, *Three Generations, No Imbeciles*; Anna Stubblefield, "'Beyond the Pale': Tainted Whiteness, Cognitive Disability, and Eugenic Sterilization," *Hypatia* 22, no. 2 (Spring 2007): 162–81; Stephen Jay Gould, "Carrie Buck's Daughter," *Natural History* 93 (July 1984): 14–18.

26. Dr. William Spratling, "An Ideal Colony for Epileptics and the Necessity for the Broader Treatment of Epilepsy," *American Medicine,* August 24, 1901, 287.

27. Goodheart, "Rethinking Mental Retardation: Education and Eugenics in Connecticut, 1818–1917," *Journal of the History of Medicine & Allied Sciences* 59, no. 1 (2004): 103.

28. Laura Skandera Trombley, "'She Wanted to Kill': Jean Clemens and Postictal Psychosis," *American Literary Realism* 37, no. 3 (Spring 2005): 225, 234; Michael Sheldon, *Mark Twain: The Man in White, His Final Years* (New York: Random House, 2010); Karen Lystra, *Dangerous Intimacy: The Untold Story of Mark Twain's Final Years* (Berkeley: University of California Press, 2004), 95.

29. Harry Hummer, "Insanity Among the Indians," *American Journal of Insanity* 69 (January 1913): 613–23; Todd Leahy, "The Canton Asylum: Indians, Psychiatrists, and Government Policy, 1899–1934" (PhD diss., Oklahoma State University, 2004), 52–76.

30. Pemina Yellow Bird, "Wild Indians: Native Perspectives on the Hiawatha Asylum for Insane Indians," available at the website of the National Empowerment Center, http://www.power2u.org, 9; Zitkala-Sa, *American Indian Stories* (1921; Lincoln: University of Nebraska Press, 1985), 55–56.

31. Scott Riney, "Power and Powerlessness: The People of the Canton Asylum for Insane Indians," *South Dakota History* 27, nos. 1–2 (Spring/Summer 1997): 56–59; Diane T. Putney, "The Canton Asylum for Insane Indians, 1902–1934," *South Dakota History* 14, no. 1 (1984): 17–20; Yellow Bird, "Wild Indians"; Bradley Soule and Jennifer Soule, "Death at the Hiawatha Asylum for Insane Indians [1908–1933]," *South Dakota Journal of Medicine* 56, no. 1 (January 2003): 15–18.

32. "'Sane' Indians Held in Dakota Asylum," *New York Times*, October 15, 1933.

33. Susan Burch, "'Dis-membered' Pasts: Histories of Removals, Institutions, and Community Lives," paper given at the January 2012 American Historical Association meeting. Cited with permission.

34. Putney, "The Canton Asylum," 28.

35. Martin Summers, "'Suitable Care of the African When Afflicted with Insanity': Race, Madness, and Social Order in Comparative Perspective," *Bulletin of the History of Medicine* 84 (2010): 70; Matthew Gambino, "'The Savage Heart beneath the Civilized Exterior': Race, Citizenship, and Mental Illness in Washington, DC, 1900–1940," *Disability Studies Quarterly* 28, no. 3 (Summer 2008). See also: Matthew Gambino, "'These Strangers within Our Gates': Race, Psychiatry, and Mental Illness among Black Americans at St. Elizabeth's Hospital in Washington, DC, 1900–1940," *History of Psychiatry* 19 (2008): 387–408. Other scholars have examined the relationship between public health policies, US imperialism, and racial segregation: Samuel Kelton Roberts Jr., *Infectious Fear: Politics, Disease, and the Health Effects of Segregation* (Chapel Hill: University of North Carolina Press, 2009); Michelle T. Moran, *Colonizing Leprosy: Imperialism and the Politics of Public Health in the United States* (Chapel Hill: University of North Carolina Press, 2007); Natalia Molina, *Fit to Be Citizens? Public Health and Race in Los Angeles, 1879–1939* (Berkeley: University of California Press, 2006).

36. Todd Benson, "Blinded with Science: American Indians, the Office of Indian Affairs, and the Federal Campaign against Trachoma, 1924–1927," in *Medicine Ways: Disease, Health, and Survival among Native Americans*, ed. Clifford E. Trafzer and Diane Weiner (Walnut Creek, CA: AltaMira Press, 2001), 54, 62.

37. Ibid., 63, 65, 67.

38. John Fabian Witt, *The Accidental Republic: Crippled Workingmen, Destitute Widows, and the Remaking of American Law* (Cambridge: Harvard University Press, 2004), 24, 38.

39. Crystal Eastman, *Work Accidents and the Law* (Pittsburgh, PA: Russell Sage Foundation, 1910), 146.

40. Ibid., 146, 148.

41. Ibid., 146, 149.

42. Ibid., 227.

43. Witt, *The Accidental Republic*, 3; Mark Aldrich, *Death Rode the Rails: American Railroad Accidents and Safety, 1828–1965* (Baltimore, MD: Johns Hopkins University Press, 2006), 2, 185; John Williams-Searle, "Cold Charity: Manhood, Brotherhood, and the Transformation of Disability" in *The New Disability History: American Perspectives*, ed. Paul K. Longmore and Lauri Umansky (New York: New York University Press, 2001), 157–86; John Williams-Searle, "Courting Risk: Disability, Masculinity, and Liability on Iowa's Railroads, 1868–1900," *Annals of Iowa* 58 (Winter 1999): 27–77; Shelton H. Stromquist, *A Generation of Boomers: The Pattern of Railroad Labor Conflict in Nineteenth-Century America* (Chicago: University of Illinois Press, 1993).

44. Witt, *The Accidental Republic,* 27; Allan Kraut, *Silent Travelers: Germs, Genes, and the "Immigrant Menace"* (New York: Basic Books, 1994), 172–78, 180; Claudia Clark, *Radium Girls: Women and Industrial Health Reform, 1910–1935* (Chapel Hill: North Carolina University Press, 1997); Jill E. Cooper, "Keeping the Girls on the Line: The Medical Department and Women Workers at AT&T, 1913–1940," *Pennsylvania History* 64, no. 4 (1997): 490–508.

45. Amy M. Hamburger, "The Cripple and His Place in the Community," *Annals of the American Academy of Political and Social Science* 77 (May 1918): 36–37.

46. Ibid., 41, 46.

47. Ana Carden-Coyne, "Ungrateful Bodies: Rehabilitation, Resistance, and Disabled American Veterans of the First World War," *European Review of History* 14, no. 4 (2007): 546. For more on disability and World War I, as well as adaptive technologies, see: Scott Gelber, "'Hard-Boiled Order': The Reeducation of Disabled WWI Veterans in New York City," *Journal of Social History* 39, no. 1 (2005): 161–80; Walter K. Hickel, "Medicine, Bureaucracy, and Social Welfare: The Politics of Disability Compensation for American Veterans of World War I," in *The New Disability History: American Perspectives,* ed. Paul K. Longmore and Lauri Umansky (New York: New York University Press, 2001), 236–67; Michael J. Lansing, "'Salvaging the Man Power of America': Conservation, Manhood, and Disabled Veterans During World War I," *Environmental History* 14, no. 1 (January 2009): 32–56; Beth Linker, "Feet for Fighting: Locating Disability and Social Medicine in First World War America," *Social History of Medicine* 20, no. 1 (2007): 91–109; Beth Linker, *War's Waste: Rehabilitation in World War One* (Chicago: University of Chicago Press, 2011); Edward Slavishak, "Artificial Limbs and Industrial Workers' Bodies in Turn-of-the-Century Pittsburgh," *Journal of Social History* 37, no. 2 (Winter 2003): 365–88.

48. "Future Ship Workers: A One-Armed Welder," 1919, Exhibit poster showing two scenes in which men with partial arm amputations are taught welding, Reproduction Number: LC-USZC4-7461, Call Number: POS—WWI—US, no. 32 (C size) [P&P], Repository: Library of Congress Prints and Photographs Division Washington, D.C. 20540 USA.

49. "The disabled man who is profitably employed is no longer handicapped," 1919, Exhibit poster, text only, calling for the extension of veterans' benefits to all injured and disabled citizens, Reproduction Number: LC-USZC4-7379 (color film copy transparency), Call Number: POS—WWI—US, no. 38 (C size) [P&P], Repository: Library of Congress Prints and Photographs Division, Washington, DC.

50. Calvin Coolidge, "1923 State of the Union Address."

CHAPTER SEVEN

1. Robert Cohen, ed., *Dear Mrs. Roosevelt: Letters from Children of the Great Depression* (Chapel Hill: University of North Carolina Press, 2002), 232–33.

2. Ibid., 233–34.

3. Paul K. Longmore and David Goldberger, "The League of the Physically Handicapped and the Great Depression: A Case Study in the New Disability History," *Journal of American History* 87, no. 3 (2000): 904, 905, 907.

4. Robert F. Jefferson, "'Enabled Courage': Race, Disability, and Black World War II Veterans in Postwar America," *Historian* 65, no. 5 (2003): 1103, 1121.

5. "Deaf" is capitalized here in the context of the self-defined cultural community, and lowercased in references to the physical condition.

6. For more on the Deaf community in this period, see Susan Burch, *Signs of Resistance: American Deaf Cultural History, 1900 to 1942* (New York: New York University Press, 2002); Michael Reis, "Student Life at the Indiana School for the Deaf During the Depression Years," in *Deaf History Unveiled: Interpretations from the New Scholarship,* ed. John Vickrey Van Cleve (Washington, DC: Gallaudet University Press, 1993), 198–223.

7. Myron Uhlberg, *Hands of My Father: A Hearing Boy, His Deaf Parents, and the Language of Love* (New York: Bantam Books, 2008), 125–26.

8. Barbara H. Baskin, "The Impact of Disability on Employment Opportunities in the Depression of the 1930s," in *The Unemployed (1930–1932),* ed. Alex Baskin (New York: Archives of Social History, 1975), 18; David Shannon, *The Great Depression* (Englewood Cliffs, NJ: Prentice Hall, 1960), 163–71. In this case the WPA interviewer did not know American Sign Language. Most of the interview was conducted via writing.

9. Uhlberg, *Hands of My Father,* 31.

10. Burch, *Signs of Resistance,* 120–28.

11. Ibid., 126.

12. Ibid., 35–39. See also: Carolyn McCaskill, Ceil Lucas, Robert Bayley, and Joseph Hill, *The Hidden Treasure of Black ASL: Its History and Structure* (Washington, DC: Gallaudet University Press, 2002).

13. For a lovely chronicle of life at the North Carolina State School for the Colored Blind and Deaf, see: Mary Herring Wright, *Sounds Like Home: Growing Up Black and Deaf in the South* (Washington, DC: Gallaudet University Press, 1999); Kim E. Nielsen, ed., *Helen Keller: Selected Writings* (New York: New York University Press, 2005), 183–84.

14. Monika Deppen-Wood, Mark R. Luborsky and Jessica Scheer, "Aging, Disability and Ethnicity: An African-American Woman's Story," in *The Cultural Context of Aging,* 2nd ed., ed. Jay Sokolovsky (Westport, CN: Bergin and Garvey, 1997), 444.

15. R. J. Altenbaugh, "Where Are the Disabled in the History of Education? The Impact of Polio on Sites of Learning," *History of Education* 35, no. 6 (November 2006): 710. For more on the history of polio and the experiences of polio survivors, see: Daniel J. Wilson, *Living with Polio: The Epidemic and Its Survivors* (Chicago: University of Chicago Press, 2005); Daniel J. Wilson, *Polio: Biographies of Disease* (Westport, CT: Greenwood Press, 2009); Naomi Rogers, *Dirt and Disease: Polio Before FDR* (New Brunswick, NJ: Rutgers University Press, 1992); Susan Richards Shreve, *Warm Springs: Traces of a Childhood at FDR's Polio Haven* (Boston: Houghton Mifflin, 2007); Anne Finger, *Elegy for a Disease: A Personal and Cultural History of Polio* (New York: St. Martin's, 2006).

16. Daniel J. Wilson, "Psychological Trauma and Its Treatment in the Polio Epidemics," *Bulletin of the History of Medicine* 82, no. 4 (Winter 2008): 871.

17. Altenbaugh, "Where Are the Disabled?" 721; Sucheng Chan, *In Defense of Asian American Studies: The Politics of Teaching and Program Building* (Chicago: University of Illinois Press, 2005), 35–36.

18. For more on FDR as well as an analysis of the implications of the erasure of his disability, see: Hugh Gregory Gallagher, *FDR's Splendid Deception* (New York: Dodd Mead, 1994); Rosemarie Garland-Thomson, "The FDR Memorial: Who Speaks from the Wheelchair?" *Chronicle of Higher Education,* January 26, 2001, B11–B12; Amy L. Fairchild, "The Polio Narratives: Dialogues with FDR," *Bulletin of the History of Medicine* 75, no. 3 (2001): 488–534;

John Duffy, "Franklin Roosevelt: Ambiguous Symbol for Disabled Americans," *Midwest Quarterly* 29, no. 1 (1987): 113–35.

19. Daniel J. Wilson, "Polio," in *Encyclopedia of American Disability History*, vol. 2, ed. Susan Burch (New York: Facts on File, 2009), 725–29. For more on Kenny, see: Naomi Rogers, "'Silence Has Its Own Stories': Elizabeth Kenny, Polio, and the Culture of Medicine," *Social History of Medicine* 21 (2008): 145–61.

20. Naomi Rogers, "Race and the Politics of Polio: Warm Springs, Tuskegee, and the March of Dimes," *American Journal of Public Health* 97, no. 5 (May 2007): 787, 791; Stephen E. Mawdsley, "'Dancing on Eggs': Charles H. Bynum, Racial Politics, and the National Foundation for Infantile Paralysis, 1938–1954," *Bulletin of the History of Medicine* 84, no. 2 (Summer 2010): 227.

21. Rogers, "Race and the Politics of Polio," 791, 793; Bruce Watson, *Freedom Summer: The Savage Season That Made Mississippi Burn and Made America a Democracy* (New York: Viking, 2010), 246; Fannie Lou Hamer's Testimony before the Credentials Committee, Democratic National Convention, Atlantic City, NJ, August 22, 1964. More research needs to be done on race and the vaccination process. For more on race, civil rights activism, and the March of Dimes, see: Mawdsley, "'Dancing on Eggs.'"

22. Doris Zames Fleischer and Frieda Zames, *The Disability Rights Movement: From Charity to Confrontation* (Philadelphia: Temple University Press, 2001), 33.

23. Allison C. Carey, *On the Margins of Citizenship: Intellectual Disability and Civil Rights in Twentieth-Century America* (Philadelphia: Temple University Press, 2009), 107; Kathleen Jones, "Education for Children with Mental Retardation: Parent Activism, Public Policy, and Family Ideology in the 1950s," in *Mental Retardation in America*, ed. Steven Noll and James W. Trent (New York: New York University Press, 2004), 327.

24. Jones, "Education for Children with Mental Retardation," 325.

25. For example, see: *Where's Molly* (San Francisco: SFO Productions, 2007); Trent, *Inventing the Feeble Mind*, chap. 7; Carey, *On the Margins*, chap. 6; Harold Pollack, "Learning to Walk Slow: America's Partial Policy Success in the Arena of Intellectual Disability," *Journal of Policy History* 19, no. 1 (2007): 95–112; Jones, "Education for Children with Mental Retardation"; Katherine Castles, "'Nice, Average Americans': Postwar Parents' Groups and the Defense of the Normal Family," in *Mental Retardation in America*, ed. Steven Noll and James W. Trent (New York: New York University Press, 2004), 351–70; Barbara Bair, "The Parents Council for Retarded Children and Social Change in Rhode Island, 1951–1970," *Rhode Island History* 40, no. 4 (1981): 144–59; Melanie Panitch, *Disability, Mothers, and Organization: Accidental Activists* (New York: Routledge, 2008).

26. Carey, *On the Margins*, 112, 115–16; Gerald O'Brien, "Rosemary Kennedy: The Importance of a Historical Footnote," *Journal of Family History* 29, no. 3 (July 2004): 225–36; David Braddock, "Honoring Eunice Kennedy Shriver's Legacy in Intellectual Disability," *Intellectual and Developmental Disabilities* 48, no. 1 (February 2010): 63–72; Edward Shorter, *The Kennedy Family and the Story of Mental Retardation* (Philadelphia: Temple University Press, 2000).

27. Carey, *On the Margins*, 190; written remembrances of Jane Birk, Minnesota ARC Papers, Minnesota Historical Society.

28. Steven J. Taylor, *Acts of Conscience: World War II, Mental Institutions, and Religious Objectors* (Syracuse, NY: Syracuse University Press, 2009), 2, chap. 7; Frank Leon Wright, ed., *Out of Sight, Out of Mind* (Philadelphia: National

Mental Health Foundation, 1947). Another such example is Albert Deutsch's *The Shame of the States* (New York: Arno Press, 1973).

29. Burton Blatt and Fred Kaplan, *Christmas in Purgatory* (New York: Allyn and Bacon, 1966).

30. Steven J. Taylor, "*Christmas in Purgatory*," in *Encyclopedia of American Disability History*, vol. 1, ed. Susan Burch (New York: Facts on File, 2009), 175. See also: David Mechanic and Gerald N. Grob, "Rhetoric, Realities, and the Plight of the Mentally Ill in America," in *History and Health Policy in the United States: Putting the Past Back*, ed. Rosemary A. Stevens, Charles E. Rosenberg, and Lawton R. Burns (New Brunswick, NJ: Rutgers University Press, 2006): 229–49; Darby Penney and Peter Stastny, *The Lives They Left Behind: Suitcases from a State Hospital Attic* (New York: Bellevue Literary Press, 2008).

31. Bay Crockett, Pueblo, CO, to Franklin D. Roosevelt, October 23, 1942, FDR Papers as President, Official File, 4920 gasoline rationing, 1942, Hyde Park, New York, FDR Presidential Library and Museum.

32. Victor L. Lee, Los Altos, California, to Franklin D. Roosevelt, January 29, 1942, FDR Papers as President, Official File, 4740 tire industry, FDR Presidential Library and Museum.

33. Julia O'Brien, Seneca Falls, New York, to Franklin D. Roosevelt, August 9, 1942, FDR Papers as President, Official File, 4740 tire industry, July–Dec 1942, FDR Presidential Library and Museum.

34. Ibid.; Letter from Julia O'Brien to Mrs. Beady, White House Executive Office, undated, FDR Papers as President, Official File, 4740 tire industry, July–Dec 1942, FDR Presidential Library and Museum.

35. Harlan Hahn, "Public Support for Rehabilitation Programs: The Analysis of US Disability Policy," *Disability, Handicap and Society* 1, no. 2 (1986): 127; R. K. McNickle, *Rehabilitation of Disabled Persons: Editorial Research Reports*, vol. 2 (Washington, DC: Congressional Quarterly Press, 1950), retrieved from CQ Researcher, http://library.cqpress.com/cqresearcher.

36. William B. Towns, "The Physically Handicapped on the Industrial Warfront," *Crippled Child*, June 1942.

37. Ibid.

38. Kathi Wolf, "Teaching of Disability History Is Eminently Right—and FAIR," *Independence Today*, August 2011, http://www.itodaynews.com, accessed November 11, 2011.

39. Andrew Edmund Kersten, *Labor's Home Front: The American Federation of Labor during World War II* (Chicago: University of Illinois Press, 2009), 166, 167.

40. Legislation passed after World War I includes the 1916 National Defense Act, the 1917 Smith-Hughes Act, which created the Federal Board of Vocational Education, and the 1918 Smith-Sears Veterans Rehabilitation Act. For more on this and debates surrounding emerging programs, see: Ruth O'Brien, *Crippled Justice: The History of Modern Disability Policy in the Workplace* (Chicago: University of Chicago Press, 2001), chap. 2. For more on the emerging rehabilitation profession, see: Martha Lentz Walker, *Beyond Bureaucracy: Mary Elizabeth Switzer and Rehabilitation* (Lanham, MD: University Press of America, 1985); Edward D. Berkowitz, "The Federal Government and the Emergence of Rehabilitation Medicine," *Historian* 43 (1981): 530–45.

41. O'Brien, *Crippled Justice*, 76–77.

42. Ibid., 77–78; Audra Jennings, "'The Greatest Numbers . . . Will Be Wage Earners': Organized Labor and Disability Activism, 1945–1953," *Labor: Studies in Working Class History of the Americas* 4, no. 4 (2007): 37–52.

43. Jennings, "'The Great Numbers,'" 66–67; Audra Jennings, "Picnics, Parties, and Rights: US Disability Activism, 1940–1960," American Historical Association conference presentation, January 2012 (used with author's permission). For more on disability as a labor issue, see: Sarah F. Rose, "'Crippled' Hands: Disability in Labor and Working-Class History," *Labor: Studies in Working-Class History of the Americas* 2, no. 1 (2005): 27–54.

44. Jennings, "'The Great Numbers," 56–57. For more on this, see: O'Brien, *Crippled Justice*; Buchanan, *Illusions of Equality;* Richard Scotch, "American Disability Policy in the Twentieth Century," in *The New Disability History: American Perspectives*, ed. Paul K. Longmore and Lauri Umansky (New York: New York University Press, 2001), 375–92.

45. Thomas L. Stokes, "'Bravest of the Brave' Fight Prejudice Caused by Extent of their Sacrifice" *State Journal* (WI), August 17, 1946.

46. Jennings, "'The Great Numbers," 72, 81.

47. David A. Gerber, "In Search Of Al Schmid: War Hero, Blinded Veteran, Everyman," *Journal of American Studies* 1995 29, no. 1 (1995): 12, 19; David Gerber, "Anger and Affability: The Rise and Representation of a Repertory of Self-Presentation Skills in a World War II Disabled Veteran," *Journal of Social History* 27, no. 1 (1993): 5–27; David Gerber, "Blind and Enlightened: The Contested Origins of the Egalitarian Politics of the Blinded Veterans Association" in *The New Disability History: American Perspectives*, ed. Paul K. Longmore and Lauri Umansky (New York: New York University Press, 2001), 313–74; David Gerber, "Memory of Enlightenment: Accounting for the Egalitarian Politics of the Blinded Veterans Association," *Disability Studies Quarterly* 18 (Fall 1998): 257–63.

48. Jefferson, "Enabled Courage," 1122–24. For more on African American disabled veterans, see: Ellen Dwyer, "Psychiatry and Race during World War II," *Journal of the History of Medicine and Allied Sciences* 61(2006): 117–43.

49. See, for example, Felicia Kornbluh, "Disability, Antiprofessionalism, and Civil Rights: The National Federation of the Blind and the 'Right to Organize' in the 1950s," *Journal of American History* (March 2011): 1023–47; Jacobus tenBroek, "The Right to Live in the World: The Disabled in the World of Torts," *California Law Review* 54, no. 2 (1966); Albert A. Herzog Jr., "From Service to Rights: The Movement for Disability Rights in the American Methodist Tradition," *Methodist History* 38, no. 1 (1999): 27–39; Edward Abrahams, "Randolph Bourne on Feminism and Feminists," *Historian* 43, no. 3 (1981): 365–77; Paul K. Longmore and Paul Steven Miller, "'A Philosophy of Handicap': The Origins Of Randolph Bourne's Radicalism," *Radical History Review* 94 (2006): 59–83; Amy L. Fairchild, "Leprosy, Domesticity, and Patient Protest: The Social Context of a Patients' Rights Movement in Mid-Century America," *Journal of Social History* (2006): 1011–42.

CHAPTER EIGHT

1. "Disabled Miners Threaten Stronger Tactics," *Beckley (WV) Post-Herald,* September 6, 1971, 6.

2. "President of Disabled Miners Claims Strike Imminent," *Uniontown (PA) Morning Herald*, September 30, 1971; Robert Payne obituary, *Beckley (WV) Register-Herald*, October 29, 2009; William Graebner, *Coal-Mining Safety in the Progressive Period: The Political Economy of Reform* (Lexington: University Press of Kentucky, 1976), 91.

3. Barbara Ellen Smith, *Digging Our Graves: Coal Miners and the Struggle over Black Lung Disease* (Philadelphia: Temple University Press, 1987), 14; Graebner, *Coal-Mining Safety,* 56. For more on coal mining and the strikes of the 1970s, see: Smith, *Digging Our Graves;* Paul F. Clark, *The Miners' Fight for Democracy: Arnold Miller and the Reform of the United Mine Workers* (Ithaca, NY: New York State School of Industrial and Labor Relations, Cornell University, 1981); Robert L. Lewis, *Black Coal Miners in America: Race, Class, and Community Conflict, 1870–1980* (Louisville: University Press of Kentucky, 1987); Richard A. Brisbin, *A Strike Like No Other Strike: Law and Resistance during the Pittston Coal Strike of 1989–1990* (Baltimore, MD: Johns Hopkins University Press, 2002); Robyn Muncy, "Coal-Fired Reform: Social Citizenship, Dissident Miners, and the Great Society," *Journal of American History* 96, no. 1 (2009): 72–98.

4. Brisbin, *A Strike Like No Other,* 82; Graebner, *Coal-Mining Safety,* 92.

5. "President of Disabled Miners Claims Strike Imminent," *Uniontown (PA) Morning Herald;* "Disabled Miners Threaten Stronger Tactics," *Beckley (WV) Post-Herald.*

6. Lewis, *Black Coal Miners,* 184; Graebner, *Coal-Mining Safety,* 92; Smith lived in Rhodell, also near Beckley, West Virginia. He credited Arnold Miller with securing him a wheelchair during this period.

7. "Clara Clow," *Frederick (MD) News,* August 15, 1990.

8. Ibid.

9. Ibid.

10. Scholarship on the disability rights movement includes, but is not limited to: Paul K. Longmore, "The Disability Rights Movement," in *Why I Burned My Book and Other Essays on Disability* (Philadelphia: Temple University Press, 2003), 101–15; Sharon Barnartt and Richard Scotch, *Disability Protests: Contentious Politics, 1970–1999* (Washington, DC: Gallaudet University Press, 2001); Doris Zames Fleischer and Frieda Zames, *The Disability Rights Movement: From Charity to Confrontation* (Philadelphia: Temple University Press, 2001); Jacqueline Vaughn Switzer, *Disabled Rights: American Disability Policy and the Fight for Equality* (Washington, DC: Georgetown University Press, 2003); Joseph P. Shapiro, *No Pity: People with Disabilities Forging a New Civil Rights Movement* (New York: Random House, 1993); Richard K. Scotch, *From Good Will to Civil Rights: Transforming Federal Disability Policy,* 2nd ed. (Philadelphia: Temple University Press, 2001).

11. Shapiro, *No Pity,* chap. 2; Barnartt and Scotch, *Disability Protests,* 42–44. Roberts noted that some of the most treasured care attendants were conscientious objectors, assigned to what a military official thought would be a miserable and punishing job. Like the conscientious objectors who brought public attention to the abuses at institutions for people with developmental disabilities, these young men quickly became valuable allies. Roberts said, "These were the kind of people we wanted to work with. We were very lucky." Fleischer and Zames, *The Disability Rights Movement,* 39.

12. Fleischman and Zames, *The Disability Rights Movement,* 41.

13. Rick Mayes and Allan V. Horwitz, "DSM III and the Revolution in the Classification of Mental Illness," *Journal of the History of Behavioral Sciences* 41, no. 3 (Summer 2005): 255; Gerald Grob, *The Mad Among Us: A History of the Care of America's Mentally Ill* (Boston: Harvard University Press), 287.

14. Michael A. Rembis, "The New Asylums: Madness and Mass Incarceration in the Neoliberal Era." Work in progress. Cited with the author's permission.

15. Lindsey M. Patterson, "Building Communities and Breaking Down Barriers: Disability Rights Activism 1959–1968," paper presented at a meeting of the American Historical Association, Chicago, January 2012. Cited with author's permission.

16. Scotch, *From Good Will to Civil Rights*, 54. See also Fleischman and Zames, *The Disability Rights Movement*, chap. 4.

17. Scotch, *From Good Will to Civil Rights*, 56–57.

18. "Handicapped People Draw Notice," *Denton (TX) Record Chronicle*, January 8, 1971; "Question Line" of the *Charleston (WV) Daily Mail*, May 15, 1972; *Greeley (CO) Daily Tribune*, March 25, 1977; "Helena Handicapped to Organize," *Independent Record* (Helena, MT), August 30, 1977; "The Handicapped Join Push for Equality," *Kennebeck Journal* (Augusta, ME), September 22, 1977; *Lima (OH) News*, August 12, 1973.

19. Department of Education, *History: Twenty-Five Years of Progress in Educating Children with Disabilities through IDEA* (Washington, DC: Office of Special Education Programs, 2008), available on the website of the US Department of Education, www.ed.gov.

20. Flesichman and Zames, *The Disability Rights Movement*, 51, 59.

21. Scotch, *From Good Will to Civil Rights*, 111–16; Barnartt and Scotch, *Disability Protests*, 165–66; Fleischman and Zames, *The Disability Rights Movement*, 53–56; *Independent Press Telegram* (Long Beach, CA), April 9, 1977; *Independent Press Telegram*, April 16, 1977.

22. Susan Schweik, "Lomax's Matrix: Disability, Solidarity, and the Black Power of 504," *Disability Studies Quarterly* 31, no. 1 (2011); Scotch, *From Good Will to Civil Rights*, 111–16; Barnartt and Scotch, *Disability Protests*, 165–66; Fleischman and Zames, *The Disability Rights Movement*, 53–56; Shapiro, *No Pity*, 64–70.

23. "Disabled Woman Claims Bias by Sheriff," *Syracuse (NY) Post-Standard*, April 22, 1975.

24. *Greeley (CO) Daily Tribune*, March 25, 1977.

25. *Zanesville (OH) Times Recorder*, July 16, 1976.

26. Shapiro, *No Pity*, 28; Paul S. Miller obituary, *Washington Post*, October 21, 2010; Paul S. Miller obituary, *New York Times*, October 21, 2010.

27. Paul K. Longmore, "Why I Burned My Book," in *Why I Burned My Book and Other Essays on Disability* (Philadelphia: Temple University Press, 2003), 231, 249, 253.

28. Shapiro, *No Pity*, 26; "Parents without Powers," *Los Angeles Times*, July 26, 1992; Jay Mathews, *A Mother's Touch: The Tiffany Callo Story* (New York: Henry Holt, 1992).

29. *Termination of Parental Rights* (Minneapolis: Center for Advanced Studies in Child Welfare, University of Minnesota, 2011), available at http://www.cehd.umn.edu/ssw, accessed November 27, 2011; Elizabeth Lightfoot, Katharine Hill, Traci LaLiberte, "The Inclusion of Disability as a Condition for Termination of Parental Rights," *Child Abuse & Neglect* 34, no. 2 (December 2010): 927–34; "Bill Seeks to Amend Law to Terminate Parental Rights Due to Mental Illness," *Mental Health Weekly* 19, no. 10 (March 3, 2009), 7; Christine Breeden, Rhoda Olkin, Daniel J. Taube, "Child Custody Evaluations When One Divorcing Parent Has a Physical Disability," *Rehabilitation Psychology* 53, no. 4 (November 2008): 445–55.

30. September 9, 1974, press release, United Handicapped Federation Records, Box 5, Minnesota Historical Society. Emphasis in original.

31. Audrey Benson to Lionel Lewis, January 9, 1975, United Handicapped Federation Records, Box 4, Correspondence, 1974, Minnesota Historical Society. The CIC handled records and finances for the UHF through at least part of 1974. See June 3, 1975, letter from Ronnie Stone, Box 4, Correspondence, June–Dec 1975, United Handicapped Federation, Minnesota Historical Society; Nancy Sopkowiak, "Bjerkesett Honored," *Access Press* 19, no. 7 (July 10, 2008), http://www.accesspress.org, accessed November 27, 2011.

32. Michael Bjerkesett to John Mykelbust, February 12, 1975, United Handicapped Federation Records, Box 4, Correspondence, 1975, Minnesota Historical Society; Michael Bjerkesett to Hubert H. Humphrey, January 31, 1975, United Handicapped Federation Records, Box 4, Correspondence, 1974, Minnesota Historical Society.

33. Michael Bjerkesett to Rep. Russell Stanton, St. Paul, February 14, 1975, United Handicapped Federation Records, Box 4, Correspondence, 1974, Minnesota Historical Society.

34. Audrey Benson to Donald Engle, president, Minnesota Orchestral Association, July 11, 1975, United Handicapped Federation Records, Box 4, Minnesota Historical Society; press release, August 8, 1975, United Handicapped Federation Records, Box 5, Minnesota Historical Society; press release, November 21, 1974, United Handicapped Federation Records, Box 5, Minnesota Historical Society.

35. Press release, January 23, 1976, United Handicapped Federation Records, Box 5, Minnesota Historical Society; Mary Johnson and Barrett Shaw, eds., *To Ride the Public's Buses: The Fight that Built a Movement* (Louisville, KY: Advocado Press, 2001), 140. The latter does a great job of telling the story of disability activism on transit issues.

36. Thomas Junilla to Northwestern Bell Telephone Company, October 13, 1976, United Handicapped Federation Records, Box 4, 1976; Harry G. Lang, *A Phone of Our Own: The Deaf Insurrection Against Ma Bell* (Washington, DC: Gallaudet University Press, 2000); Audrey Benson to Minnesota Teamsters Public Employees Union Local 320, Minneapolis, June 18, 1976, United Handicapped Federation Records, Box 4, Minnesota Historical Society.

37. United Handicapped Federation Records, Box 10, Minnesota Historical Society; Stephan Marincel to William Mahlum (UHF attorney), September 1977, United Handicapped Federation Records, Box 4, Minnesota Historical Society.

38. Scott Rostron, "The Progress," August 1977, United Handicapped Federation Records, Box 2, Minnesota Historical Society.

39. United Handicapped Federation, July 14, 1978 delegate assembly notes, United Handicapped Federation Records, Minnesota Historical Society; Peg Edel, Director of Rape and Sexual Assault, Neighborhood Involvement Program, Minneapolis, to Frances Strong, January 9, 1979, United Handicapped Federation Records, Box 4, Minnesota Historical Society. For more on the early emerging relationship between feminism and disability rights, see: Marian Blackwell-Stratton et al., "Smashing Icons: Disabled Women and the Disability and Women's Movements," in *Women with Disabilities: Essays in Psychology, Culture, and Politics,* ed. Michelle Fine and Adrienne Asch (Philadelphia: Temple University Press), 306–32; Pamela Brandwein and Richard K. Scotch, "The Gender Analogy in the Disability Discrimination Literature," *Ohio State Law Journal* 62, no. 465 (2001).

40. Frances Strong, conference report, July 14, 1979, Conference on Sexual and Physical Assault of Disabled People, United Handicapped Federation Records, Minnesota Historical Society; press release, March 23, 1982, United Handicapped Federation Records, Box 5, Minnesota Historical Society.

41. Letter to the Editor, September 2, 1975, *Minneapolis Star*, United Handicapped Federation Records, clippings, Minnesota Historical Society.

42. Barnartt and Scotch, *Disability Protests*, 197–201.

43. Steve Bailey, *Athlete First: A History of the Paralympic Movement* (Hoboken, NJ: Wiley, 2008); Victoria Ann Lewis, "Radical Wallflowers: Disability and the People's Theater," *Radical History Review* 94 (2006): 84–110; Victoria Ann Lewis, ed., *Beyond Victims and Villains: Contemporary Plays by Disabled Playwrights* (New York: Theatre Communications Group, 2006).

44. For more on the ADA, see: Barnartt and Scotch, *Disability Protests*, 169–74; Edward D. Berkowitz, "A Historical Preface to the Americans with Disabilities Act," *Journal of Policy History* 6, no. 1 (1994): 96–119; H. McCarthy, "A Belated Appreciation of Justin Dart (1930–2002)," *Rehabilitation Counseling Bulletin* 46, no. 4 (June 2003): 242–44.

45. Eli Clare, *Exile and Pride: Disability, Queerness, and Liberation* (Boston: South End Press, 2009), 160.

46. Ibid., 107.

INDEX

Able-Disabled Club, 167
Ableism, xii, xiv, 48, 154–56, 179,
     181–83; and citizenship, 52; educa-
     tion, 137; and immigration, 106,
     109–10; and labor, 46–47, 74,
     109–10, 128–29, 134–35, 151–52
Abolition, 52, 58–60, 67–68
Accessibility, 74, 146–47; Architectural
     Barriers Act, 165; disability rights
     movement, 150, 151, 161, 163, 165,
     174–78, 181; Warm Springs, 140
ADA. *See* Americans with Disabilities
     Act (ADA)
Adams, John, 33, 49
ADAPT, 176
Adaptive equipment, 129, 146; canes,
     85; prostheses, 80, 85–86, 126–27;
     wheelchairs, 80, 139–41, 161, 163,
     171, 180
African Americans, 80, 93, 100, 112,
     136–38, 140–41, 160–62, 169; civic
     life, 50, 96; institutionalization,
     91–93, 122–23; war, 82–83, 85–87,
     133, 146. *See also* slavery
Alabama, 75, 91–92
Alabama Insane Hospital, 91–92
Alabama School for the Deaf, 98
Alcott, Louisa May, 79
Algonquin, 16–17
American Asylum for the Deaf, 67
American Federation of Labor. *See*
     AFL-CIO
American Federation of the Physically
     Handicapped (AFPH), 150–54
American Revolution, 38–39, 49–50,
     52–56, 65–66, 68–69, 75–76, 80, 86
American Sign Language (ASL), 98,
     133, 137, 177, 179

Americans with Disabilities Act (ADA),
     161, 180; ADA Amendments Act, 181
Amputation, 128, 149–50, 170; and
     industrialization, 125–26; and
     slavery, 59; and veterans, 53–54,
     79, 84–85, 87
Apache, 4–5
Arc, 143–44
Architectural Barriers Act (ABA), 165,
     180
Arkansas, 87, 92
Asian Americans, 3, 103, 105, 140. *See
     also* Chinese Americans
ASL. *See* American Sign Language (ASL)
Asylums, 35, 37, 66–67, 69–75, 92, 96,
     98–99, 102, 115, 144, 164. *See also*
     individual asylums
Aztec, 41

Barnum, P. T., 89–90
Bassoff, Sylvia Flexer, 132–33
Beecher, Catharine, 94
Bell, Alexander Graham, 97
Benson, Audrey, 173, 175
Berkeley's Center for Independent
     Living, 163
Berry, James H., 87
Biard, Pierre, 13, 19
Bjerkesett, Michael, 173–74
Blackham, Sandra, 170
Black Lung Association (BLA), 159
Black lung disease, 158–60
Black Panthers, 169
Blackwell's Island, 144
Blatt, Burton, 145
Blind Veterans Association (BVA), 153–56
Blindness, 32, 54, 77, 84, 115, 151,
     162, 178; and epidemics, 15, 18, 39,